# Zen Masters
## *of* China

# Zen Masters
## *of* China

## The First Step East

ZEN STORIES COLLECTED AND RETOLD BY

## Richard Bryan McDaniel

FOREWORD BY **ALBERT LOW**
DIRECTOR AND TEACHER, MONTREAL ZEN CENTER

**TUTTLE** Publishing
Tokyo | Rutland, Vermont | Singapore

## The Tuttle Story: "Books to Span the East and West"

Most people are surprised to learn that the world's largest publisher of books on Asia had its humble beginnings in the tiny American state of Vermont. The company's founder, Charles E. Tuttle, belonged to a New England family steeped in publishing. And his first love was naturally books—especially old and rare editions.

Immediately after WW II, serving in Tokyo under General Douglas MacArthur, Tuttle was tasked with reviving the Japanese publishing industry. He later founded the Charles E. Tuttle Publishing Company, which thrives today as one of the world's leading independent publishers.

Though a westerner, Tuttle was hugely instrumental in bringing a knowledge of Japan and Asia to a world hungry for information about the East. By the time of his death in 1993, Tuttle had published over 6,000 books on Asian culture, history and art—a legacy honored by the Japanese emperor with the "Order of the Sacred Treasure," the highest tribute Japan can bestow upon a non-Japanese.

With a backlist of 1,500 titles, Tuttle Publishing is more active today than at any time in its past—inspired by Charles Tuttle's core mission to publish fine books to span the East and West and provide a greater understanding of each.

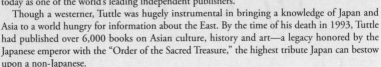

Published by Tuttle Publishing, an imprint of Periplus Editions (HK) Ltd.

www.tuttlepublishing.com

**Library of Congress Cataloging-in-Publication Data**

Zen masters of China : the first step east : Zen stories / collected and retold by Richard Bryan McDaniel ; foreword by Albert Low, LLD, Director and Teacher, Montreal Zen Center. -- First edition.

   pages cm

Includes bibliographical references and index.

ISBN 978-0-8048-4282-2 (hardcover)

1. Zen stories--China. 2. Koan. I. McDaniel, Richard Bryan, editor of compilation. II. Low, Albert, writer of added commentary.

  BQ9291.4.C6Z46 2012

  294.3'927092251--dc23

        2012003310

ISBN 978-0-8048-4282-2

**Distributed by**

**North America, Latin America & Europe**
Tuttle Publishing
364 Innovation Drive
North Clarendon, VT 05759-9436 U.S.A.
Tel: 1 (802) 773-8930;
Fax: 1 (802) 773-6993
info@tuttlepublishing.com
www.tuttlepublishing.com

**Asia Pacific**
Berkeley Books Pte. Ltd.
61 Tai Seng Avenue #02-12
Singapore 534167
Tel: (65) 6280-1330
Fax: (65) 6280-6290
inquiries@periplus.com.sg
www.periplus.com

First edition
16 15 14 13 12
10 9 8 7 6 5 4 3 2 1        1205RP

Printed in China

# Contents

*List of Illustrations* ................ 8
*Foreword by Albert Low* ....... 10
*Preface* ................................ 15

Prologue in India .............. 25

CHAPTER ONE
**Bodhidharma** ....................35

CHAPTER TWO
**Four Patriarchs**....................47
   Huike ................................48
   Jianzhi Sengcan .................51
   Dayi Daoxin ......................53
   Niutou Farong ...................54
   Daman Hongren................55

CHAPTER THREE
**Huineng**.............................59

CHAPTER FOUR
**The Rise of the Southern
School** ...................................69
   Shenxiu .............................70
   Huineng (continued) .........72
   Nanyang Huizhong............73
   Yingzhen ...........................77
   Qingyuan Xingshi............. 78

Nanyue Huairang..............79
Heze Shenhui.....................79

CHAPTER FIVE
**Mazu Daoyi** .........................83

CHAPTER SIX
**Shitou Xiqian and His
Disciples** .............................93
   Shitou Xiqian.....................94
   Layman Pang (Pangyun) ..100
   Tianhuang Daowu ..........102
   Tanxia Tianran ...............103
   Cuiwei Wuxue.................105

CHAPTER SEVEN
**Yaoshan Weiyan and His
Descendants**.......................109
   Yaoshan Weiyan ...............110
   Yunyan Tansheng.............116
   Daowu Yuanjie.................116
   Chunzi Decheng...............119
   Jiashan Shanhui...............120

CHAPTER EIGHT
**Dongshan Liangjie**.............125
   Dongshan Liangjie...........126
   Caoshan Benji.................134

CHAPTER NINE

**The Heirs of Mazu** ............139

Yanguan Qian ..................140

Xingshan Weikuan ...........141

Dazhu Huihai ..................142

Guizong Zhichang ...........143

Panshan Baoji...................144

Shigong Huicang .............146

Damei Fachang ................148

CHAPTER TEN

**The Poets** ...........................153

Hanshan...........................157

Shide ................................158

CHAPTER ELEVEN

**Nanquan Puyuan and
Baizhang Huaihai** ..............163

Nanquan Puyuan .............164

Baizhang Huaihai.............169

CHAPTER TWELVE

**Zhaozhou Congshen**..........177

Zhaozhou Congshen........178

Zui Jiao ............................188

CHAPTER THIRTEEN

**Zhaozhou's Contemporaries** . 191

Huangbo Xiyun ...............192

Changsha Jingcen.............195

Hangzhou Tianlong .........198

Jinhua Juzhi .....................199

Guishan Lingyou .............200

CHAPTER FOURTEEN

**Guishan's Descendants**.......205

Yangshan Huiji.................207

Xiangyan Zhixian.............210

Chanqing Daan ...............214

CHAPTER FIFTEEN

**Linji Yixuan**.......................217

CHAPTER SIXTEEN

**Deshan Xuanjian and His
Students** ............................229

Deshan Xuanjian..............230

Yantou Quanhuo .............235

Xuefeng Yicun..................235

Qinshan Wensui ..............235

CHAPTER SEVENTEEN

**The Linji Line** ...................243

Dingzhou Shizang............244

Sansheng Huiran..............245

Xinghua Cunjiang............246

Nanyuan Huiyong ...........246

Fengxue Yanzhao..............247

Shoushan Xingnian..........250

Fenyang Shanzhao............251

Shishuang Chuyuan.........253

Yangqi Fanghui ...............254

Huanglong Huinan..........254

CHAPTER EIGHTEEN

**The Fayan House** ..............257

Xuansha Shibei.................258

Luohan Chichen ..............259
Fayan Wenyi .....................259
Tiantai Deshao.................265
Yongming Yanshou ..........265
Daoyun ............................266

CHAPTER NINETEEN
**Yunmen Wenyan**................**269**

Yunmen Wenyan..............270
Muzhou Daozong.............270
Xuefeng Yicun...................271
Dongshan Shouchu..........277
Baling Haojian.................278
Xianglin Chengyuan ........279

CHAPTER TWENTY
**The Song Dynasty**.............**283**

Huitang Zuxin.................285

Wuzu Fayan .....................287
Yuanwu Keqin.................292

CHAPTER TWENTY-ONE
*Wu!* .....................................**295**

Dahui Zonggao................296
Yuelin Shiguan .................298
Wumen Huikai ................299

*Epilogue in Japan* ..............304
*Acknowledgments* ..............306
*Appendix: Wade-Giles and*
*  Japanese Variants of the*
*  Zen Masters' Names* ..........308
*Notes*.................................312
*Bibliography*.......................314
*Index of Stories*..................316

# List of Illustrations

Chapter One: Nineteenth-century Japanese woodblock portrait of Bodhidharma

Chapter Two: *Portrait of Huike* by Shi Ke, Song dynasty

Chapter Three: *Portrait of Huineng Chopping Bamboo* by Liang Kai, Southern Song dynasty

Chapter Four: *Lofty Hermitage in Cloudy Mountains* by Fang Fanghu, fourteenth century

Chapter Five: *The Solitary Angler* by Ma Yuan (1170–1260)

Chapter Six: *Two Zen Masters*

Chapter Seven: *Zen Master and Tiger* by Shi Ke, Song dynasty

Chapter Eight: *Walking on a Path in Spring* by Ma Yuan (1170–1260)

Chapter Nine: *Monk* by Liang Kai, Southern Song dynasty

Chapter Ten: Portraits of Shide and Hanshan by Yen Hui (1280–1368)

Chapter Eleven: The *Ox Herding Pictures*, sometimes called the *Ten Bulls*, are a series of ten pictures portraying the stages of growth in Zen. The set portrayed in this book are copies of now lost twelfth-century Chinese originals by the fifteenth-century Japanese artist, Tensho Shubun. The first picture is entitled *Searching for the Ox*.

Chapter Twelve: Second *Ox Herding Picture, Finding the Footprints of the Ox*

Chapter Thirteen: Third *Ox Herding Picture, Glimpsing the Ox*

Chapter Fourteen: Fourth *Ox Herding Picture, Catching the Ox*

Chapter Fifteen: Fifth *Ox Herding Picture, Taming the Ox*

Chapter Sixteen: Sixth *Ox Herding Picture, Riding the Ox Home*

Chapter Seventeen: Seventh *Ox Herding Picture, Ox Forgotten*

Chapter Eighteen: Eighth *Ox Herding Picture, Ox and Self Forgotten*

Chapter Nineteen: Ninth *Ox Herding Picture, Returning to the Source*

Chapter Twenty: Tenth *Ox Herding Picture, Going Among the People in the Marketplace*

Chapter Twenty-One: Southern Song dynasty portrait of a Zen priest

# Foreword

by
Albert Low, LLD.,
Director and Teacher, Montreal Zen Center

According to the French philosopher and mathematician Blaise Pascal, "The heart has its reasons that reason knows not of." The stories that follow in this book address those reasons of the heart. For thousands of years human beings have used stories to convey a message that the intellect can neither grasp nor communicate. Perhaps the earliest of these was the story of Gilgamesh. Since then the Hindus (through the *Mahabharata*, of which the *Bhagavad Gita* forms a part), the Sufis (through the stories of Mullah Nasrudin), Jesus (through his many parables), the Hassidic Jews, and the Chinese (through koans and *mondo*), and countless others have taught the wisdom of the heart to an ever receptive humanity.

Why should stories be able to do what even the keenest intellect is unable to achieve? Why do spiritual teachers of all kinds resort to stories to get across subtle yet vitally important teachings?

It is a matter of common knowledge that the mind operates on at least two different levels, a so-called "conscious" level and an "unconscious" level. In the West this is a comparatively recent discovery made popular by Sigmund Freud and the psychoanalytical school of psychology. But in the East the idea of a Higher Self, an Over Self, or a True Self that presides over and gives direction to a lower self has been present since the beginning of civilization.

Generally speaking, for the Westerner, the unconscious is considered to be inferior to the conscious mind. As Freud would have it, "Where there is id there shall be ego." The picture that Freud drew of the client's ego absorbing or reclaiming the unconscious was similar to the one we have of the Dutch with their system of dikes and dams reclaiming the land from the Zuider Zee. Jung drew a radically different picture of the unconscious that was more favorably inclined towards it. The unconscious, according to Freud, was a sea of dark, uncontrolled passions ready to erupt into consciousness with dire results. But Jung saw it more as a repository of ancient wisdom in the form of Archetypes. Nevertheless, he was still inclined to put the conscious mind in the role of the director whose function it was to interpret and make sense of the messages received from the unconscious.

For the East the roles of conscious and unconscious are reversed. The "unconscious" mind was the real mind or true self, and the conscious mind, in a well regulated individual, was the servant carrying out the dictates of the real self. Unfortunately, in most people the real self has fallen asleep and the conscious mind has abandoned its role as servant and elevated itself into the role of master and director, to the detriment of the individual.

Our task in life is to awaken as the true self and reclaim our rightful heritage. But how can this be accomplished? The rational intellectual mind is a product of consciousness. It is dependent upon forms coming from the senses and upon symbols—words, numbers, and signs—by which to organize the forms. It is at home with abstractions, distillations of experience into the barest essentials, and only knows a linear form of reasoning. On the other hand, true self is at home with direct experience, unmediated or filtered by thoughts and ideas. It deals with wholes and with what is present in a concrete, real way. When awake, instead of operating in the dream world of the intellect, it is at home in the real, concrete world and can act accordingly.

To try to communicate with true self via reason alone is doomed to failure, as true self does not understand the language of reason. This is where stories as well as symbols, rituals, images in the form of icons, and ceremonies come in. By their means the obstructions of the rational mind are bypassed and the message arrives unfiltered.

The Chinese and Persians were particularly adept at converting ordinary, entertaining, and simple stories into profound spiritual statements. An example is the use the Sufis make of the exploits of Mullah Nasrudin, a wise fool. On one occasion the mullah, coveting his neighbor's pears that were growing on a tree in a garden surrounded by a high wall, decided to scale the wall and help himself to a few of the choicest pears. To accomplish this he moved a ladder up against the wall, climbed the ladder, and, while sitting on top of the wall, hauled the ladder up and placed it securely on the other side of the wall. He then climbed down the ladder into the neighbor's garden, and, turning to go to the tree, collided with the irate neighbor. "What are you doing?" yelled the neighbor. "Selling ladders," replied the mullah. "Don't be ridiculous, you can't sell ladders here," spluttered the neighbor. "It's you that is being ridiculous. You can sell ladders anywhere" was the mullah's response. Across Asia, and down the centuries, stories about the mullah's adventures have been passed on from mouth to mouth, challenging people to no longer take for granted their fixed opinions, beliefs, and theories and to awaken to a more reality-based awareness.

The stories told by the Chinese and Sufis have much in common with jokes, and some are indistinguishable from them. The surest way to ruin a joke is to try to explain why it is funny, and the surest way to obscure the teaching in these stories is also to try to explain them. Most jokes are funny because the words describing the situation can be interpreted in two quite contradictory ways. For example, the following notice appeared on a church bulletin board: "Thursday at 5:00 p.m. there will be a meeting of the Little Mothers Club. All wishing to become Little Mothers, please see the minister in his study." But this is true of the stories also. The mullah is right: you can sell ladders anywhere. The neighbor is right: he could not sell ladders in an orchard. The conscious mind is baffled, and the only way out of the impasse is for the higher consciousness to intervene. The intervention of higher consciousness to resolve the impasse of two contradictory situations is the basis of creativity, humor, scientific discovery; it is also the basis of spiritual awakening.

The Chinese, however, have taken to the highest level the art of using storytelling as a spiritual way. One sees this in what are called *mondo* and koan, and much of the following book is devoted to these two forms. Mondo are questions and answers. The questioner and the one answering may be a novice, or he or she may be a person advanced on the Way, and when one is reading the mondo this must be firmly kept in mind, as the meaning will change depending on the level of the protagonists.

Sometimes the mondo will take the form of a *dharma duel.* A dharma duel takes place between two people who are well advanced along the Way. Each is asking the other to show the workings of the higher mind. For example, someone asked Zen Master Zhaozhou Congshen, "What is my essence?" Zhaozhou said, "The tree sways, the bird flies about, the fish leaps, the water is muddy." The questioner is asking, "What is the higher mind?" and Zhaozhou responds from the higher mind.

However, it is with the koan that the true value of the story is revealed. Everyone has surely heard of the Sound of One Hand. The full koan reads, "You know the sound of two hands clapping. What is the sound of one hand clapping?" A number of collections of koans have been made; among the most popular are *The Mumonkan, The Hekiganroku*, and *The Book of Serenity*. Many koans are indeed simply mondo that have been stripped down to the essential. Comments are added to the koan to help the student gain an entry into it. Each koan therefore is a miniature drama. To "work" with the koan—that is, to plumb its meaning—one must *inhabit* the koan. We must understand the conflict, twist, or incongruity described and dwell with the contradiction, and so allow the higher mind to awaken.

The above explanation gives the direction in which to go when reading this book. We do not read a book like this for information or knowledge but to awaken a higher part of the mind, a part that in most of us is asleep. A certain amount of information is given in the book, but this simply provides a framework within which to contain the essential part of the book: the stories, mondo, and koans.

Koan practice is more properly called koan *appreciation*. We appreciate what is being said in the same way that we appreciate music, poetry, or drama. To do so is to dwell in the situation described in much the same way we dwell in a drama. By doing so we will not only gain a richer understanding of the stories or mondo, we will also gain a richer appreciation of life itself.

Rick McDaniel is well qualified to write a book such as this. He has been a long time member of the Montreal Zen Center and has attended many intensive retreats at the Center. He has worked on koan for much of his time with the center and draws on this experience in the writing of this book.

# Preface

It was the stories of Zen that brought me to the practice of Zen—not the theory or teachings of Buddhism, not the philosophy or dogma, but the stories.

Once one takes up the practice, one encounters these stories again, in *teishos* (the talks given by the teacher during Zen retreats called *sesshin*) and *dokusan* (personal meetings with the teacher). But now they are teaching aids, *upaya*, "skillful means" by which the teacher seeks to help the student attain the experience called "awakening," deepen it, and integrate it into his or her life. That is, after all, the purpose of the stories, the reason they have been preserved.

Still, when one first encounters them—when they are still not so much even stories as anecdotes—they have a freshness that is entrancing. In all the scriptures of this multicultured planet, nowhere else does one find tales like these—beguiling, often humorous, frequently irreverent.

The lore of religion begins in myth, passes through legend, and only slowly comes to verifiable historical narrative. One sees this pattern in the dominant religious traditions of the West. First there are the tales of the Bible, followed by the legends of Christian saints and Jewish folklore. And only in the later centuries do we have what might be considered objectively accurate information.

The stories of Zen likewise begin with the anecdotes of sixth century China, pass through the legends of the Tang and Song dynasties as well as of Japan, and continue in the records of the Zen teachers of more recent centuries, including those pioneers who brought the tradition to the world outside of Asia.

The spread of the teaching has been steadily eastward. It has been said that Zen (*Chan* in Chinese) is the product of the encounter between Indian Buddhism and Chinese culture, especially Daoism and Confucianism. From China, various schools of Buddhism, including Chan, spread to Korea, Vietnam, and Japan (where it was called Zen). While over time the Chan school declined in China, it continued to flourish in Japan, where it had its fullest flowering. Finally, at the end of the nineteenth century, Zen took its longest stride east, across the Pacific Ocean to the shores of North America.

In this, the first of three projected volumes, I retell some of the most significant Zen stories to come from China. The second and third volumes will recount the Zen tales of Japan, the United States, and Canada.

For some people, the stories in this collection form a kind of Zen canon. Even today certain teachers accept them as historically accurate. Scholarship, however, has not only called into question the historicity of individuals such as Bodhidharma but even details about the lives of historically verifiable individuals such as the Sixth Patriarch, Huineng. The story of the Buddha's flower sermon and the transmission of the dharma (the teaching) to Mahakasyapa does not appear in any Indian source; it is a Chinese invention first recorded in the eleventh century.

The stories, however, were not originally collected as historical records. They were collected because they had the potential to help Zen practitioners attain "awakening" or "enlightenment," the same experience that Siddhartha Gautama had had and because of which he came to be called the Buddha—the "Awakened One." Insofar as they accomplished that end, it did not matter whether they described actual events or not—in much the same way that the significance of the parables of Jesus were not dependent upon whether the stories he told were based on events that had actually taken place or not. To be too concerned with the historical accuracy of the events described would probably result in one failing to understand the purpose of the stories.

Compared with the writings of other religious traditions, including the sutras of Indian Buddhism, Chinese Zen stories are refreshingly unique. One does not find in them exhortations to morality or discussions of points of doctrine. When first encountering them, one may fail to see any religious, philosophical, or moral content at all. For example, the story is told of a new student who came to work with the ninth-century master, Zhaozhou Congshen. He presented himself, saying, "I have just entered the monastery, and I beg you to accept me as a disciple and teach me."

Zhaozhou asked him, "Have you had anything to eat yet?"

"Yes, I have. Thank you."

"Then you had better wash your bowl," Zhaozhou told him. And we are informed that upon hearing those words, the new monk attained awakening.

Whether one understands how this conversation brought about the result it claims to have done or not, one certainly recognizes that the method being described is exceptional in both global religious and philosophical traditions.

D. T. Suzuki was the Japanese Zen scholar primarily responsible for introducing Zen to the non-Asian world. He posited that the character of Zen was the result of the way Indian Buddhism adapted itself to the Chinese mentality in order to be relevant in that land. To demonstrate what he meant, he compared stories used by Indian and Chinese Buddhism to convey certain basic doctrines:

> Buddhism . . . is a religion of freedom and emancipation, and the ultimate aim of its discipline is to release the spirit from its possible bondages so that it can act freely in accordance to its own principles. This is what is meant by non-attachment. . . . The idea is negative inasmuch as it is concerned with untying the knots of the intellect and passion, but the feeling implied is positive, and the final object is attained only when

the spirit is restored to its original activity. The spirit knows its own way, and what we can do is to rid it of all the obstacles our ignorance has piled before it. "Throw them down" is therefore the recurring note in the Buddhist teaching.

The Indian Buddhist way of impressing the idea is this: a Brahman named Black-nails came to the Buddha and offered him two huge flowering trees that he carried each in one of his hands through his magical power. The Buddha called out, and when the Brahman responded the Buddha said, "Throw them down!" The Brahman let down the flowering tree in his left hand before the Buddha. The latter called out again to let them go, whereupon Black-nails dropped the other flowering tree in the right hand. The Buddha still kept up his command. Said the Brahman: "I have nothing now to let go. What do you want me to do?" "I never told you to abandon your flowering plants," said the Buddha. "What I want you to do is to abandon your six objects of sense, your six organs of sense [sight, touch, taste, smell, hearing, and mind], and your six consciousnesses. When these are all at once abandoned and there remains nothing further to be abandoned, it is then that you are released from the bondage of birth-and-death."

In contrast to this plain, though somewhat roundabout, talk of the Buddha, the following case of Joshu [Zhaozhou] is direct and concise and disposes of the matter in a most unequivocal manner. A monk came and asked the master, "How is it when a man brings nothing with him?" "Throw it away!" was Joshu's immediate response. "What shall he throw down when he is not burdened at all?" "If so, carry it along!"[1]

In a second example, Suzuki dealt with the question of who or what the Buddha was. This was a question that naturally arose in China as the teaching associated with him struggled to establish itself alongside native traditions such as Confucianism and Daoism. Suzuki's example from India told of a woman, during the Buddha's lifetime, who had formed an aversion to him and went out of her way to avoid him. However, no matter in which direction she turned, there he miraculously appeared. Finally, in desperation, she covered her eyes with her hands only to find him in her own mind.

The contrasting Chinese story is one of my favorite Zen tales, one of the tales that first drew me to this tradition. An inquirer asked Yanguan Qian, "Who was the Buddha?"

Yanguan replied by requesting of his visitor, "Would you please pass me that water pitcher."

The inquirer looked around, saw the pitcher, and passed it to the master. Yanguan poured himself a cup of water and then asked the visitor to replace the pitcher. The visitor did so, then, thinking that perhaps Yanguan had not heard his original question, put it again: "About the Buddha—who was he?"

"Oh, yes," Yanguan said. "Well, you know, he's been dead a long time now."

The contrast between the Indian and Chinese stories does more than demonstrate cultural differences between the two peoples. It emphasizes a difference in perspective. The Indian stories seek to make a point, to convey information. The Chinese stories, even when making a point, do so without trying. The Chinese stories are not about conveying information but about helping one achieve a different way of seeing things, an experience.

That experience has traditionally been associated with the practice of meditation. The terms *Chan* and *Zen* are derived from the Sanskrit word *dhyana*, which means "meditation." The Zen tradition as it developed in China, Japan, and now in North America is not a doctrine so much as it is, and always has been, a practice. It is the meditation school of Buddhism. And to that extent, it is—as Bodhidharma was supposed to have defined it—a teaching outside the scriptures, not dependent upon words or letters.

Words and letters, on the other hand, can be intriguing, and it is in that spirit that these stories are retold. Collected together as they are here, the stories are little more than the folklore of Zen, but perhaps that folklore will draw those who encounter it to the practice of Zen.

There is no new material in this collection. All the stories collected here have been told in English elsewhere (they can be found, for example, in the books listed in the bibliography). My only contributions—minor ones at that—have been to arrange them in roughly chronological sequence and to present them in a style more in accord with Western narrative traditions than the originals were. Written Chinese is a much more terse language than English, often implying as much as it states. In order to retell the tales in English, I have given myself the storyteller's prerogative of making minor embellishments.

This is not a work of scholarship, but one academic issue needed to be addressed early in the process of writing. Although Zen originated in China, it comes to North America and Europe as a Japanese tradition. Educated Japanese can read Chinese characters, but they do not pronounce them as the Chinese do. To confuse matters further, the way in which the Chinese pronunciations are rendered into the Roman alphabet has undergone a recent change. The name of the individual who originated the koan that is often first presented to Zen students (the same individual who asked the new monk if he had eaten yet) is written 趙州從諗. When receiving this first koan, it is probable that the student will be told that the individual is Joshu Jushin (the Japanese rendering). In older books on Zen, he may be called Chao-chou Ts'ung-shen, the Chinese rendering according to the Wade-Giles manner of transliterating Chinese. Current scholars prefer the newer Pinyin rendering, which is Zhaozhou Congshen.

Because the Japanese and Wade-Giles romanizations are often more familiar to actual practitioners of Zen, my original inclination had been to give all names in their Japanese forms, which would also have allowed consistency throughout the three volumes of stories. On reflection, this seemed inappropriate, and so I follow current usage and give them in the Pinyin form. In the appendix, however, I provide a table in which the names are presented in all three forms.

I have chosen, however, to retain the more familiar Japanese forms for other terms that come from these original languages. So the tradition is called Zen, not *Ch'an* [Wade-Giles] or *Chan* [Pinyin]. Where appropriate, I will first introduce a term in Chinese (*gongan*) followed by the Japanese form (*koan*), which will then become the usual form in the text.

Finally, Zen is, above all, a practice. These stories may lead one to the practice, as they did me, but on their own they do not provide the necessary instruction. For those readers who are interested in the actual practice of Zen, I recommend either Albert Low's *Zen Meditation: Plain and Simple* (originally published as *An Invitation to Practice Zen*) or Robert Aitkin's *Taking the Path of Zen*. Both are admirable for their clarity and brevity.

"Why did the First Patriarch come east?"

# Zen Masters
## *of* China

# Prologue in India

The story goes that one day the Buddha's disciples were gathered at the Bamboo Grove to listen to one of his dharma talks. *Dharma* is a word with several meanings. At times it simply means "phenomenon" or the way things are, the laws governing existence. When used in Buddhist texts, however, it usually refers to the general content of the Buddha's teachings.

Among the disciples gathered that day was one named Kasyapa. To distinguish him from another disciple with the same name, he came to be known as Mahakasyapa or the "Great Kasyapa." Mahakasyapa was the son of the richest man in the kingdom of Magadha, located in what is now the northeastern corner of India. His father's wealth was so great that it exceeded that of the king. But wealth alone does not necessarily bring contentment or security.

Mahakasyapa was drawn to religious life after waking one morning to find a poisonous snake creeping along the bed beside his wife. Mahakasyapa froze in terror, unable to brush the serpent away for fear that if he startled it, it would bite his wife and cause her death. When at last the snake moved off the bed, onto the floor, and out of the bedchamber, Mahakasyapa woke his wife and told her of the danger in which they had been. The two of them were sensitive and reflective individuals, and the incident made them ponder the fragile nature of human life. It became clear to Mahakasyapa that he should look for a teacher who would help him understand the significance of life. So he sought out the Buddha, who accepted him as a pupil.

Those who gathered about the Buddha were referred to as the *sangha*. They lived collectively, following a strict discipline that included the practice of *dhyana*, or meditation. Kasyapa adapted to sangha life easily.

On the day in question, the disciples who gathered to listen to the Buddha probably expected him to discuss one of the many themes he returned to time and again—such as the origin of suffering and the path to freedom from suffering, or the chain of causation, or the doctrine of impermanence. However, on this occasion, instead of speaking the Buddha simply sat before the assembled monks and twirled a flower between his fingers. Some disciples shifted in their seats uneasily, some felt impatient, others wondered if there were some hidden significance in the Buddha's silence; but Mahakasyapa smiled—even though, it is said, he attempted to control his expression because it was, after all, a solemn occasion.

The Buddha noticed that smile and finally spoke: "I have the eye of the true teaching," he told the assembly, "the heart of nirvana—or liberation—the true aspect of no-form, the unquestionable dharma. Today I have passed these on to Mahakasyapa."

*Buddha* is not a name but rather a title meaning "the awakened one." The man now known as the Buddha had been a prince named Siddhartha Gautama. At his birth, astrologers predicted that he would either grow up to become a great secular or great religious leader. His father, King Suddhodana, naturally hoped the boy would succeed him on the throne, so he tried to shield his son from those sorrows that often draw people to the religious life.

The child was raised in luxury and seclusion. The accounts of his early life insist that he had no contact with sickness, old age, or death until he was nearly thirty years old, by which time he was already married and his wife was pregnant.

However, the ease and privileges of his life had eventually begun to pall, and he grew curious about what life was like beyond the grounds of the palace. So one day he ordered his charioteer, Channa, to take him to see the kingdom he was to inherit. On that first outing, they encountered an old man. The prince stared at him in wonder, then turned to Channa and asked:

"Tell me, Channa, what kind of being is that over there, moving so slowly and with such great effort? Can it be a man? He does not look like other men I have seen. His hair is sparse and white, unlike that of other men. His skin is wrinkled and hangs loosely on his neck and arms, unlike that of other men. His mouth is sunken, and he appears to lack the teeth of other men. His back is stooped, and he supports himself on that stick, unlike other men. His movements are halting, and his limbs quiver, unlike those of other men. What kind of being, O Channa, is he?"

"Prince, he is only a man like yourself who has grown old and frail with the passing of the years."

"Is it perhaps, Channa, that only this man is subject to this deterioration of age, or are all men so subject?"

"All men, my Prince, are subject to the deterioration of their powers and faculties as they grow older. Even you, sir."

Distressed by this information, Prince Siddhartha ordered Channa to return to the palace. But not long after, he felt compelled to go out into the kingdom once again. On this occasion, they encountered a man sick with fever, emaciated but with a swollen belly, covered with flies, and soiled by his own filth.

"What kind of being, O Channa," Prince Siddhartha asked the charioteer, "is that over there? Surely his body is not like that of other men. His shaking and sweating are not like the behavior of other men. The moans and incomprehensible sounds proceeding from his mouth are not like the words other men speak. What kind of being is he?"

"Prince, he is only an unfortunate man, such as yourself, who has fallen ill with a fever."

"Is it perhaps, Channa, that only this man is subject to the ravages of illness, or are all men so subject?"

"All men, my Prince, are subject to the ravages of illness. Even you, sir."

"Then how can humankind bear this burden, knowing this to be their fate? If physical beauty and good health are so fragile and fleeting, how can one take any joy in entertainments and the pleasures of the senses?" And once again, he ordered Channa to return to the palace.

For a time, the prince tried to lose himself in the pleasures and privileges of his station, but eventually he once more felt compelled to venture out of the palace grounds. On this occasion, they came upon a funeral procession.

"Why, O Channa," Siddhartha asked, "are these people wailing and lamenting so? And what kind of being is that which they carry on that litter? He does not move as other men do. The odor that comes from him is not like that of other men. Even the mottled color of his skin is not like that of other men."

"Prince, that is a corpse. The man has died. The breath has left his body, and he will never again be with his family and friends to share their joys and sorrows. The ones who carry him are those same friends and family, mourning him as they take his body to be burnt."

"And is it perhaps, Channa, that only this man is subject to death, or are all men so subject?"

"All men, my prince, are inevitably subject to death. Even you, sir."

Siddhartha returned to the palace, but by now had lost all interest in the distractions his father provided. He was so devastated by what he had discovered that he was unable to rest. And so, for a final time, he ordered his charioteer to take him from the security of the palace to the world beyond. On this occasion they came upon a figure with a shaved head, walking with serenity and dignity. He wore a robe that left one shoulder bare, and he carried a begging bowl. He went up to the door of a house, knocked, and waited calmly until the housewife looked out at him. Wordlessly, he bowed and proffered the empty bowl, into which she placed a small ball of rice.

"Tell me, O Channa, what kind of being is that over yonder? He has a serenity and dignity I have not seen in other men."

"He is a *bhikku*, my Prince, a monk. He is one who has left his home and given up all of his possessions. He has learned to control his passions and his ego. He spends his time in meditation and devotional activities seeking to learn the secrets of Being."

When he heard these words, Siddhartha felt as if a door had opened. He sensed for the first time the purpose of his life and the destiny for which he had come into the world. So it was that he gave up his royal position to become a wandering monk. In doing so, he sought to understand the purpose of his existence and to find a way to escape the bondage of a life subject to illness, age, and final dissolution.

In that culture, it was commonly believed such concerns could best be resolved not by reasoning but through the practice of meditation. Accordingly, Gautama studied with two of the most celebrated meditation masters of his time, but he was dissatisfied with what they were able to teach him. Leaving them, he went on to practice severe austerities with a group of ascetics for six years. These practices also failed to help him achieve what he was seeking and brought him to the brink of starvation. He had become so weak from this lifestyle that one day he collapsed. A young girl, sent to take a food offering to the spirits of the forest, found him and offered him a bowl of milk. He accepted her gift and from that moment gave up the practice of asceticism. His former companions considered this a betrayal of their way of life and abandoned him.

Left on his own, he retired to a grove of fig trees, where he sat under a tree that would later be known as the Bodhi Tree, or Tree of Enlightenment. There he vowed he would remain meditating until he came to full and complete enlightenment.

Even after years of practice with meditation teachers and further years of ascetic activity, the future Buddha still did not have complete control over his thoughts and emotions. As he sat beneath the tree, he was assailed by sexual images, anxieties, and fantasies of accomplishment. But not allowing these to distract him, he remained focused, seeking an answer to the questions of life and death, of existence and human experience.

He sat through the night, focused on these questions, and ignoring the random distractions that arose in his mind. Then as dawn broke he saw the planet Venus on the horizon, and at that moment he became awakened—he came to full and complete enlightenment. Tradition has it that at the moment of his enlightenment, he exclaimed: "O wonder of wonders! All beings just as they are are whole and complete! All beings are endowed with Buddha-nature!" All beings, in other words, have the inherent capacity to realize that their most basic nature, their fundamental nature, is no different from that of all existence.

This was a well-known experience in the traditions current in Buddha's time. It was experience of what in Sanskrit was called *advaya*, which can be translated as "nonduality." While most people have a sense of themselves as an entity within the world confronting other entities through their six senses (the Asian tradition considers thought a sixth sense), in the experience of *advaya* there is no sense of self separate from all else. For this reason, the experience came to be called, in Buddhism, *sunyata* or "emptiness."

The newly awakened Buddha remained beneath the Bodhi Tree for forty-nine days after his enlightenment, during which time he contemplated his experience and reflected on the laws of causality to which humankind is subject. On the forty-ninth day, the Buddha reflected that, although he had found the Path of Liberation he had sought so diligently, he was uncertain whether he would be able to communicate what he had discovered to others. The next morning, as he went to the river to bathe, he paused to observe the lotus flowers growing there. The flowers were at different stages of development. Some were little more than roots buried in the mud; others had stems that still had not risen to the surface of the water; still others had emerged but their leaves remained curled shut; the buds of yet others were just opening; and finally there were flowers in full bloom. In like manner, he reflected, people were at various stages of development, but in each person there existed the seed of enlightenment—their inherent Buddha-nature. With proper cultivation, all persons are capable of realization and enlightenment. So the Buddha decided to share the dharma (the teaching) with others.

Spiritual teachers were common in that era. The Buddha became one teacher among many. He was known by many names. One of his most common titles was Shakyamuni, or "sage of the Shakya clan." The clarity and simplicity of what he taught quickly attracted followers, and, within a short time, he had a large following. Because the Buddha was recognized as an enlightened being, many people came to him hoping he would be able to help them with their problems. While a few may have wanted to achieve their own awakening, most considered that beyond their capacities and simply sought the assistance of one who had attained that height. They brought to him the type of concerns that humankind has always turned to religion to address. They wanted explanations for why things were the way they were. Others sought guidance on how they should live their lives. Some, no doubt, were looking for that companionship which is found in being a member of a community with shared beliefs. And, of course, there were those who wanted magic, who came in hopes of miracles.

He responded to those questions that came from the heart, which needed to be answered if the individual were to attain peace, but he ignored questions that were purely theoretical—such as those posed by the monk Malunkyaputta, who asked whether the world was eternal or finite, whether the soul and body were one or separate, whether or not there was an existence after death, and so on. To be concerned about such things, the Buddha told Malunkyaputta, was to be like a man wounded by an arrow who refused to have the arrow withdrawn until he knew who had crafted it, what type of wood was used, or what feathers were used in the fletching. Malunkyaputta's questions were about issues that do not matter and are probably unanswerable, so the Buddha refused to offer an opinion on them.

But to those who sought answers to basic questions such as why there was so much suffering in the world, the Buddha provided teachings such as the Four Noble Truths, which explain that suffering is inherent in the human condition because of desire and that only by letting go of desire can one overcome suffering. To those seeking guidance about how they should live their lives, he offered the Eightfold Path, the last two steps of which are "correct mindfulness" and "correct meditation." And to those seeking miracles—such as the woman Kisagotami whose infant son had died from a snakebite—he responded with compassion and kindness. In Kisagotami's case he told her that if she could find a household that would give her a single mustard seed, he would cure her child; but, he added, the household must be one wherein no one had ever died. Through this gentle method, he led her to recognize the reality of suffering, the Four Noble Truths, and the Eightfold Path.

The wisdom the Buddha demonstrated in his teachings was the result of his enlightenment, but the achievement of that wisdom was not the content of his enlightenment. He was not enlightened because he understood the laws of causation or realized the formula of the Four Noble Truths. The enlightenment experience, which led him to understand these things, was beyond verbal formulae and logical structures; it could not be expressed in words. The Buddha's insights, which were the result of his enlightenment, were recorded—and no doubt elaborated upon by others—in the scriptures called sutras. What the Buddha transmitted to Mahakasyapa was not dependent upon words and letters but something outside the scriptures. What he transmitted to Mahakasyapa was the experience of awakening itself. Mahakasyapa's realization was the same as the Buddha's. And when the Buddha recognized Mahakasyapa's awakening, it was not as a result of anything the disciple had said but by how he behaved, the way in which he reacted.

In the centuries after the Buddha's death, several schools based on his teachings arose. There was a very strict brotherhood of monks focused on personal liberation and salvation. But over time there also developed schools that focused upon specific sutras and composed elaborate commentaries on them. This resulted in an intellectual Buddhism that was, perhaps, more philosophical than religious. Eventually a popular devotional Buddhism also evolved, in which the Buddha came to be seen as a celestial being and in which devotees recited sutras, made offerings, and undertook good deeds in order to acquire merit that would lead to future auspicious rebirths.

These schools transmitted the Buddha's instructions and teachings. But parallel to them, according to the Zen tradition, a school of meditation descended from Mahakasyapa in which the enlightenment experience was transmitted.

No doubt thousands of individuals attained awakening, but in each generation there was one individual whose experience was so deep that he was identified as a patriarch of the meditation, or *dhyana*, school. The names of twenty-eight individuals are recorded, spanning a thousand years, beginning with the Buddha and Mahakasyapa and continuing until Bodhidharma, the man credited with bringing the school to China. There the term *dhyana* was translated as *chan*. Some six hundred years later when the school proceeded on to Japan, the Japanese read the Chinese character for *Chan* as "Zen."

*Nineteenth-century Japanese woodblock portrait of Bodhidharma*

# CHAPTER ONE

# BODHIDHARMA

The traditional list of Zen patriarchs is probably as accurate as the list of early popes in Christian lore. After the Buddha and Mahakasyapa, third in succession was the Buddha's cousin and attendant, Ananda, who did not achieve awakening until after the Buddha's death. Others in the list include historical figures such as Asvaghosha, the reputed author of *The Awakening of the Faith in the Mahayana* (twelfth patriarch) and Nagarjuna, the founder of the Madhyamaka school of Buddhism (fourteenth patriarch). The twenty-eighth in this lineage was Bodhidharma—a man whose name consists of the terms for wisdom/enlightenment (*Bodhi*) and teaching (*dharma*). Bodhidharma is credited with bringing the meditation school to China and is also considered the first patriarch of Chinese Zen.

Bodhidharma is a favorite subject of Zen painting, in which he is portrayed with exaggerated features emphasizing that to the sixth-century Chinese he would have been considered a barbarian. He is shown bearded, with prominent shaggy eyebrows, large, round eyes, and often a stern expression.

It is said that he was the third son in a prominent Brahmin family from southern India. The Brahmin were the priestly caste in the Hindu tradition, the caste that studied the various scriptures and were responsible for carrying out the intricate religious rituals associated with them. But rather than assuming the role of his caste, Bodhidharma was drawn to the practice of Buddhism and eventually became a master in the meditation school under the twenty-seventh patriarch, Prajnatara.

Whereas the Hindu faith was grounded in written texts such as the *Vedas* and even the Buddhism of the day was transmitted through the recorded sutras, or sermons attributed to the Buddha, Bodhidharma would describe Zen in a four-line poem as:

> A special transmission outside the scriptures;
> Not dependent on words or letters;
> By direct pointing to the mind of man,
> Seeing into one's true nature and attaining Buddhahood.

Buddhism was a thousand years old when Bodhidharma became a member of the sangha, and, in the land of its birth, the faith had deteriorated over that time, becoming more speculative and abstract. Monks spent as much or more time analyzing the sutras as in meditating. Their faith had become theoretical rather than grounded in the experience of awakening, what the Japanese would later term *kensho* (*ken*, "seeing into or understanding something"; *sho*, "one's true nature").

Nor was Buddhism a single system any longer. Competing theories and interpretations of the sutras led to a proliferation of schools, including the establishment of two broad traditions: the conservative Theraveda (the Teaching of the Elders), which spread to Sri Lanka, Burma, and Thailand, and the more liberal but also at times more fanciful Mahayana, which spread north to Tibet as well as into China, Vietnam, and Korea. It was out of the Mahayana tradition (and partially in reaction to it) that Zen would evolve.

Saddened by the condition of Buddhism in India, Prajnatara suggested that Bodhidharma travel to China and determine if that land were a suitable environment in which to revitalize Zen. It was also their intention to correct the form of Buddhism then prevalent in the Celestial Kingdom.

Buddhism had been practiced in China for over four hundred years by the time of Bodhidharma's journey, but it was largely an academic Buddhism. Chinese scholars translated the Indian sutras and composed elaborate commentaries on them. A variety of competing schools had evolved that based their teachings on one or the other of these scriptures. Devotional Buddhism was popular with the masses. There were meditation teachers as well, but none belonged to the line of transmission descended from Mahakasyapa.

Bodhidharma was an old man when he set out for China, and it took him three long, hard years to complete his journey, traveling over both land and sea, during which time he must have learned to speak Chinese. Finally, around the year 520, he landed on the southern shore of China and from there he continued his travels on foot.

Evidence of a historical basis to the story of Bodhidharma is found in a document written by an official named Yang Xuanzhi in 547. He recorded that when he visited the temple of Yongning in Luoyang, he came upon an elderly Indian monk named Bodhidharma who claimed to be over a hundred years old. Yang noted that the monk expressed great admiration for the beauties of the shrines and other buildings he found in China.

The story of the legendary Bodhidharma does not include the visit to Luoyang but does say that eventually the Indian monk's pilgrimage brought him to the capital city of the emperor Wu, founder of the Liang dynasty.

This emperor had been the third son of a noble family and as a young man pursued a career in military and government service, distinguishing himself as a general in the army of the emperor Ming of the Han dynasty. After Ming's death, however, Wu led a rebellion against Ming's son and successor. Following a prolonged siege, during which the young emperor died, Wu successfully occupied the royal palace. He had potential rivals to the throne executed, then declared himself emperor.

Although the new emperor had come to his throne by means of contrivance and violence, he proved to be a competent ruler, commended by his contemporaries for the modesty of his personal lifestyle. Around 517 he became a Buddhist, although he continued to respect the native Confucian rites as well. As a Buddhist, he adopted vegetarianism and went so far as to substitute vegetable offerings in place of the usual animal sacrifices that were ritually presented to the ancestors. In 527 he formally dedicated himself to the service of the Buddha, a commitment he renewed three more times. He even authored a repentance ritual still in use by Chinese Buddhists.

When the emperor learned that a monk from the land of the Buddha's birth was in his kingdom, he had Bodhidharma brought to his court. The monk, however, was probably not what the emperor had expected. The naturalist, writer, and Zen practitioner Peter Matthiessen imagines Bodhidharma presenting an uncouth appearance in the court:

Cowled, round-shouldered, big-headed, bearded, broken-toothed, with prominent and piercing eyes, sometimes said to be blue—one can all but smell his hard-patched robes, stained with ghee butter from India, the wafting reek of cooking smoke and old human leather. One imagines him slouched there scratching and belching, or perhaps demanding, *What time do we eat?*[2]

The emperor was concerned about the misdeeds of his younger years and had tried to compensate for them through a variety of devotional acts. He had sponsored the translation of Buddhist texts, supported large numbers of monks and nuns, and assumed the cost of building temples. Like many devotional Buddhists, the emperor believed in karma, the concept that one's actions bore consequences both in this life and in future lives. Eager to know if his religious activities balanced the crimes of his past, he described to Bodhidharma all he had done to promote Buddhism in his country, then asked, "What is your opinion? What merit have I accumulated as a result of these deeds?"

Bodhidharma, rejecting this simplistic understanding of Buddhism, replied bluntly and tactlessly: "No merit whatsoever."

It was a courageous statement, because the emperor, for all his good qualities, was also known to have a temper and had the power of life and death over his subjects. A story is told that once Wu was engaged in a board game with a courtier when a monk paid him a visit. The emperor, preoccupied with his play, did not notice the monk. Making a strong move in the game, he exclaimed, "Kill!" His bodyguard misunderstood what he was saying and executed the unoffending monk before the emperor could prevent them from doing so.

On this occasion the emperor controlled himself, although he must have been angered by the old and shabbily dressed Indian's reply. He limited himself to inquiring, "Why no merit?"

"Motives for such actions are impure," Bodhidharma told him. "They are undertaken solely for the purposes of attaining future rebirth. They are like shadows cast by bodies, following those bodies but having no reality of their own."

"Then what is true merit?" the emperor asked.

"It is clear seeing, pure knowing, beyond the discriminating intelligence. Its essence is emptiness. Such merit cannot be gained by worldly means."

This was unlike any exposition of the Buddhist faith the emperor had heard before, and he asked, "According to your understanding, then, what is the first principle of Buddhism?"

"Vast emptiness and not a thing that can be called holy," Bodhidharma replied at once.

Wu spluttered: "What does that mean? And who are you who now stands before me?"

To which Bodhidharma replied: "I don't know." Then he left the court.

The courtiers were outraged by the barbarian's behavior, and it is even possible his life may have been in danger after this encounter. He traveled south, crossing the Yangtze River, some claim by floating on a reed.

After Bodhidharma had left, the emperor discussed the Indian with a local Buddhist monk named Chih Kung. Chih Kung expressed the opinion that Bodhidharma may have been the reincarnation of a bodhisattva (roughly the equivalent of a Buddhist saint), perhaps even the reincarnation of the bodhisattva of compassion, Guanyin.

The emperor, abashed that he had not recognized this possibility himself, wanted to send soldiers to retrieve Bodhidharma and bring him back to the court. But Chih Kung dissuaded him, remarking, "It will be of no use, your majesty. Were all the people of your kingdom to appeal to him, he still won't retrace his steps."

After crossing the Yangtzi, Bodhidharma proceeded to the Shaolin Temple located in the Songshan mountain range, which would later become famous for its affiliation with the martial arts. Bodhidharma built a hermitage on the peak of Mount Shaoshi and there practiced silent meditation while facing the wall of the cliff that rose in front of his hut. He came to be known locally as *Biguan*, the wall-gazing Brahmin, and the hut was known as the Wall-Gazing Hermitage.

Popular legends, not taken seriously in the Zen tradition, recount that he sat so long in meditation that his legs withered and fell off (for which reason the round-bottomed dolls weighted so that they always return upright when pushed over are known as Bodhidharma—or Daruma—dolls in Japan). Another story asserts that he became so angered after falling asleep during meditation one day that he cut off his eyelids, which then fell to the earth and grew to become the first tea plants.

Word of Bodhidharma's audience with the emperor spread throughout the kingdom, and most members of the Buddhist community avoided the barbarian monk, leaving him in isolation. There was, however, a Confucian scholar named Ji who was searching for a teacher to help him resolve the concerns that weighed heavily on his mind—the same type of concerns that had driven the young Siddhartha Gautama to abandon his princely state in order to become a monk. Ji had visited many teachers, Confucian, Daoist, and Buddhist. He studied all three traditions and was well versed not only in the Confucian classics but also in the doctrines of both the Theravada and Mahayana schools of Buddhism. Nothing, however, had brought him peace of mind. In desperation he sought out the old barbarian monk who had come from the land of the Buddha.

When Ji presented himself at Mount Shaoshi, Bodhidharma suspected his visitor was another who came seeking an intellectual explanation of Buddhist doctrine rather than the experiential insight that comes from the practice of meditation. So, for a long while he ignored Ji. The Confucian, however, remained patiently outside the hut, waiting several days for Bodhidharma to acknowledge him.

One night, it began to snow. The snow fell so heavily that by morning, it was up to Ji's knees. Seeing this, Bodhidharma finally spoke to his visitor, asking, "What is it you seek?"

"Your teaching," Ji told him.

"The teaching of the Buddha is subtle and difficult. Understanding can only be acquired through strenuous effort, doing what is hard to do and enduring what is hard to endure, continuing the practice for even countless eons of time. How can a man of scant virtue and great vanity, such as yourself, achieve it? Your puny efforts will only end in failure."

Ji drew his sword and cut off his left arm, which he presented to Bodhidharma as evidence of the sincerity of his intention.

"What you seek," Bodhidharma told him, "can't be sought through another."

"My mind isn't at peace," Ji lamented. "Please, master, pacify it."

"Very well. Bring your mind here, and I'll pacify it."

"I've sought it for these many years, even practicing sitting mediation as you do, but still I'm not able to get hold of it."

"There! Now it's pacified!"

And at these words—as when Mahakasyapa saw the Buddha twirling the flower between his fingers—Ji came to awakening. He came to the same experiential understanding that the Buddha, Mahakasyapa, and all the patriarchs before Bodhidharma had attained—that his basic nature, his "Buddha-nature," was no different from that of all existence. In acknowledgment of this attainment, Bodhidharma told him that henceforth his name would be Huike, which means "his understanding will do."

Bodhidharma remained at Shaolin for nine years, during which time only a few aspirants sought him out. His teaching was based on the practice of meditation and the attainment of awakening, but (in spite of his emphasis that Zen was a tradition "outside the scriptures and not dependent on words and letters") he also introduced his students to the *Lankavatara Sutra*. It would be his followers and descendents who would mold the old Brahmin's teaching into something thoroughly grounded in Chinese practicality.

In spite of the fact that he had only a handful of disciples, his teaching angered members of other Buddhist sects, and it is said that six attempts were made to poison him, all of which he thwarted.

Eventually Bodhidharma decided to return to India, and, in preparation for his departure, he called his chief disciples together and asked each of them to give him their understanding of the teaching of the meditation school.

The first to reply was a monk named Dao Fu, who said, "Reality is beyond yes and no, beyond all duality."

Bodhidharma told him, "You have my skin."

The second to speak was a nun, Zong Chi. "To my mind, truth is like the vision Ananda had of the Buddha-lands, glimpsed once and forever."

Bodhidharma told her, "You have my flesh."

Next came Dao Yu: "All things are empty. The elements of fire, air, earth, and water are empty. Form, sensation, perception, ideation, and consciousness—all of these also are empty."

Bodhidharma told him, "You have my bones."

Finally, there was only Huike. When Bodhidharma turned to him, Huike bowed and remained silent.

"Ah," Bodhidharma exclaimed in admiration. "You have my marrow."

Some accounts put Bodhidharma's age at 150 by the time he decided to return to India. In one account, he died en route and was buried by Huike in a cave on the banks of the Luo River.

One more story, however, is told of him.

A government official named Song Yun claimed that as he was returning to China from a visit to Central Asia he met Bodhidharma proceeding in the opposite direction, barefoot and carrying one sandal in his hands. When Bodhidharma's disciples heard this account, they opened the patriarch's tomb and found it empty except for a single sandal.

*Huike meditating*

CHAPTER TWO

# FOUR PATRIARCHS

Bodhidharma was Indian, but his disciples were not, and they began the process that resulted in the development of a Zen tradition that was uniquely Chinese. Earlier Buddhists in China had noted similarities between their teachings and native Daoism—which sought to bring its adherents into harmony with the Way (*Dao* or *Tao*) of nature and all being. Bodhidharma's disciples recognized that realizing the Dao was essentially the same thing as achieving Awakening or realizing one's Buddha-nature. As they adapted the Zen tradition to the Chinese temperament, they naturally assimilated Daoist terms and concepts.

## HUIKE

Huike had been forty years old when he met Bodhidharma, and he remained with the first patriarch for six years. When Bodhidharma decided to return to India, he formally acknowledged Huike as his successor by presenting him with his robe and begging bowl.

Huike accompanied his master as he set out on his return journey and may have buried Bodhidharma when he died before reaching India. After that, Huike became a wandering monk. He did not profess to be a teacher and contented himself with living among ordinary people. Over time, however, he was recognized as a man of deep spiritual awakening and began to acquire his own disciples.

Conditions had changed in China since Bodhidharma first landed on its shores. The emperor Wu had been removed from his throne and starved to death while under house arrest in 549. Wu's successors were traditional Confucianists who considered both Daoism (which had originated in China) and Buddhism (which they dismissed as something foreign) to be disruptive elements in society. Emperor Wu's vegetarian offerings to the ancestors may have contributed to that feeling, but in particular the celibate life of monks and nuns in Buddhist monasteries was repugnant to Confucianists, who put great value on family life and social responsibility. They argued that the monks and nuns living in temples such as Shaolin were parasites who contributed nothing to society.

An edict was passed that banned the practices of Buddhism and Daoism. Religious texts and artwork were destroyed. Monks and nuns, such as those formerly supported by the Emperor Wu, were ordered to return to lay life. During the height of this persecution, Huike, with the aid of another monk named Tanlin, concealed sutras and images of the Buddha from the authorities. Tanlin had also been a disciple of Bodhidharma and had written a biography of his teacher. For a while, Tanlin was a dedicated Zen practitioner.

While the persecution was raging, Huike and Tanlin retired together to the mountains by the Yangtze River. There it happened that Tanlin lost his arm during an encounter with brigands. Huike (who had sacrificed his own arm to gain the dharma) nursed Tanlin, cauterizing the wound with fire, and wrapping the stump in silk. All through the night, however, Tanlin bewailed his fate.

During the day, Huike went into the village to beg for food, which he brought back to share with Tanlin. But when he offered Tanlin a portion, the wounded man snapped that he could not take it up because he now only had one hand. Huike pointed out, gently, that it was no different with him. Tanlin failed to be comforted, however, and eventually fell away from the practice of Zen, complaining that his fate must be due to a karmic debt he had incurred in the past.

While in the mountains, Huike was approached one day by a layman with leprosy. The layman hoped that Huike could free him of the sins that he believed were the cause of his condition. Echoing his own teacher, Huike told the man, "Bring your sins here, and I'll rid you of them."

"When I reflect on my sins," the man admitted, "I'm not sure what they are."

"Then you're cleansed," Huike told him. "Now all that remains is for you to take refuge in the Buddha, the Dharma, and the Sangha."

"I understand that you are a member of a group known as the Sangha, but what are the Buddha and the Dharma?"

"Mind is Buddha. Mind is Dharma. Dharma and Buddha are not two. So it is with Sangha."

The leper then made one of those intuitive leaps of understanding only possible when one has been considering a problem, as he had been considering the problem of sin, for a long time: "Now I understand that sins are neither within nor without," he exclaimed. "Just as the Mind is, so is Buddha, so is Dharma. They aren't two."

Huike recognized that here was the man who would be his successor and gave him the name Sengcan, which means "jewel monk."

When the persecution began to abate, Huike returned to the capital, where he once again attracted disciples, much to the irritation of other teachers in the city. A meditation teacher named Dao Huan, in particular, resented the second patriarch's popularity. Desiring to find out what Huike was teaching, Dao Huan ordered one of his own disciples to go to Huike and pretend to ask for instruction. But once the disciple met the second patriarch he was so impressed that he took up Zen practice in earnest. When Dao Huan did not hear back from his disciple, he sent several messengers to fetch him, but each came back without the disciple. Some time later Dao Huan encountered his former disciple in the market and asked, "Why is it that I had to send so many messengers to bring you back? Why are you behaving in such an ungrateful manner? Didn't I exhaust myself in opening your eye to the truth?"

To which the former disciple replied, "My eye was right from the beginning. It was only because of you that I came to squint."

Dao Huan stormed off, even more angry with Huike than before.

For several years, Huike continued in this manner, living unostentatiously and teaching those who sought him out. One day he was talking to a group of people gathered in front of a Buddhist temple wherein the local priest was giving a discourse on the *Nirvana Sutra*. The priest's lecture was not very interesting, and some of those near the door, who could hear Huike speaking outside, stepped out to listen to him. The temple priest, annoyed by the situation, later denounced Huike to the authorities, asserting that the Zen master was promoting heresy. The charge would no doubt have been seconded by Dao Huan and others. The priest must have had some political influence because Huike was arrested and condemned to death. He did not resist being taken into custody and faced his execution with equanimity, remarking only that—like Tanlin—he no doubt had a karmic debt to repay.

He was one hundred and seven years old at the time of his death.

## JIANZHI SENGCAN

After the leper Jianzhi Sengcan had been ordained by Huike, he also lived in obscurity. When presenting him with Bodhidharma's robe and bowl, Huike had warned Sengcan of the civil unrest coming to the country. "Now that you have my teaching," Huike had instructed him, "it is your responsibility to preserve it. Don't make your dwelling in the cities and towns where you will draw the attention of the authorities, but go to the mountains."

Little is known of Sengcan's activities in the mountains, but he is recognized as the author of the *Xinxin Ming* (*Inscription on the Believing Mind*), a verse composition still popular with Zen practitioners. The following passages, "liberally" translated by D. T. Suzuki, show how Daoist terminology had been united with Buddhist principles:

> The Perfect Way [Tao or Dao] knows no difficulties
> Except that it refuses to make preference:
> Only when freed from hate and love,
> It reveals itself fully and without disguise.

A tenth of an inch's difference,
And heaven and earth are set apart;
If you want to see it manifest,
Take no thought either for or against it.

To set up what you like against what you dislike—
This is the disease of the mind:
When the deep meaning of Tao is not understood
Peace of mind is disturbed and nothing is gained.

The Tao is perfect like unto vast space,
With nothing wanting, nothing superfluous:
It is indeed due to making choice
That suchness is lost sight of.

Pursue not the outer entanglements,
Dwell not in the inner void;
When the mind rests serene in the oneness of things,
The dualism vanishes by itself.
. . . .
When we return to the root, we gain the meaning. . . .
. . . .
Try not to seek after the true,
Only cease to cherish opinions.

Tarry not with dualism,
Carefully avoid pursuing it;
As soon as you have right and wrong,
Confusion ensues, the mind is lost.
. . . .
The object is an object for the subject,
The subject is a subject for an object:
Know that the relativity of the two
Rests ultimately on the oneness of the void.
. . . .

The infinitely small is as large as large can be,
When external conditions are forgotten;
The infinitely large is as small as small can be,
When objective limits are put out of sight.

. . . .

One in all
All in one—
If only this is realized;
No more worry about your not being perfect!

The believing mind is not divided,
And undivided is the unbelieving mind—
This is where words fail,
For it is not of the past, future, or present.[3]

## DAYI DAOXIN

Regardless of how reclusive Zen masters were, highly motivated students continued to seek them out. So it was that Dayi Daoxin tracked down Sengcan. The third patriarch asked his visitor what he was looking for, and Daoxin replied: "Please show me the way to achieve liberation."

"Who is it that holds you in bondage?" Sengcan asked.

"Well, no one," Daoxin admitted.

"Then why are you seeking liberation?"

These words startled the young man, and he became Sengcan's disciple. After many years, he too attained awakening and Sengcan declared him his successor, giving him the robe and bowl that had been passed down from Bodhidharma.

By the time of Daoxin, the suppression of Buddhism had abated and monasteries were once again open. A formal tradition of Zen training was starting to evolve. Daoxin instructed his disciples to be earnest in their practice of *zuo chan* (*zazen* in Japanese) or sitting meditation. "Zazen is basic to all else. Don't bother reading the sutras; don't become involved in discussions. If you can refrain from doing so and concentrate instead on zazen, for as much as thirty-five years or more, you will benefit. Just as a monkey will eat a nut still in its shell although it's only satisfied when it has patiently extracted the nut from that shell, so there are only a few who will bring their zazen to fulfillment."

Zazen was brought to fulfillment in the "emptiness" of which Bodhidharma had spoken to Emperor Wu. But Daoxin warned, "When those who are still young in the practice see emptiness, this is seeing emptiness, but it isn't real emptiness. To those who are mature in the practice and who have attained emptiness, they see neither emptiness nor non-emptiness."

## NIUTOU FARONG

Two schools of Zen are said to have descended from Daoxin's teaching. The first was the Niutou, or Ox-head School, which only survived for a few generations. The actual founder of this school was the hermit Farong who lived in a small temple in the Niutou Mountains. He lived such a holy life that birds brought him offerings of wild flowers. Farong's fame was such that Daoxin's curiosity was aroused and he determined to visit the recluse; others, however, warned him that Farong was so committed to his practice of meditation that he would not even acknowledge the presence of people who sought him out.

Undiscouraged, Daoxin made his way into the mountains and at length found Farong, just as he had been described, sitting in meditation on a stone outside the small temple he maintained.

Daoxin sat opposite the hermit and when, at last, the hermit glanced at him, Daoxin asked: "Reverend Sir, may I ask what you're doing?"

"I'm contemplating Mind," Farong answered.

"Ah. May I ask: *who* is he who is contemplating, and what mind is it that's being contemplated?"

Farong was taken aback, uncertain how to answer these questions. Suspecting that his visitor might be someone more accomplished than himself, he rose from the stone on which he had been sitting and greeted Daoxin formally, inviting him to stay and have a cup of tea.

While they were chatting, Daoxin heard the roar of a wild beast in the woods, and he was startled. Farong smiled and remarked, "I see it's still with you."

Daoxin made no comment, but, when Farong went into his dwelling to prepare the tea, Daoxin took the opportunity to write the name of the Buddha on the stone where Farong had been sitting. When he returned, Farong saw the sacred name on his stone and hesitated to desecrate it by sitting down.

"Mmm," Daoxin murmured. "I see it's still with you."

On hearing these words, Farong came to genuine awakening, and the birds no longer brought him wildflowers.

## DAMAN HONGREN

The second school to descend from Daoxin was the East Mountain School of his successor, the fifth patriarch, Hongren.

The story is told that an elderly tree-planter heard Daoxin speaking one day and felt a great longing to become his disciple. But because of his age, he believed he was too old to begin the practice of Zen. Somewhat despondent, he returned to his home and along the way came upon a young woman washing clothes on the bank of a river. He spoke to her, telling her that he sought to be reborn in order to become a disciple of the fourth patriarch and asked if she would be willing to be his mother in his new life. As odd a proposition as this was, the girl agreed to do so. The tree planter then died, and the young laundress found herself pregnant. When her child was born, the girl's parents tried to conceal their daughter's disgrace by throwing it into the river. But the newborn floated on the water and survived to be raised by others.

Now named Hongren, the child came to visit Daoxin when he was only six years old and asked to be admitted to the sangha. Daoxin asked the boy what his family name (*xing*) was, and Hongren replied with a clever pun: "I have a nature (*xing*) but it is not an ordinary one." Although the characters for "name" and "nature" are different, they are pronounced the same.

"What is it then?" Daoxin inquired, still asking for the precocious child's name.

"It is Buddha-nature [*fo xing*]."

"So you have no name [*xing*]?"

"No, master," the boy continued the pun, "because it [referring to his nature] is empty."

Daoxin accepted Hongren as a disciple, despite his age, and the boy dedicated himself to the practice with fervor. Zen chroniclers record that he worked in the monastery during the day and then often remained up until dawn sitting in meditation.

When Daoxin retired, he named Hongren his successor, passing on Bodhidharma's robe and bowl. The fifth patriarch then moved to East Mountain. He was already famous and quickly attracted a large group of disciples. There were even invitations from the emperor to come to the city, which Hongren declined, saying that he would refuse even if threatened with execution—an answer it is said the emperor admired.

On East Mountain, Hongren taught his disciples Daoxin's discipline of zazen. The Zen School was still small, and some of Hongren's students wondered why he hid away in the mountains rather than teaching in the cities, where more students might be attracted. Hongren offered this analogy: "Where are the trees found that are used for making the pillars and beams of a large building? They aren't found in populated areas where they may be cut down for trivial reasons such as for firewood. They're found in secluded mountain valleys where they're free to grow as large as they can. In the same way, those who seek to grow in the dharma must live apart from the large population centers so that they too may grow unmolested, undistracted by trivialities. Studying in this manner, away from distractions, they grow strong."

It was to this isolated mountain temple that a young, illiterate woodcutter named Huineng would make his way.

*Huineng (who had been a woodcutter as a child)*
*chopping bamboo*

# CHAPTER THREE

# HUINENG

The story of Dajian Huineng is one of the best known in the Zen tradition and is recorded in a document entitled *The Platform Sutra of the Sixth Patriarch*. This purports to be a transcript of statements made by Huineng from his seat on the platform in the meditation hall. It begins with his account of how he came to be Hongren's successor.

He tells his disciples that his father had been a disgraced government official who had died when Huineng was only three years old, leaving his wife and child in extreme poverty. Once the boy was old enough, he took on the responsibility of supporting his mother by gathering and selling firewood. As a commoner, he had no schooling, and, in the chronicles of Zen, stress is put on the fact that he was not able to read or write.

When he in his mid-twenties, he was going about his rounds and happened to hear a man chanting a sutra. Although Huineng was unfamiliar with the sutra, when he heard the phrase "let thought arise without resting it anywhere" he came to a deep spontaneous awakening. He asked the man what he was reciting and was told that it was the *Diamond Sutra*.

"How did you come by this sutra?" Huineng inquired.

"I visited the East Mountain Monastery," the man explained, "and the master there gave it to me."

"And who's that master?"

"He's Master Hongren, who is called the Fifth Patriarch, and he has one thousand monks studying with him. But he encourages even laypeople to recite this sutra so that they might realize their true nature, their Buddha-nature, for themselves. If you want to learn about this sutra, he's the man you should go to see."

Huineng was eager to visit the Fifth Patriarch, but he first needed to arrange for his mother's care. Fortunately, a villager who learned of his desire to travel to East Mountain provided him with a sum of money that ensured his mother's security. Once the appropriate arrangements had been made, he set out on the journey that took thirty days to complete.

The Fifth Patriarch received Huineng formally, asking his name and inquiring where he had come from. The young man replied that he was a commoner from Guangdong in the South and that he had come to East Mountain in order to attain Buddhahood.

The patriarch tested Huineng by asking: "How is it possible for someone like you to attain Buddhahood? Southerners are barbarians and don't have Buddha-nature."

Undeterred, Huineng responded: "There may be Southerners and there may be Northerners, but what has that to do with Buddha-nature?"

"You are a very clever barbarian," Hongren said. "But you aren't a monk, so you can't stay in the monastery. Report to the granary. You may begin work there."

The young man was put to work hulling rice and splitting firewood. It is said that he was so slight that he had to have a stone tied to his belt in order to give him enough weight to trample the rice.

He worked without any instruction from Hongren for eight months before the master came to see how he was doing. At that time, the patriarch confirmed Huineng's awakening. "Among the monks in this monastery there are none who have attained what you have attained," he added. "Instead of striving to open their mind's eye, they seek only to accumulate merit in hopes of obtaining a more auspicious rebirth in the future. If they heard that a layman, an illiterate lad at that, had achieved awakening, they wouldn't believe it, and they might do you harm. Or they might come to lose respect for the teachings of Buddhism altogether. So for a while, you and I will keep this secret."

Huineng agreed to do as the master instructed. He kept away from the monks' quarters and the meditation hall, and he pursued his chores in the granary.

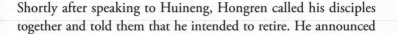

Shortly after speaking to Huineng, Hongren called his disciples together and told them that he intended to retire. He announced

that he needed to identify a successor to follow him as Sixth Patriarch, and he challenged the monks to submit their understanding
of the dharma in a short poem, or *gatha*. The one whose poem
demonstrated the deepest insight, he told them, would receive the
bowl and robe of Bodhidharma.

The monks consulted among themselves and decided that surely
it would be the senior monk, Shenxiu, who should succeed the master and therefore there was no point in anyone else submitting a
poem for consideration. Shenxiu, however, was not confident of his
own understanding of the dharma, so he decided to submit his poem
anonymously. If Hongren approved it, Shenxiu would acknowledge
having written it, but if the patriarch did not, then Shenxiu would
be able to retain face by keeping silent. "If that's the case, however,"
he reflected, "then I've wasted many years in this monastery and have
gained the admiration of others without just cause."

There were three corridors in the meditation hall that had been
whitewashed in preparation for a series of murals. An artist from
the capital had been commissioned to portray significant events in
the lives of the four patriarchs who had come before Hongren for
the edification of the monks and visiting laypeople. That midnight,
Shenxiu inscribed his poem on one of these walls. He wrote:

> The body is like the Buddha-tree,
> the mind a stand with a mirror bright.
> Take care to wipe it clean,
> and don't let dust or dirt alight!

The next morning, Hongren met with the artist who was to do
the murals. When they found the gatha inscribed on the wall, Hongren told him, "I'm sorry to have inconvenienced you by asking you
here today, but your presence is no longer necessary. These walls
don't need to be painted now."

Then he called the monks together and, in their presence, he
had incense lit and burnt in front of the poem to honor it. "We will
leave this stanza here so that all may read and benefit from it," he

announced. "All those who practice as it describes will undoubtedly acquire great merit by doing so."

Then he signaled Shenxiu to meet with him privately. When they were alone, Hongren told Shenxiu that he suspected him to have been the author of the gatha, and the head monk admitted that was the case. "I'm not so vain that I expect to be declared your successor," he said. "But would you be kind enough to tell me whether I've shown any indication of wisdom."

"The enlightenment of the Buddha comes when one realizes one's true-self, the self that is neither born nor dies," Hongren told him. "You haven't achieved this yet. You've come to the gate, but you still need to pass through. Go to your quarters and reflect on this. When you come to complete realization, submit another poem, and, if it demonstrates true understanding, I'll transmit the robe and bowl to you."

Shenxiu bowed and took his leave. He meditated on the Fifth Patriarch's words for days but was unable come to any clearer understanding.

Meanwhile, the other monks had taken to reciting Shenxiu's stanza as a mantra. It so happened that, while he was hulling rice, Huineng heard one of them do so. The young man asked the monk about the gatha, and the monk replied disdainfully, "You Southerner, how is it that you alone of everyone in this monastery don't know of this gatha composed by our chief monk, who's surely to become our new master when the present patriarch retires. It's inscribed on the wall of the corridor in the meditation hall for all to read and admire."

Huineng explained that he had not yet visited the meditation hall. "But I'd be grateful if you'd show me the stanza so that I can honor it as well as everyone else."

The monk directed Huineng to the spot where Shenxiu had written his poem. When Huineng got to the corridor, he found a district official there as well. The young man asked the official to read the poem to him, explaining that he could not read himself. After hearing Shenxiu's poem once more, Huineng said: "I've also composed a poem. Could you write it on the wall for me?"

The district officer expressed surprise that someone who could not read would be able to compose a lyric, but he agreed to do so, asking only, "If you're successful in acquiring the dharma, please don't forget me."

The response that Huineng made to Shenxiu's poem went:

> The body is not a tree,
> nor the mind a mirror bright.
> Since from the beginning not a thing exists,
> where can dirt and dust alight?

There is a significant difference between Huineng's and Shenxiu's gathas. Shenxiu's remains dualistic. He compares the mind to a mirror reflecting a world external to it. For Huineng there is no separation, no mirror distinct from what it reflects and no world distinct from its reflection in mind. The reason for this difference is that Shenxiu's understanding, as Hongren pointed, was theoretical, while Huineng's was grounded in his awakened mind.

Later that day, Hongren found a group of monks gathered before the two verses, discussing who the author of the second could be. The patriarch read the new verse, then slipped off his shoe and used it to erase the new lines from the wall. The monks supposed this to mean that he disapproved of them. But when no one was observing him, Hongren went to the granary. There he told Huineng, "Those who seek the Way must be prepared to risk their lives for it." Huineng had nothing to say in reply. Then, the patriarch asked, "Is the rice ready?"

"Ready long ago," Huineng said.

Hongren told the young man to come to his quarters later that night. Huineng visited the Fifth Patriarch at midnight. When he did so, Hongren acknowledged Huineng as his successor and passed over Bodhidharma's bowl and robe to his keeping. "But you need to understand that there will be those who will object to you having these. So you must leave East Mountain and conceal yourself until the time is ready for you." The patriarch also told him that it would no longer be necessary to continue the practice of transmitting the robe and bowl. "The real transmission," he explained, "is from mind to mind. It's because of that transmission, and not because of these relics, that you'll be known as the Sixth Patriarch of our school."

Hongren accompanied Huineng to a landing on the river where they found a boat. The Fifth Patriarch seated himself in the boat and took up the oars. When Huineng offered to take the oars himself, the older man said, "It's appropriate that I be the one to ferry you across."

"When I was in illusion, then I needed the guidance of another," Huineng replied. "But now that my mind's eye is open, it's appropriate for me to cross the waters of birth and death by my own efforts."

So Hongren turned the oars over to Huineng and got out of the boat, and the younger man set out on his own.

Three days later, a rumor went through the monastery that an illiterate layman had stolen the sacred relics of the First Patriarch and fled south with them. Outraged at this sacrilege, a group of monks went in pursuit of the thief. They were led by a monk named Ming, who, before entering the sangha, had been a general of the fourth rank. In spite of his time at the monastery, Ming still had a soldier's manner and temperament. For two months the group followed Huineng. As the chase went on, the other pursuers, one after another, gave up until Ming alone continued undaunted.

Eventually Ming caught up with Huineng at a pass in the mountains. When the new patriarch saw the former soldier approaching, he placed the robe and bowl on a rock and waited for his pursuer to come nearer.

"You've come for these," he called when Ming was within hearing distance. "These are merely symbols of our tradition. They have no other value. If you want them, take them."

But when Ming tried to pick up the items, he was unable to lift them. Shaken by this inability, Ming paused a moment, then said:

"If that's so, I have no use for them. What I've come for is the dharma. So if you are indeed the successor of Hongren, please dispel my ignorance."

"If you've come for the dharma, then please compose yourself in meditation and refrain from thinking about anything. When your mind is still and receptive, I'll teach you."

Ming did as he was told, and when Huineng saw that the monk was in a state of concentration, he commanded him: "Without thinking about good or bad, *show* me your face before your parents were born."

As soon as he heard these words, Ming also attained awakening. He bowed before the younger man, saying, "Besides this, is there anything else? Are there other secret doctrines?"

"Nothing I've said is secret. If you look within, you'll find all the secrets within your own mind."

"I spent many years on the East Mountain," Ming said, "but was unable to realize my self-nature. Now, thanks to your guidance, I realize it in the same way that one who drinks water knows whether it is hot or cold. You're now my master, and I your disciple."

"Let's, rather, say that both of us are disciples of Master Hongren," Huineng suggested.

Four years after acknowledging Huineng as his successor, Hongren died in 675. He was seventy-four years old. The Sixth Patriarch was still residing in seclusion in the mountains. He lived for a while with a group of hunters, secretly freeing the animals the hunters trapped in their nets.

When he was thirty-nine years old, he decided it was time to assume his responsibilities, and he made his way to Fat Shin Temple. As he approached it, he saw a group of monks observing and discussing a flapping pennant. The first monk said, "It's the pennant that moves." Another objected, "The pennant is an inanimate object and has no power to move; it is the wind that moves." Then a third said, "The flapping of the pennant is due to the combination of flag and wind."

Huineng interrupted the discussion, telling the monks, "It's neither wind nor pennant that moves; rather it's your own minds that move."

When the temple master, Yin Zong, overheard this encounter, he was impressed by Huineng's authoritative manner and invited him to describe the teachings he brought from the Master of the East Mountain.

"My master had no special teaching," Huineng said. "He stressed only the need to see into one's true nature through one's own efforts."

After this, Huineng established himself at the Baolin Monastery in the mountains of the South, and here it is said thousands of people came seeking to become his disciples. His fame spread as far as the capital, where the emperor invited him to move, but Huineng declined the invitation as his master, Hongren, had done before him.

Meanwhile, in the north, Hongren's chief monk, Shenxiu was gathering his own following.

雲山高隱

金門羽客方二壺為
天岸上人畫

Lofty Hermitage in Cloudy Mountain *by Fang Fanghu*

# CHAPTER FOUR

# THE RISE OF THE SOUTHERN SCHOOL

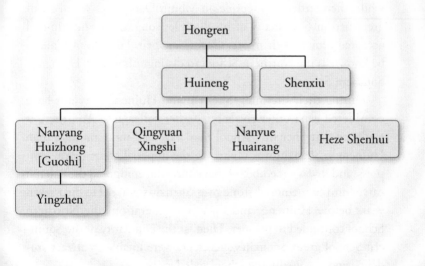

## SHENXIU

Today Huineng is the last of the Chinese Zen teachers to be referred to as a patriarch, but this was not an uncontested title. In Shenxiu's epitaph, he also is identified as Hongren's successor and Sixth Patriarch.

In contrast to Huineng, who was portrayed as an illiterate woodcutter, Shenxiu was a scholar before being drawn to the Zen tradition. Although he was ordained a monk at the age of twenty, he was fifty by the time he came to study with Hongren. He distinguished himself by his knowledge of the Confucian and Daoist texts as well as by the breadth of his understanding of Buddhism, and he quickly rose to the rank of chief monk. He stayed with Hongren for six years.

After leaving Hongren, Shenxiu lived as a hermit for a long while, then settled at a temple on Mount Dangyang. When Hongren died in 674, many of his disciples sought out Shenxiu and accepted him as their master's legitimate heir. His school came to be known as the Northern School to distinguish it from Huineng's Southern School.

During their lifetimes, Shenxiu and Huineng may not have considered each other rivals but rather colleagues. And there is evidence that Shenxiu's school may have had more prestige than Huineng's. Shenxiu was invited to the imperial court by the empress, and it was a member of that court who composed the epitaph carved in the memorial stone over Shenxiu's grave. He died seven years before Huineng, and for a few generations the Northern School continued to prosper. Then, as the popularity of the Southern School grew, Shenxiu's successors were unable to attract students, and eventually the school faded away.

Both history and legend are recorded by those who survive, so regardless of what Shenxiu's school actually taught, the version of those teachings we now have is presented by Huineng's followers. According to them, the primary difference between the schools had to do with the issue of whether one comes to awakening gradually or suddenly. As Shenxiu's gatha suggests, he viewed awakening as something acquired gradually, comparable to the process of burnishing a metal surface so that it slowly reflects a clearer and sharper image. Huineng's school, on the other hand, insisted that true awakening necessarily occurred suddenly and immediately. Although there may be activity leading up to that experience, the experience itself comes all at once. The Southern School might compare the process to chipping away at a stone barrier. While it could take a long while to pierce the barrier, once one does, the view on the other side becomes visible immediately.

Because of its emphasis on gradual "polishing," Shenxiu's school advocated prolonged periods of meditation, but it also promoted sutra study and chanting as well as other ritual activities that Huineng's school did not value as highly. Even more so than the Northern School, the Southern School focused on meditation, but it also recognized that the enlightenment experience could be acquired—as Huineng had acquired it—during activities as mundane as chopping and hauling wood.

The story is told of one of Shenxiu's students who paid a visit to Huineng. When Huineng asked him to describe what he had learned so far, he said: "My teacher asserts that the teaching of all the Buddhas is found in one's own mind, and that to seek the teaching outside of one's self is the same as running away from one's father and abandoning one's home." This much Huineng could agree with. But the student went on to say: "We're taught to stop the workings of our minds, to control our wandering thoughts, and to sit in meditation for long periods of time without moving."

"To stop the working of the mind and to sit without moving isn't Zen," Huineng snapped back. "It's a disease. There's no profit to be found in such a method."

The visitor asked, then, how one should practice.

"While alive, one sits and doesn't lie down," Huineng told him. "When one is dead, one lies down but doesn't sit."

## HUINENG (CONTINUED)

According to a story from the Southern School, shortly after Huineng left Hongren, the governor of the district happened to hear that an illiterate commoner had been chosen to succeed the Fifth Patriarch. Curious about this choice, he went to see Hongren.

"You have a thousand disciples," he said. "In what way does this Huineng distinguish himself from the others that you should bestow upon him the honor of possessing the bowl and robe of Bodhidharma?"

"Nine hundred and ninety-nine of my disciples have a good understanding of Buddhism," the master replied. "The only exception is Huineng. He isn't to be compared with the others, and for that reason I've transmitted the bowl and robe to him."

In another story, a monk asked Huineng, "Who now has the secret teachings of Master Hongren?"

"Someone who understands Buddhism," Huineng said.

"Do you, then, have them, sir?"

"I don't understand Buddhism," declared Huineng.

On another occasion, Huineng came upon a Buddhist nun who was chanting selections from the *Maha Parinirvana Sutra*. Huineng asked her if she understood the significance of the words she chanted, and she admitted that she found the sutra difficult to understand. So Huineng started to explain it to her. Pleased with his commentary, she brought out a copy of the text with the intention of asking him to help her understand other passages she found obscure.

She pointed to one with her finger, and Huineng told her: "I'm not an educated man, and I can't read. But if you read the passage to me, I'll do my best to help you with it."

"How is that?" she asked in wonder. "How can you understand the meaning of the text if you can't read the words?"

"The teaching of the Buddhas isn't found in written language," he answered.

The nun was so impressed by the Sixth Patriarch that she organized the local village to help him rebuild an old, abandoned temple and supplied him with food and other necessities while he lived there. This was the Baolin Temple, where Huineng would eventually deliver the *Platform Sutra*.

## NANYANG HUIZHONG

Instead of identifying a single individual to carry on his teaching, Huineng had three major heirs. The first was Nanyang Huizhong, more popularly known to later generations as the "National Teacher" (Guoshi) because, like his master, he was invited to the imperial court, but, unlike Huineng, he accepted the invitation. Huizhong was not the only Zen master to be given this title, but he is the one with whom it is most commonly associated.

After completing his work with Huineng, Huizhong retired to a temple on Mount Baiya, where he remained for forty years. Although he never left the temple during that period, his fame extended to the court, and the emperor invited him to come to the capital. Huizhong deferred twice before finally agreeing to a third invitation. It is said that the emperor was so pleased with his acceptance that when the carriage carrying Huizhong approached the palace, the emperor himself went out to grasp its shaft and help pull it the final distance.

An inquirer once asked Huizhong how he could attain Buddhahood. Huizhong told him that Buddhahood was attained only by the use of "no mind" (*wuxin* or *wu-shin* in the Wade-Giles Romanization).

"But if no mind is used, who can attain Buddhahood?" the inquirer asked.

> Hui-chung [Huizhong]: "By no-mind the task is accomplished by itself. Buddha, too, has no mind."
>
> Inquirer: "The Buddha has wonderful ways and knows how to deliver all beings. If he had no mind, who would ever deliver all beings?"
>
> Hui-chung: "To have no mind means to deliver all beings. If he sees any being who is to be delivered, he has a mind (*yu-shin*) and is surely subject to birth and death."
>
> Inquirer: "'No-mind-ness' (*wu-shin*) is then already here, and how was it that the Buddha appeared in the world and left behind ever so many sermons? Is this a fiction?"
>
> Hui-chung: "With all the teachings left by him, the Buddha is *wu-shin* (no-mind)."
>
> Inquirer: "If all his teachings come from his no-mind-ness, they must be also no-teachings."
>
> Hui-chung: "To preach is not (to preach), and not (to preach) is to preach."
>
> Inquirer: "If his teachings come out of his no-mind-ness, is my working karma the outcome of cherishing the idea of a mind (*yu-shin*)?"
>
> Hui-chung: "In no-mind-ness there is no karma. But (as long as you refer to working out your karma) karma is already here, and your mind is subjected to birth and death. How then can there be no-mind-ness (in you)?"
>
> Inquirer: "If no-mind-ness means Buddhahood, has your Reverence already attained Buddhahood, or not?"
>
> Hui-chung: "When mind is not (*wu*), who talks about attaining Buddhahood? To think that there is something called

Buddhahood which is to be attained, this is cherishing the idea of a mind (*yu-shin*); to cherish the idea of a mind is an attempt to accomplish something that flows out . . . ; this being so, there is no no-mind-ness here."

Inquirer: "If there is no Buddhahood to be attained, has your Reverence the Buddha-function?"

Hui-chung: "Where mind itself is not, whence its functioning?"

Inquirer: "One is then lost in outer no-ness (*wu*); may this not be an absolutely nihilistic view?"

Hui-chung: "From the first there is (no viewer and) no viewing; and who says this to be nihilist?"

Inquirer: "To say that from the first nothing is, is this not falling into emptiness?"

Hui-chung: "Even emptiness is not, and where is the falling?"

Inquirer: "Both subject and object are negated (*wu*). Suppose a man were all of a sudden to make his appearance here and cut your head off with a sword. Is this to be considered real (*yu*) or not real (*wu*)?"

Hui-chung: "This is not real."

Inquirer: "Pain or no pain."

Hui-chung: "Pain too is not real."

Inquirer: "Pain not being real, in what path of existence would you be reborn after death?"

Hui-chung: "No death, no birth, and no path."

Inquirer: "Having already attained the state of absolute no-ness, one is perfect master of oneself; but how would you use the mind (*yung-hsin*), when hunger and cold assail you?"

Hui-chung: "When hungry, I eat, and when cold I put on more clothes."

Inquirer: "If you are aware of hunger and cold, you have a mind (*yu-hsin*)."

Hui-chung: "I have a question for you: Has the mind you speak of as a mind a form?"

Inquirer: "The mind has no form."

Hui-chung: "If you already knew that the mind has no form, that means that from the first the mind is not, and how could you talk about having a mind?"[4]

When he felt his death approaching, Huizhong determined to identify a successor and chose his attendant, Yingzhen. However, as a final test, he called the attendant by name one day: "Yingzhen!"

The attendant presented himself at the door and bowed. "Yes, sir!"

"Mmm. You're here. Very well, you may return to your room."

But as soon as the attendant departed, Huizhong called again: "Yingzhen!"

"Yes, sir!" the attendant answered, returning at once and bowing in the doorway.

"Return to your room," Huizhong instructed him.

But when the attendant had departed, Huizhong called a third time: "Yingzhen!"

Once more, the attendant returned to the doorway and bowed. "Yes, sir."

Huizhong said: "For a long time I feared that I'd been betraying you, but really it was you who were betraying me."

After this, Huizhong paid a final visit to his imperial patron. The emperor could see that the Zen master was in failing health and asked, "After you have departed from this world, what can I do to honor your memory?"

"Build a seamless tower for me," Huizhong told him.

Unsure of what Huizhong meant, the emperor asked, "What design do you wish us to follow in building this tower?"

Huizhong sat silent a while, then asked, "Do you understand?"

"No, I don't," the emperor admitted.

"After my death, Yingzhen will understand the matter."

The National Teacher died on January 4, 776. After the funeral ceremonies, the emperor summoned Yingzhen before him and described his final conversation with Huizhong. "And then he told me," the emperor concluded, "that after his death you'd understand this matter."

Yingzhen sat silent before the emperor for a while, then asked, "Do you understand?"

"No, I don't understand," the emperor said.

Yingzhen then recited a verse:

> South of the [Xiang]
> And north of the [Tan]
> Is a country abounding in gold.
> Under a shadowless tree, a ferry boat,
> In the Emerald Pavilion, no one who knows.[5]

## YINGZHEN

After his encounter with the emperor, Yingzhen went off to live and teach on Mount Tan Yuan. On the first anniversary of Huizhong's death, Yingzhen arranged a memorial banquet. One of his monks (perhaps whimsically, perhaps to make a point) asked if they could expect the National Teacher to attend.

"No, he won't," Yingzhen admitted.

"In that case, why are we offering this banquet?"

"So the truth will not be lost."

## QINGYUAN XINGSHI

Although Yingzhen gathered his own students, no lasting school followed him. It was from Huineng's two other heirs, Qingyuan Xingshi and Nanyue Huairang, that the Five Houses of Zen would descend.

Qingyuan began his search for the dharma as a young man, but it was several years before he came to study with the Sixth Patriarch. At their initial interview, Qingyuan asked, "In what I do, how can I avoid falling into the stages of spiritual development?"

"What is it that you do?" Huineng asked.

"I don't even know the Four Noble Truths."

"And what stages have you fallen into?"

"If I don't even know the Four Noble Truths, what stages could I fall into?"

Huineng was pleased with the answer and accepted Qingyuan as a disciple.

Qingyuan was the author of this famous description of Zen: "Before I began the study of Zen, mountains were mountains and waters were waters. When I first achieved some insight into the truth of Zen through the benevolence of my teacher, mountains were no longer mountains and waters no longer waters. But now that I've attained full enlightenment, I'm at rest, and mountains are once again mountains and waters are waters."

Three of the five schools would derive from his descendants: the Caodong (J: Soto) School, founded by Dongshan Liangjie (J: Tozan Ryokai), the largest existing Zen school today; the Yunmen School, founded by Yunmen Wenyan; and the Fayan School, founded by Fayan Wenyi.

## Nanyue Huairang

When Nanyue first came to see Huineng, the patriarch asked him where he had come from.

"From Dongshan," the visitor replied.

Huineng then asked: "*What* is it that's come from Dongshan?"

It took Nanyue six years to resolve this question, and when he did, he stated, "Even when it's said to be something, it's off the mark!"

Like his predecessors in the Zen tradition, Nanyue was a meditation teacher, and yet, like Huineng, he stressed that meditation was not something limited to the practice of sitting. It is recorded that he told his students: "Are you here to learn zazen or sitting Buddhahood? If you seek to learn zazen, know that Zen isn't sitting or lying down. If you seek to learn sitting Buddhahood, know that Buddha isn't a fixed form. The teaching of non-attachment instructs you neither to accept nor to reject, neither to adopt nor refuse. If you labor to become a sitting Buddha, you kill the Buddha. If you are attached to sitting, you won't attain awakening."

The two houses to descend from Nanyue were the Guiyang School founded by Guishan Lingyou, and the Linji (J: Rinzai), founded by Linji Yixuan (J: Rinzai Gigen).

## Heze Shenhui

Although another heir of Huineng, Heze Shenhui, is not remembered in the traditional Zen tales that have come down to us, he played an important historical role in that chain of tales. He originally studied the Daoist teachings of Laozi and Zhuangzi, then trained with Shenxiu of the Northern School. When Shenxiu was summoned to serve at court, he suggested that Shenhui, who was still just a boy at the time, join Huineng's assembly in the south.

During one of his dharma talks, Huineng told the assembly, "There is something without name or description. It doesn't have eyes or ears, head or tail, neither front nor back, inside or outside. It's neither cause nor effect. What is it?"

When none of the older monks replied, Shenhui said, "It's the Buddha-nature, the source of all things."

"If it has neither name nor description," Huineng retorted, "how can you call it the Buddha-nature?"

"Buddha-nature has neither name nor description, but because my master asked what it was, name and description are used. However, even named and described, it remains without name or description."

Huineng struck the boy and dismissed the assembly. Later, however, Huineng sent for Shenhui and asked, "Today I struck you. Was it you or Buddha-nature that felt the blow?" When confronted with this question, Shenhui came to awakening. After this he served as Huineng's attendant until the Sixth Patriarch's death.

Huineng taught for thirty-seven years and, according to the codicil at the end of the *Platform Sutra*, the number of his disciples who achieved some degree of enlightenment was too large to count.

In August of 712, Huineng sensed the end of his life was approaching. He directed his disciples to start the construction of a stupa where his remains would be interred. A year later, on the 28th of July, he gave a last sermon in which he told his followers not to mourn his passing but rather to continue their practice just as they would if he were still alive. In spite of this command, the disciples wept openly. Only the young attendant, Shenhui did not show any outward emotion. Huineng praised him, saying, "Although you're young, you alone have attained the awareness that good and bad are the same; you alone are moved neither by praise nor by blame."

Then, at seventy-six years old, Huineng died. Bodhidharma's robe and bowl, along with other gifts Huineng had received during his life time, were buried with him.

It was only after Huineng's death that a rivalry broke out between his heirs and those of Shenxiu regarding which of the two men was Hongren's legitimate successor. Shenhui became a vociferous supporter of Huineng's claim to be the Sixth Patriarch, and to support his position he called together an assembly of Buddhist teachers. Here he told the others the story of the Sixth Patriarch as it is now known. The former attendant dismissed the legitimacy of Shenxiu and the school that descended from him, even accusing Shenxiu's heirs of trying to steal the relics of Hongren. The representative from the Northern School, not expecting the assembly to focus on this issue, was ill-prepared to counter Shenhui's assertions.

Several factors contributed to the eventual demise of the Northern School, but Shenhui's advocacy of Huineng was certainly one of them. All existing Zen schools today trace their lineages back to the Sixth Patriarch. However, none of those lineages pass through Shenhui. Unlike Qingyuan Xingshi and Nanyue Huairang, Shenhui had no heirs of note.

Solitary Angler *by Ma Yuan*

*During the Song dynasty, a style of painting evolved in China that was influenced by Zen sensibilities. These works were greatly admired by the Japanese pilgrims who visited China and brought the Zen tradition back with them. They also brought back samples of the art they found, and many of these pieces are now considered national treasures in Japan.*

*Ma Yuan (1175–1225) was one of the most influential of these Chinese artists. His style of painting, which made use of large amounts of empty space, would come to be imitated by Japanese admirers.*

# MAZU DAOYI

Within fifty years of the Sixth Patriarch's death, Zen was fully established on Chinese soil. At the end of the eighth century, two Zen masters in particular were revered. One was a student of Qingyuan, Shitou Xiqian, also known as Stone Head. The other was Nanyue's disciple, Mazu Daoyi, popularly referred to as the Great Solitary One. In their day it was said no one could be considered a serious student of Zen if they had not visited these two masters. Between them, they completed the slow process of the sinoization of the Buddhist meditation tradition that had originated in India.

Mazu is the first teacher to be associated with those unique behaviors that have since become associated in popular literature with Zen—such as striking his students or responding to questions with the meaningless shout, "*Ho!*" (J: *Kwatz!*). He was described as having the stride of a bull and the glare of a tiger and is recorded to have had the questionably useful ability to extend his tongue out so far that he could cover his nose with it.

He began his Zen training under one of Hongren's disciples who seems to have been more in sympathy with the Northern than the Southern School. That instructor taught him to strive to keep an empty mind during meditation. When Mazu came to Nanyue's monastery, he continued to practice as he had been shown. Nanyue happened to notice the young man's dedicated sitting and recognized he had the potential to become a strong monk. Nanyue asked him, "What is it that you're trying to accomplish by sitting like this?"

Probably surprised by the question, Mazu replied, "I want to attain Buddhahood."

Nanyue nodded his head, then, without a word, picked up a piece of broken tile that was lying on the ground and began to rub it vigorously. He kept this up so long that Mazu eventually inquired, "Master, if I may ask, what are you doing?"

"I'm polishing this tile to make it into a mirror."

"But no amount of polishing will turn a tile into a mirror!"

"Neither will any amount of meditation, as you practice it, make you into a Buddha."

"What should I do then?" Mazu asked.

"If you were driving a cart and it stopped, what would you do? Would you strike the cart or the ox?"

Mazu did not know how to reply.

"Consider your intention," Nanyue continued. "Is it to become a master of Zen (sitting meditation)? Or is it to attain Buddhahood. If what you wish is to study Zen, then know that Zen isn't a matter of sitting or lying down or any other position. If you wish to become a Buddha, then know that the Buddha is formless. Buddha has no particular posture, such as sitting in the cross-legged position. Buddha doesn't abide here or there. You can neither take hold of nor let go of Buddha. Trying to become a Buddha by sitting cross-legged kills the Buddha. Cling to this practice and you'll never attain the truth."

Hearing these words, Mazu felt refreshed, as if he had had a cool drink on a warm day. Bowing, he asked: "How should I strive to come into accord with the *samadhi* [concentration] of formlessness?" (In other words, how does one concentrate on formlessness— or the Dao.)

"Training yourself in the study of Mind is like sowing seeds in the ground," Nanyue said. "My instructions are like the rain watering these seeds. When conditions are appropriate, you'll find the Dao."

"If Dao has no form, how, then, can it be found?"

"There is a dharma-eye that is able to see Dao. This is the samadhi of formlessness."

"Is Dao subject to creation and destruction?"

"If you apply notions such as these, you'll never attain it."

The dialogue resembles that which took place between Huineng and Shenxiu's disciple. Although both appear to question the value of sitting meditation, what is actually being challenged is the style of meditation being practiced. It is not by "wiping the mirror of the mind" clear and sitting passively that one comes to awakening but rather through seeing into the nature of Mind, which is identical with one's Buddha-nature (the Indian term) or the Dao (the traditional Chinese term). And, of course, the action of Mind is not limited to a specific posture, such as sitting.

The goal of Zen training is to bring the practitioner to awakening, but that awakening must be sought within oneself rather than outside of oneself or from something acquired from another. A third-generation descendent of Mazu, Xiangyan Zhixian, would compare the relationship between the Zen teacher and his student to that of a hen and a chick still in its egg. It is the chick that must strive to break free of the shell, pecking at it from within. Only when the chick makes some progress can the hen assist by pecking at the outside of the shell. When the student is ready, the Zen teacher makes use of what Buddhism calls skillful means (*upaya*) to assist him to attain the final breakthrough. The skillful means used with one student are not necessarily appropriate to another; the choice of upaya employed by the teacher is dictated by the stage the student is at and the particular conditions of that student's quest for awakening. The stories of the Tang dynasty masters such as Mazu are stories about the wide variety of skillful means Zen masters developed during that age to assist their disciples to achieve awakening.

Once Nanyue confirmed Mazu's enlightenment, the latter sought to live a quiet and solitary life in an obscure rural district. He changed locations several times after students sought him out, but, wherever he went, people committed to achieving awakening found him.

Setting a pattern that would be repeated by other Zen teachers throughout what is called the Classic Period of Zen, Mazu's methods were challenging and often bizarre. His teaching was later described as "strange words and extraordinary actions." He did not comment on the sutras or engage in religious rites but rather took advantage of situations that arose during ordinary daily activities. In this manner, he helped 139 of his disciples achieve the status of Zen master.

A monk, for example, was engaged in trimming a wisteria vine with Mazu one day. The monk took the opportunity to pose the question, "Why did the First Patriarch come from the west?" This was a formula question meaning "what was the significance or content of Bodhidharma's teaching?"

The monk expected a verbal answer, but Mazu responded by motioning to him and whispering: "Come a little nearer, and I'll tell you."

When the monk went over to Mazu, the master kicked him so hard that the student fell over. As he hit the ground, the monk came to awakening, and he sat up laughing heartily.

"What is the meaning of this laughter?" Mazu asked.

"How strange! How odd! The teachings of the Buddha are so vast they can't be numbered. And yet I now see them all revealed on the tip of a single hair."

When the monk was asked about this episode later, he said that ever since he had been kicked by Mazu he had been unable to stop laughing.

The skillful means, the kick, used in this instance would have been both ineffective and cruel if the student had not attained a certain level of readiness through traditional meditation and other ritual practices.

When another monk asked Mazu, "How does one come into accordance with Dao?" Mazu replied by saying he himself had not come into accordance with it.

"In that case," the monk persisted, "what's the meaning of Zen?"

Mazu struck the monk, saying, "If I didn't hit you, I'd be laughed at from every direction."

A scholar who visited Mazu also needed only a nudge to come to awakening. Before coming to Mazu, the scholar had spent a long time studying the Buddhist scriptures. There were matters, however, which he still did not understand, and he hoped that Mazu would be able to resolve them. When the scholar presented himself, Mazu greeted him with the words: "What a magnificent structure with no Buddha in it!"

The scholar ignored this odd remark and asked permission to put a question: "I'm fairly well acquainted with the literature of Buddhism that has been translated into our language, but I still haven't been able to understand why it is that the Zen school claims that mind is Buddha."

"The very mind that doesn't understand is Buddha; there isn't any other," Mazu told him.

Still not grasping what Mazu was saying, the scholar persisted: "It's said that your First Patriarch brought a secret teaching from India, from where all the scriptures originate. Will Your Reverence please reveal that secret to me?"

"Well, I'm very busy just now. Perhaps you could come again at a later time."

Disappointed, the scholar bowed and turned to leave. Before he reached the door, however, Mazu called out: "Scholar!"

The scholar turned back to him.

"*What is it?*" Mazu demanded sharply.

The scholar came to awakening and at that moment understood the secret teaching of Bodhidharma. Full of gratitude, he bowed to Mazu.

"Don't be foolish," Mazu said. "What use is there in bowing?"

A similar story, however, did not have as happy an ending, demonstrating that, like all teachers, Mazu was not always able to help those who came to him. Another scholar sought an audience with him and asked what teaching he provided. Mazu avoided the question, asking the scholar about his own teaching.

"I lecture on more than twenty volumes of sutras," this scholar said proudly.

"So much!" Mazu said. "Are you a young lion?"

"I can't claim to be."

Mazu roared like a lion.

"Ah," the scholar murmured, "that, of course, is a teaching."

"What teaching is it?"

"The teaching of the lion coming forth from its den."

Mazu made no reply, and the scholar commented, "That, too, is a teaching."

"And what teaching is it?" Mazu asked.

"The teaching of the lion remaining in his den."

"If you know so much," Mazu said, "tell me then: neither going nor staying, what teaching is that?"

The scholar did not have an answer to the question and turned to leave.

"Scholar!" Mazu shouted. The scholar turned back. "What is it!?" Mazu demanded.

The scholar did not know how to reply and left.

"What a dull-witted fellow," Mazu commented.

When another monk came to Mazu saying that he sought awakening, Mazu asked, "Why have you come to me? You have your own treasure house. Look there for what you seek."

"Where is this treasure house of mine?" the monk inquired.

"What you're asking is your treasure house."

Pangyun, a lay Buddhist convert from Confucianism, asked, "Who is the man who has no companions among the ten thousand things of the world?" (In other words, who is the self-sufficient man?)

Mazu's answer was: "I'll tell you when you have swallowed up all the waters of the West River in a single gulp."

"I've already done so," Pangyun claimed.

"Then I've already told you!" Mazu shot back.

Mazu's remarks in each of these encounters were appropriate to the condition of the one asking instruction of him. Outside the specific context of the situation in which teacher and student were at the time, the answers make little sense. Stories such as these, as well as those told of the other Tang dynasty Zen masters, came to be used by later Zen masters as subjects assigned to their students for meditation. They were called *gongan* (J: *koan*), a term that meant "a public record" in the sense of the records kept by a court of law, records that establish precedent in jurisprudence. Koans came to be another skillful means by which teachers could help their students come to awakening. In order to do so, the meditator needed to put himself imaginatively into the situation of the student posing the original question and discover how the master's response was appropriate in those circumstances.

The events described in koans can be very peculiar. One day Mazu's disciple, Deng Yinfeng, was pushing a cart along a path beside which Mazu was sitting. The master's legs were extended into the path, and Yinfeng asked Mazu to draw back his legs.

"Once a thing is stretched out," Mazu said, "it can never be contracted."

"If that's the case," the disciple said, "then once a thing is pushed it can never be stopped." And he pushed the cart over Mazu's legs.

Later in the day, when it was time for the monks to assemble in the meditation hall, Mazu limped in, carrying an axe. "Where's the one who wounded this old man's legs with his cart?" he demanded.

Yinfeng stepped forward and knelt in front of his master, stretching out his neck as if presenting himself to be beheaded. Mazu set the axe down and withdrew.

The essence of Mazu's teaching was that Mind is Buddha. It is a simple statement but one that is easily misinterpreted. Mazu meant it literally. In one of his recorded sermons, he told the assembled monks: "Your very mind is Buddha. When Bodhidharma came from India to China, this was his teaching. There is no Buddha apart from Mind. Apart from Mind there is no Buddha."

When a monk asked, "What is the fundamental meaning of Buddhism?," Mazu asked, "What is the fundamental meaning of this moment?"

During Mazu's final illness, he received a visitor who inquired about his health. Mazu replied frankly, saying, "It will be odd if this old body is not carried to the graveyard within three days." The visitor, nonplussed, did not know how to respond. Mazu, referring to a passage in one of the sutras, said, "Sun-faced Buddha. Moon-faced Buddha."

The Sun-faced Buddha lives for one thousand eight hundred years. The Moon-faced Buddha lives only a single day and night. But whether one's lifetime is short or long, Buddha-nature is immeasurable.

Two Zen Masters

# CHAPTER SIX

# SHITOU XIQIAN AND HIS DISCIPLES

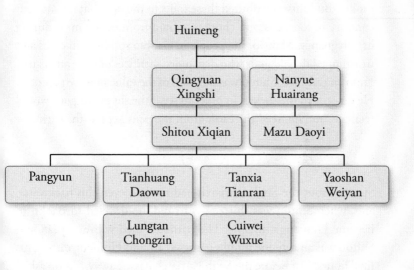

Huineng

Qingyuan Xingshi — Nanyue Huairang

Shitou Xiqian — Mazu Daoyi

Pangyun — Tianhuang Daowu — Tanxia Tianran — Yaoshan Weiyan

Lungtan Chongzin — Cuiwei Wuxue

## SHITOU XIQIAN

Mazu's great contemporary was Shitou Xiqian, whose name meant "Stone Head" or, more literally, the "Monk Who Lives on Top of the Stone." This referred to the location where he had built a small hut for himself. Shitou's fame rivaled that of Mazu during their lifetimes. Both of them gathered disciples in rural rather than urban settings, Mazu "west of the river" and Shitou in Hunan "south of the lake." The establishment of monasteries in the countryside was one of the factors that protected the Zen tradition during later persecutions of Buddhism in China.

Shitou had been born in Gaoyao, which at that time was a very primitive area. He was described as being a well-behaved and generous child who was bright and self-confident beyond his years. Orthodox Buddhists attributed these traits to the fact that his mother, contrary to local custom, chose to refrain from eating meat during her pregnancy. Many of the people in Gaoyao still lived in caves and worshipped the old gods who demanded sacrifices of wine and cattle. From an early age, Shitou was skeptical of the value of these practices. He desecrated the shrines in order to see if the supposed gods would retaliate, and he freed the cattle from the pens kept at the shrines.

Stories about the Sixth Patriarch had reached even this backwater, and, when Shitou was thirteen years old, he traveled to Baolin to become Huineng's disciple. The patriarch died within a year, and Shitou was among the monks gathered around Huineng during his final hours. Just before the Sixth Patriarch passed away, Shitou asked him, "Master, what should I do?"

"You should go to Xingshi," Huineng instructed him. But Shitou misunderstood him to say "*xinsi*" or "to seek thoughts." Shitou interpreted this to mean he should observe his thoughts during the practice of meditation, a technique advocated by certain teachers of the day. Seeking to follow what he understood to be Huineng's advice, Shitou dedicated himself to sitting in meditation, observing his thoughts as they rose and passed away. One day an older disciple of Huineng asked Shitou how he was practicing.

"I'm following our master's instructions; I'm observing the rise and fall of my thoughts," he replied.

The older monk gently suggested that Shitou may have misunderstood the Sixth Patriarch and told him he should seek out their master's heir, Qingyuan Xingshi.

Qingyuan had several monks studying with him, but when Shitou presented himself, the master remarked, "I have many cattle with two horns among my followers, but just one unicorn will do." It was a local belief that the appearance of a unicorn presaged a particularly auspicious occasion.

Qingyuan's students not only practiced meditation but also studied the Chinese translations of Buddhist texts from India as well as Indian and Chinese commentaries on those scriptures. Shitou's awakening came about as a result of a passage he read that declared: "Only those can be called holy who view the world in such a way that they see themselves in all things." Shitou had a sudden insight that this statement did not go far enough. He slammed his fist on the table, exclaiming: "Only those are holy who have no selves, for everything is their self. Who, then, can speak of you and me, of one's self and another's self?"

After Qingyuan recognized Shitou as one of his successors, the younger man retired to a temple on Mount Heng. It was there that he built his hut on the large, flat rock from which he derived his name. Here he attracted his own disciples and taught for twenty-three years. As the number of those disciples grew, Shitou moved to more spacious quarters.

Shitou's style of teaching lacked the dramatic elements—the "strange words and extraordinary actions"—employed by Mazu. And he was more open to the value of traditional devotional practices. In an often quoted sermon, he sounds more like Mazu's teacher, Nanyue, than he does like the Great Solitary One.

"I received my dharma, my teaching, from a preceding Buddha [Qingyuan]. It doesn't matter what method one uses—zazen or chanting sutras or other means of devotion. All that matters is attaining Buddha-wisdom. This very mind—this is Buddha. Mind, Buddha, sentient beings, pure wisdom, even defiling passions, these are all different names for one reality; they're all names for one and the same substance.

"What you must discover is your own Mind-essence. Realize that it's separate from creation and destruction, from permanence and extinction. Its nature is neither stained nor pure. It's absolutely still and completely whole. It makes no distinction between sacred or profane. It has countless ways of responding to circumstances. And although I call it Mind, it's distinct from both mind and consciousness. The various modes of being and the different manners of birth are all only appearances that have been produced by Mind, like the reflection of the moon in water or of images in a mirror. How can Mind be subject to birth and death? If you understand this, you won't lack anything."

One of the disciples present during this dharma talk was Tianhuang Daowu, who later acquired fame in his own right as a Zen master. The meditation tradition was already starting to divide into a number of different schools, and, during this talk, Tianhuang asked Shitou which teachers carried on the authentic tradition that could be traced back to Huineng. "Who obtained the essential teaching of the Sixth Patriarch?" he asked.

Shitou replied, "One who understands Buddha-dharma obtained it."

"Did you obtain it, master?" Tianhuang persisted.

"I don't understand Buddha-dharma," Shitou answered, echoing the Sixth Patriarch.

Likewise, when another monk asked, "What about liberation then?" Shitou's answer was the same as that given by Bodhidharma to Huike: "Who has put you in bondage?"

"No one."

"In that case, why do you need liberation?"

"Very well, then," another asked, "what about the Pure Land?" The Pure Land is a heaven where devotional Buddhists hope to be reborn. It is a place where all defilements are absent; therefore Shitou responded to this question by asking, "Who defiles you?"

"What about nirvana? What about seeking release from the wheel of birth and death?"

"Who has placed you on this wheel of birth and death?"

When a monk asked the purpose of Bodhidharma's coming from the west, Shitou instructed him, "Go ask the temple pillar."

"I don't understand," the monk complained.

"Neither do I," Shitou said.

In this way, one by one, he dealt with the various traditional Buddhist teachings, forcing his students to turn away from speculation and search within themselves for their true nature.

Shitou shared with Mazu the habit of making use of ordinary activities during the course of the day as opportunities to bring his students to understanding. One day as he was walking in the mountains with the disciple Shandao, their way was blocked by the branches of a tree growing over the pathway.

"Clear them away," Shitou told Shandao.

"I didn't bring a knife with me," the other said.

Shitou took out his own knife and presented it, blade outward, to his student.

Shandao was reluctant to take hold of the sharp blade and asked, "Please give me the other end."

"What are you going to do with the other end?" Shitou asked.

It is said that this was all that was necessary to help Shandao come to awakening.

Shitou described his dharma in a poem still chanted in the Soto Zen sect. The title in Chinese is *Cantongqi* (J: *Sandokai*), "In Praise of Sameness and Difference":

The mind of the great Indian Immortal [Gautama Buddha]
moves seamlessly between East and West.
It is human nature to be quick or slow,
but in the Way there are no northern or southern ancestors.
The mysterious source of the bright is clear and unstained;
branches of light stream from that dark.
Trying to control things is only delusion,
but hanging onto the absolute isn't enlightenment, either.
We and everything we perceive
    are interwoven and not interwoven,
and this interweaving continues on and on,
while each thing stands in its own place.
In the world of form, we differentiate Substances and Images;
in the world of sound, we distinguish music from noise.
In the embrace of the dark, good words and bad words are
    the same,
but in the bright we divide clear speech from confusion.
The four elements return to their natures
    like a child to the mother.
Fire is hot, the winds blow,
water is wet, the earth solid.

The eye sees form, the ear hears voices,
the nose smells fragrance, the tongue tastes salt and sour.
Everything, depending on its root, spreads out its leaves.
Both roots and branches must return to their origin,
and so do respectful and insulting words.
The darkness is inside the bright,
but don't look only with the eyes of the dark.
The brightness is inside the dark,
but don't look only through the eyes of the bright.
Bright and dark are a pair,
like front foot and back foot walking.
Each thing by nature has worth,
but we notice it is shaped by its circumstances.
Things fit together like boxes and lids,
while the absolute is like arrows meeting in mid-air.
When you let these words in, you encounter the ancestors;
don't limit yourself to your own small story.
If you don't see the Way [Dao] with your own eyes,
you won't know the road even as you're walking on it.
Walking the Way, we're never near or far from it:
deluded, we are cut off from it by mountains and rivers.
You who seek the mystery,
in daylight or in the shadows of night, don't throw away your
    time.[6]

Shitou died in 790 at the age of ninety-one. He had several successors, stories of whom were prized by later generations of Zen masters and students. One of his most interesting disciples was Pangyun,
or Layman Pang as he came to be known.

## LAYMAN PANG (PANGYUN)

Pang began his study of Zen with Mazu, and it was he who had asked, "Who is the man who has no companions among the ten thousand things?" Pang came to a degree of awakening with Mazu, after which that master suggested he would profit from spending time with Shitou. When Pang first approached Shitou, he intended to put the same question he had asked Mazu. Before he could get the words out, however, Shitou clasped his hand over Pang's mouth. That was enough to bring the layman to full awakening.

Along with Pang, his wife and daughter also attained awakening. And it is said that when all three were awakened, they put their belongings in a small boat that they sank in the river. After that, Pang and his family earned their living by weaving baskets and selling them in the local market.

Pang continued to work with Shitou in order to deepen his understanding of Zen. Because he was a layman, he did not participate in the devotional activities of those who were ordained but spent his days carrying out the various menial chores required to maintain the temple. One day Shitou came upon him as he was at work on the grounds, and the master asked him how he had been filling his time. Pang replied with a verse:

> Daily, nothing particular,
> Only nodding to myself,
> Nothing to choose, nothing to discard.
>
> No coming, no going,
> No person in purple,
> Blue mountains without a speck of dust.
>
> I exercise occult and subtle power,
> Carrying water, shouldering firewood.[7]

The final couplet of the poem, variously translated, has become one of the best known in the literature of Zen:

> How miraculous! How wondrous!
> Hauling water and carrying wood!

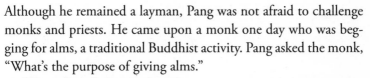

Although he remained a layman, Pang was not afraid to challenge monks and priests. He came upon a monk one day who was begging for alms, a traditional Buddhist activity. Pang asked the monk, "What's the purpose of giving alms."

"You tell me," the monk said.

"Very few people know," Pang told him.

"I don't understand."

"*Who* is it that doesn't understand?" Pang demanded.

On another occasion, he happened to hear a monk lecturing on the *Diamond Sutra*. When the monk came to the lines that speak of "no self, no other," Pang interrupted him to ask, "If there's no self and no other, then who's speaking, and who's hearing?"

The monk did not know how to reply. "What do you think?" he asked.

"Of course, I'm just a layperson, but I'll tell you what I think:

> No self, no other,
> Then how could there be intimate and estranged?
> I advise you to cease all your lectures.
> They can't compare with directly seeking truth.
> The Diamond Wisdom nature
> Erases even a speck of dust.
> 'Thus I have heard,' and 'Thus I believe,'
> Are but so many words."[8]

During the layman's final illness, the local governor paid him a visit to inquire about his health.

Pang told him, "Recognize that all things are empty and don't give substance to that which has none. This world is no more than reflections on water or echoes in the hills." Then he laid his head in the governor's lap and died.

## TIANHUANG DAOWU

Tianhuang Daowu, who had participated in the discussion following Shitou's dharma talk described above, had a teaching style similar to his master's. He is remembered for a conversation he had with his own disciple, Lungtan Chongzin. Lungtan served Tianhuang as his personal attendant. After he had been in that position for several years, he approached his master and complained, "Since I came here, I haven't had any instruction in the study of mind."

"That isn't so," Tianhuang said. "Since the day you first arrived, I haven't missed an opportunity to show you how to study mind."

"In what way, sir?"

"When you brought me a cup of tea, didn't I drink it? When you bowed to me, didn't I return the bow? When did I ever neglect instructing you?"

Lungtan sat for a moment with his head down. "If you want to see it," Tianhuang snapped, "see it directly! When you just think about it, it's lost!"

With those words, Lungtan came to awakening. He asked, in marvel, "How does one maintain it?"

"Live in accordance with conditions as they arise moment to moment," Tianhuang instructed him. "Surrender to everyday mind. There's nothing sacred except this."

## TANXIA TIANRAN

The stories told of Tanxia Tianran, another of Shitou's disciples, have contributed to the iconoclastic reputation Zen has acquired. Tanxia had been successful in school as a young man, and it was his intention to take the civil service examinations that would earn him a position within the Chinese bureaucracy. But he encountered a Zen monk who convinced him that seeking the dharma was a better use of his talents than functioning as a government official. Tanxia spent some time with Mazu but did not go through the ritual of having his head shaved or taking the precepts, which would symbolize his commitment to the life of a monk.

After a while, Mazu advised Tanxia to visit Shitou. When Tanxia arrived at Shitou's temple, Shitou saw from his hair and mode of dress that he was not a monk, so Shitou assigned him to work in the kitchen and allowed him to stay in a shed separate from the monks' quarters. Tanxia lived like this for three years, until one day when the members of the community were all engaged in cutting grass in front of the Buddha Hall. Instead of joining the others in their work, Tanxia poured a pail of water over his head and squatted in front of Shitou's quarters. Shitou understood that Tanxia was presenting himself to be received in the sangha. He called for a razor and shaved the younger man's head. But as Shitou chanted the precepts, Tanxia put his hands over his ears.

After completing his work with Shitou, Tanxia returned to pay his respects to Mazu; however, before presenting himself to the master, Tanxia went into the meditation hall, climbed up the altar and onto the shoulders of the statue of Manjusri. Manjusri was believed to have been a disciple of the Buddha (although there is no record of him in early Indian scriptures) who came to be recognized as the Bodhisattva who presides over the meditation hall. He is generally portrayed seated on a lion and carrying a sword with which he dispels illusion.

The monks in the meditation hall were shocked by Tanxia's behavior and rushed to inform Mazu. Mazu came out and, when he recognized Tanxia, greeted him by saying, "My natural [*tianran*] disciple has returned."

Tanxia slid from the statue's shoulders and bowed before Mazu. After this, he was known as Tanxia Tianran.

Mazu asked him where he had come from.

"I come from Shitou."

"The road of Shitou is slippery. Did you fall?"

"If I'd fallen, I wouldn't have returned here," Tanxia said.

He remained with Mazu until the latter's death, after which he went on a pilgrimage visiting Zen masters throughout China to test his, and their, understanding of the dharma. During this journey the most famous episode of his life occurred one winter's night when he took shelter at an empty temple in the capital. The weather was very bitter, and Tianran struggled to keep warm. Eventually he took one of the three wooden Buddhas he found on an altar and broke it into pieces that he used to make a fire. Noticing smoke coming from the temple, the resident priest came in to see what was causing it and found Tianran contentedly warming his hands before the burning Buddha.

"What have you done!" the priest exclaimed in outrage. "This is sacrilege! Have you no respect for the Holy Buddha?"

Without answering the priest, Tianran began to poke about in the embers with a stick.

"And now what are you doing?" the priest demanded.

"I'm searching the ashes for the relics, the Buddha's bones."

"You're a madman!" the priest exclaimed. "What bones or relics would you find from a wooden Buddha!"

"In that case," Tianran said, "could I have another of those Buddhas there for my fire?"

At the age of eighty-one, Tianran settled at a temple in Hunan Province. There for four years he gathered his own disciples. He told them, "All of you who have come here to ask about Dao or to practice Zen, I have nothing for you! There's no doctrine, no dogma, only eat when you're hungry and drink when you're thirsty. Everyone does this! Understand that that old rascal Shakyamuni was an ordinary man no different from you. See it for yourself! Don't strive after the unattainable, misleading one another, lost in dualism."

One day in the year 824, he dressed as if he were once again going on pilgrimage. Grasping his walking staff in his hand, he announced, "I'm going on a journey." Then he collapsed to the ground, dead.

## CUIWEI WUXUE

Cuiwei Wuxue was a disciple of Tanxia Tianran. The story of his master burning wooden Buddhas in order to keep warm had become famous. So it was that when Cuiwei was burning incense and leaving offerings of fruit at an altar to one of the Bodhisattvas of the Mahayana tradition, a monk who observed him came forward and challenged him, asking: "Were you not a disciple of Tanxia who is known for burning the wooden Buddha? Why, then, are you leaving offerings at this altar?"

"Even when it was burned, it wasn't burned up," Cuiwei answered. "As for my offerings, let me to do as I please."

"Do you believe these offerings will be eaten by the Bodhisattvas?"

"What about you? Do you eat everyday or not?"

The monk, suspecting a trap in this question, was not sure how to answer.

Cuiwei remarked, "It's difficult to find ones with intelligence."

There are several stories about Cuiwei's encounters with students. On one occasion, a monk asked Cuiwei the traditional question: "Why did the First Patriarch come from India?"

Cuiwei looked about then said, softly, "Wait until no one else is around and I'll answer your question then."

Sometime later, the man saw Cuiwei in the garden by himself, so he approached him again. "We're alone now. So, please, tell me: why did the first patriarch come from India?"

Without speaking, Cuiwei indicated the nearby grove of bamboo with a wave of his hand.

The monk looked at the grove, then turned back to Cuiwei. "I'm sorry; I don't understand."

"Look!" Cuiwei told him. "There's a tall bamboo and here's a short one!"

This brought the monk to awakening.

Another monk came up to Cuiwei as he was walking in the garden and posed the same question, "What is the meaning of Bodhidharma's coming from the west?"

Cuiwei paused in his walking without speaking. The monk continued, "Please instruct me."

"Do you need a second helping?" Cuiwei asked. Then he continued his walk, saying over his shoulder, "Don't neglect it."

On a third occasion, when a monk asked, "Why did the Patriarch come from the west?" Cuiwei answered by asking the monk to pass him the wooden headrest that was beside him. When the monk did so, Cuiwei hit him with it.

Zen Master and Tiger *by Shi Ke*

# CHAPTER SEVEN

# YAOSHAN WEIYAN AND HIS DESCENDANTS

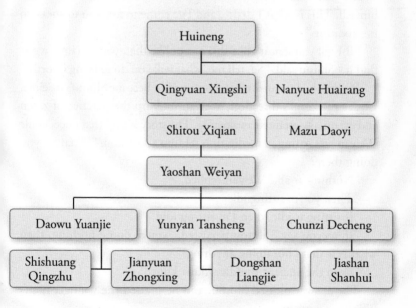

## YAOSHAN WEIYAN

Yaoshan Weiyan was born in 745. At the age of seventeen, he went to study with a Vinaya master, Xicao. Under Xicao's direction, the young man focused his study on the sutras and the many regulations that governed the life of the Buddhist religious community. But at the age of twenty-nine, Weiyan was dissatisfied with his accomplishments, and he left Xicao in order to take up the practices of the meditation school under the direction of Shitou Xiqian. There is also evidence that, like other disciples of Shitou, Weiyan spent a period of time with Mazu.

Weiyan explained to Shitou, that he was familiar with the sutras and their commentaries. "But I've been told," he said, "that in your school, instead of reading about Original Nature, you point to it in such a way that a person may see it and attain Buddhahood for himself. This is what I desire, and I've come to ask you to speak to me about it."

"If I tell you that it's like this or not like that, you certainly won't find it," Shitou said. "So, tell me, what will you do to bring it forth?"

Weiyan had no answer, and he asked to become Shitou's disciple. Under the latter's direction, Weiyan took up the practice of zazen and eventually attained awakening. The story is told that once, while Weiyan was sitting in meditation, Shitou asked him, "What are you doing there?"

"Nothing at all," Weiyan replied.

"Then you're sitting idle."

"If sitting is idle, then I'm sitting idly."

"If, as you say," Shitou persisted, "you're doing nothing, then what is it that's not doing anything?"

"Even the ancient Buddhas don't know."

The answer pleased Shitou, and he praised the younger man's insight in a poem:

> Living long together, and not knowing his name;
> Naturally you have worked along with him.

But even the ancient Buddhas did not know;
How can an ordinary soul know him?[9]

Zen practitioners continue to sit zazen after awakening and even after becoming teachers. So it was that zazen continued to be an important part of Weiyan's personal practice. One day after he had been seated in meditation for a long while, a monk asked him what he did during zazen: "What is it that you think of while you sit there as still as a mountain?"

"I think of not-thinking," Weiyan replied.

"How can you think of not-thinking?" the bewildered monk persisted.

"It isn't thought."

After receiving transmission from Shitou, Weiyan traveled to Mount Yao (Yaoshan) west of Lake Tungting in Hunan; from his residence there, he acquired the name by which he is most commonly known. Like many Zen practitioners, he sought to live in anonymity as he deepened his understanding of the dharma. His needs were modest. When he first came to the mountain village, he requested the use of an abandoned cattle barn, which was where he resided. But the very act of seeking anonymity seemed to draw the attention of others, and when he had acquired too many disciples to be housed in the barn, more appropriate accommodations were built.

Although Yaoshan's personal training had included an extensive study of the sutras, he did not advocate that route for his own students. On one occasion, a disciple found him reading the sutras and complained, "Master, you forbid us to read the sutras, so why do you read them?"

"I just keep the document before my eyes," Yaoshan replied.

"Can't we do so as well?"

"You need eyesight sharp enough to see through the binding," Yaoshan told him.

Yaoshan recognized that awakening could be deepened by reading the sutras but that reading alone would not bring one to awakening. Students inevitably begin by seeking something outside of themselves—guidance, instruction, a methodology. Yaoshan continuously insisted that students could only find what they were looking for within.

When a novice monk visited Yaoshan's temple, the master asked him where he had come from. The novice said he had come from the district of Nanyue.

"And where are you going?" Yaoshan inquired.

"To Jiangling."

"Why?"

"To be ordained a monk in the sangha."

"Why do you want to be ordained a monk in the sangha?"

"I seek to be freed from the wheel of birth-and-death."

"Didn't you know that there is one who, even without being ordained, is free from the wheel of birth-and-death?"

On another occasion, a monk came to see Yaoshan, saying: "There's something I don't understand that I hope you can help me with."

Yaoshan nodded and said, "Very well. Wait until all the monks are assembled in the hall for my dharma talk and we'll look into the matter then."

The monk bowed and left. He waited until that evening, when all the monks came together. Yaoshan took his place on the platform facing them, then asked: "Where's the monk who has something he doesn't understand?"

The monk rose from his seat and came forward, making his bows before the master. Yaoshan jumped up, seized him by the collar of his robe, and shook him. "Here, O monks, is someone who has something he doesn't understand!" Then, without another word, he released the monk and left the meditation hall.

The local governor, Li Ao, heard that a respected Zen master was dwelling in his province, so he sent an invitation requesting Yaoshan to come to the capital to meet him. Yaoshan ignored the invitation as well as several others that followed. Finally Li Ao went to visit the master himself. It is said that Yaoshan was engaged in reading the sutras when Li Ao arrived, and he paid no attention to the official or his entourage. Yaoshan's attendant, who was embarrassed by this lack of courtesy, interrupted Yaoshan's reading to announce that the governor had come to see him. Yaoshan continued reading without glancing up.

Li Ao remarked loudly, "Seeing the man himself, he turns out not to be at all like what we'd heard of him."

"And why do you value hearing over seeing?" Yaoshan asked, finally acknowledging the other's presence.

Li Ao made a formal bow, then said, "I've come to ask you: What is the Dao?"

Yaoshan pointed towards the sky with his hand and then down to the earth. "Do you understand?"

"No, Master," Li Ao admitted.

"Clouds are in the sky; water is in the jar."

The governor admired the comment but asked, "Is there any more than this?"

"Such as?"

"Such as the precepts, zazen, the attainment of wisdom?"

"My room isn't cluttered with useless items," Yaoshan told him.

Li Ao pondered that statement for a while in silence, then Yaoshan remarked, "If you seek to take this on, you must sit high on the mountain peak and walk in the depths of the ocean."

The conversation inspired the governor to become Yaoshan's disciple, and, as his duties permitted, he continued to visit the teacher.

A koan collected in the *Blue Cliff Records* shows a playful side to Yaoshan's personality.

> A monk said to Yakusan [Yaoshan], "On the grassy plain there is a herd of deer, with the king deer among them. How could one shoot the great king of the king deer?" Yakusan said, "Watch the arrow!" The monk threw himself on the floor. Yakusan called his attendant and said, "Boy! Take this dead fellow away!" The monk ran away. Yakusan said, "There is no end to these people who play with mud pies."[10]

One evening he went for a walk in the mountains. Just as he came to the summit, the clouds parted to reveal the moon. The sight evoked a laugh from Yaoshan that was so loud it was heard in a far-off village. Wondering at the source of such merriment, the villagers traced it to Yaoshan's temple, where the monks informed them, "Last night our master laughed the greatest laugh of his life at the top of the mountain." Li Ao commemorated the occasion in a poem:

> He has chosen a lonely dwelling,
>   and is content with the rustic life;
> Year after year he goes to greet no one, he sees no one off.
> Once, he climbed straight to the top of a lone peak,
> And, as the moon broke through the clouds,
>   laughed a great laugh.[11]

As Li Ao's poem noted, Yaoshan was a natural recluse, and the time came when he eventually withdrew even from his disciples. When he had failed to give a formal address to his students for some time, his head monk complained that he was neglecting his duties. Yaoshan told the monk to call the assembly together. As soon as the head monk did so, however, Yaoshan left the meditation hall and returned to his private quarters.

The head monk followed him and demanded, "I understood that you were going to speak to the monks. They're now all assembled, but you remain in your rooms. Are you going to speak to them or not?"

Yaoshan said, "There are priests who preach about the sutras. There are other priests who preach about the commandments and precepts. Why question my method? I've preached about what I myself have experienced. I've tried to say what isn't sayable in as many ways as possible. Some have heard me express what can't be expressed, and they've come to some degree of enlightenment. What more can I do? Let those who seek the truth sit alongside those who've come to enlightenment and learn from them. As for me, my work is done. Every day since the day I came to enlightenment and saw the futility of words, it's been my desire to retire in anonymity. But so many came seeking awakening that I was moved by compassion and didn't keep silent, even though that was my only wish. It isn't my words or silence that will bring another to awakening, only their own desire, their need, their thirst can do that."

One day in the year 828, at the age of eighty-four, Yaoshan shouted loudly, "The Dharma Hall is falling!" The monks, misunderstanding him, rushed to check the pillars and crossbeams of the hall.

Yaoshan laughed delightedly. "None of you understand my meaning!" he told them. Then he died.

## YUNYAN TANSHENG
## DAOWU YUANJIE

Yaoshan's two most significant heirs were the friends Daowu Yuanjie and Yunyan Tansheng. Tansheng began his study of Zen with Mazu's disciple, Baizhang Huaihai, but then, at Daowu's suggestion, he accepted Yaoshan as his teacher. Although Yunyan Tan-sheng's legacy was more significant that Daowu's, one story recounted about the two suggests that the latter perhaps had the greater insight. They were admiring a statue of the Bodhisattva of Compassion, Guan-yin (a female figure in Chinese and Japanese Buddhism who was originally a male, Avalokiteshvara, in the Indian tradition). As was common, the statue portrayed the bodhisattva with multiple arms and eyes.

Tansheng asked, "Why do you suppose the bodhisattva has so many hands and eyes."

"It's like someone in their sleep groping for a pillow," Daowu replied.

"Ah! I understand."

"Tell me what you understand."

"The whole body is covered with hands and eyes."

"That isn't bad," Daowu said, but his tone suggested that Tansheng still did not fully understand.

"How would you put it?" Tansheng asked.

"The whole body *is* hands and eyes."

On another occasion, Tansheng was making tea. Daowu asked for whom the tea was intended.

"There's someone who wants it."

"So why doesn't he make it himself?"

"Fortunately I'm here to do it."

Like Yaoshan, Tansheng acquired his name from the mountain where he lived after his master's death. He chose to dwell in a cave on Mount Yunyan. Unlike Yaoshan, Yunyan was able to remain in his mountain retreat where, instead of gathering disciples, he received traveling monks who would stay with him for a while and then go their way. The monk who would be recognized as Yunyan's successor was one of these, Dongshan Liangjie.

Yunyan once told this parable:

"Three travelers noticed a man standing on a small hill looking out over the landscape. The first traveler said, 'Look at that man. I suppose he's searching the country round for an animal that has wandered from his herd.'

"'Not at all,' the second said, 'he's simply watching out for a friend who's coming to visit him.'

"'Nonsense,' said the third. 'He's just enjoying the refreshing breeze.'

"The travelers argued among themselves but weren't able to come to agreement about why the man was standing there. When they came nearer to him, the first traveler called out to the man, 'Are you looking for a goat or sheep that has wandered from your flock?'

"'I don't have any flocks,' the man replied.

"'Then are you waiting for a friend?' the second asked.

"'No. I'm not waiting for a friend.'

"'Ah,' said the third. 'It must be as I expected, that you're just enjoying the refreshing breeze.'

"'Not particularly,' the man said.

"'Then what *are* you doing?' the three travelers demanded.
"'I'm just standing here.'"

Daowu was once asked by Wefeng Zhangguan, "Do you know the old master who resides at Yaoshan?"

Daowu said, "No, I don't."

"Aren't you his disciple? How could you not know him?

"I don't know him," Daowu insisted.

Daowu's chief disciple was Shishuang Qingzhu. He once asked Daowu, "After you've died, if someone were to ask me about the ultimate thing, how should I answer him?"

Daowu appeared to ignore Shishuang's question and called his attendant over. "Please fill this pitcher with fresh water," he instructed the attendant.

When the attendant had left with the pitcher, Daowu turned to Shishuang and said, "What was your question?"

Shishuang said, "After you've died, if someone should ask me about the ultimate thing, what answer should I give him?"

Without a word, Daowu rose from his seat and left the room.

One of the most curious and disturbing Zen stories concerns Daowu and another of his disciples, Jianyuan Zhongxing. The two went to visit a family who were mourning the death of one its members. The coffin was still at the house, and Jianyuan took the opportunity to ask his master a question. Laying his hand on the coffin he asked, "Is he alive or dead?"

"I won't say alive," Daowu told him. "I won't say dead."

"Why not?"

"I won't say."

After the visit, as they were returning to the monastery, Jianyuan was very disturbed and demanded, "Tell me, alive or dead. If not, I'll strike you down!"

"Strike me or not, I still won't tell you."

Jianyuan was unable to restrain himself, and he struck his master. Daowu did not strike back, but it was such a breach of etiquette that he told his student, "If others learn what you've done, it may cause you trouble. So it would better if you leave our monastery for a while."

Jianyuan wandered from place to place until he learned that his former master had died. Then he returned to the monastery where Shishuang was now teaching. He explained why he had been absent from the monastery for so long and told the new master about the question to which Daowu had merely said: "I won't say alive; I won't say dead."

"Can you answer my question?" he asked Shishuang.

"I won't say alive; I won't say dead," Shishuang replied.

"But why not?" Jianyuan asked.

"I won't say."

And with those words, Jianyuan finally came to awakening.

## CHUNZI DECHENG

Chunzi Decheng was a third disciple of Yaoshan and the dharma brother of Daowu and Yunyan. After he had received transmission from Yaoshan, Chunzi met with Daowu and Yunyan. He told them: "I know that both of you will eventually go your separate ways and continue our master's dharma. That isn't my path; I lack that much discipline. I enjoy nature and will follow my own way. I'm not fit to be the teacher of a great assembly. Still, if an appropriate student comes to you, please send him to me so that I may repay our teacher by passing on what little I've learned."

He then became a ferryman and was popularly known to the people he helped cross the river as the "Boatman Monk."

## JIASHAN SHANHUI

Jiashan Shanhui was a student of the sutras and was a recognized lecture master. He attracted large audiences to his presentations. At one of these, a listener asked about the Buddhist doctrine of the Three *Kayas* or the Three Bodies of the Buddha. The first of these is the *Nirmanakaya*, which is the physical incarnation of a Buddha, usually referring to Siddhartha Gautama. The second is the *Sambhogakaya*, which is the realization of Buddha-nature in oneself. The third is the *Dharamakaya* (literally "body of the dharma"), which in the Zen tradition is similar to the Chinese concept of Dao, that from which all things arise. The question put to Jiashan was: "What is the Dharmakaya?"

"It's without form," Jiashan said.

"What then is the true eye of the dharma [which, it was claimed, Buddha had passed onto Mahakasyapa]?"

"It's without flaw."

Daowu had been traveling in the region and had happened to be in the lecture hall when this exchange took place. Recognizing that Jiashan's answers came from a superficial understanding of the sutras rather than from a personal experience of his own Buddha-nature, Daowu laughed out loud.

Jiashan demanded, "Why are you laughing?"

"You might understand the sutras, but you still need a master to guide you to the discovery of your own Buddha-nature."

Jiashan was honest enough to recognize the legitimacy of the Daowu's words.

"Where would I find such a man?"

"Go see the Boatman Monk. He hasn't a tile to cover his head nor a speck of earth to stand upon."

Jiashan gave up lecturing and sought out Chunzi. It was a long trip, and Jiashan's traveling clothes were dusty and soiled by the time he finally came to the ferryman. When Chunzi saw Jiashan approaching, he shouted, "Monk, at what monastery do you reside?"

"I'm not a resident of any monastery. Otherwise I wouldn't look like this."

"So what do you look like?" the Boatman Monk asked.

"I'm beyond sight and sound and consciousness."

"Is that so?" Chunzi said, then he took hold of Jiashan and pushed him into the river, holding his head under water for a long while before letting him up. "Speak now!" Chunzi demanded, but as soon as Jiashan opened his mouth, the ferryman plunged him into the water yet again. "Speak!" Chunzi shouted. Jiashan tried again and was submerged a third time. On this occasion, he came to awakening, and when Chunzi let him up, he bowed in gratitude.

Chunzi acknowledged Jiashan as his successor and advised him to live in obscurity, developing his insight before beginning to teach but also telling him that he had an obligation to pass on the dharma if only to a single person. Then Chunzi went off and was never seen again.

Following Chunzi's recommendations, Jiashan built a hermitage on the mountain from which he derived his name. When he had been there for a while, inquirers sought him out and eventually a temple was built for him.

One day, the former lecture master was challenged by one his students, who said "I've heard you claim that although you've lived on this mountain for more than twenty years you've never preached a word of Zen. Is that so?"

"It is."

The monk then pushed Jiashan from his seat, as if challenging his authority to teach. Jiashan did not respond immediately but simply got to his feet and returned to his quarters. The next day he had his attendant dig a pit in the courtyard. Once it was prepared, he called the assembly of monks together.

Jiashan addressed the monk who had challenged him the day before. Handing him a spade, he said, "For twenty years all I've said is nonsense. It is only right that you should take this spade and kill me with it, then bury me in this pit. If you don't, then you must kill yourself and be buried here instead."

The monk withdrew from the assembly and left the monastery.

On another occasion, a monk asked, "What is the condition of Jiashan?" The question could have been understood to refer to either the teacher or the mountain (*shan*) where his temple was located. Jiashan replied in verse:

> The monkeys, clasping their young to their breasts,
> Have returned behind the blue peaks;
> A bird, holding a flower in its beak,
> Alights before the [blue cliff].[12]

The term for "blue cliff" is *biyan* (J: *hekigan*), and the master's quarters at the temple on Mount Jia came to be known by this name. Two centuries later, these were the accommodations of Yuanwu Keqin, the collector of koans now known as the *Blue Cliff Records* (J: *Hekiganroku*).

Walking on a Path in Spring *by Ma Yuan*

# CHAPTER EIGHT

# DONGSHAN LIANGJIE

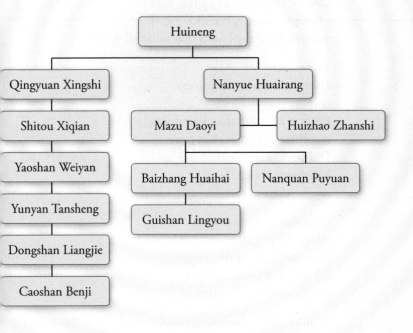

## Dongshan Liangjie

As a child, Dongshan Liangjie was sent to a local Buddhist temple to begin his education. His teacher was not a Zen master but rather a priest who served the community. He was a modest man without pretensions about his own attainments. He recited the sutras and carried out the various devotional duties expected of him, and he shared what he knew with Liangjie.

One day, as he had been instructed, the boy was reciting the *Heart Sutra*, a short text common to the schools of Mahayana Buddhism, including Zen:

> The Bodhisattva of Compassion
> from the depths of Prajna Wisdom,
> saw the emptiness of all five skandhas [form, feeling,
>     thought, choice, consciousness]
> and sundered the bonds that cause all suffering.
>
> Know then:
> Form here is only emptiness;
> emptiness only form.
> Form is no other than emptiness;
> emptiness no other than form.
> Feeling, thought and choice—
> consciousness itself—
> are the same as this.
>
> Dharmas here are empty;
> all are the primal void.
> None are born or die,
> nor are they stained or pure,
> nor do they wax or wane.
>
> So in emptiness no form,
> no feeling, thought or choice,
> nor is there consciousness.
> No eye, ear, nose, tongue, body, mind;

no color, sound, smell, taste, touch,
or what the mind takes hold of,
nor even act of sensing.
No ignorance or end of it,
nor all that comes from ignorance:
No withering, no death, no end of them.
Nor is there pain, or cause of pain,
or cease in pain,
or noble path to lead from pain;
not even wisdom to attain:
Attainment too is emptiness.

So know that the Bodhisattva,
holding to nothing whatever,
but dwelling in prajna wisdom,
is freed of delusive hindrance,
rid of the fear bred by it,
and reaches clearest nirvana.

All buddhas of past and present,
buddhas of future time,
through faith in prajna wisdom,
come to full enlightenment.
Know then the great dharani,
the radiant, peerless mantra,
the supreme, unfailing mantra,
the Prajna Paramita,
whose words allay all pain.
This is highest wisdom,
true beyond all doubt;
know and proclaim its truth:

Gate, gate,
Paragate
Parasamgate
bodhi, sva-ha![13]

When the boy came to the line that asserts that there is "No eye, ear, nose, tongue, body, mind," he paused. It seemed the most commonsense thing in the world that he did, in fact, have eyes, ears, a nose, and so on; that there were colors, sounds, smells, and taste. Confused by this, he sought out his teacher and asked him why the sutra would declare something so obviously false.

The priest, who had probably chanted those lines thousands of times without giving them much thought, was surprised by Liangjie's question. "I don't know," he admitted. "I can't give you an answer, but perhaps there is someone who can." He then suggested the boy continue his studies with one of the growing number of Zen teachers living in the mountains.

Liangjie left the temple and pursued his formation under the guidance of several Zen masters, including Nanquan Puyuan. His visit to Nanquan coincided with the anniversary of the death of Nanquan's teacher, Mazu, and the Zen master and his students were preparing a commemorative feast. Nanquan asked his students if they thought Mazu would, himself, attend the celebration; none of the students knew how to reply, but young Liangjie said, "If he has a companion, he'll come."

The answer pleased Nanquan, who remarked, "He may be young, but he shows promise. Perhaps with some carving and polishing we'll be able to make something of him."

Liangjie (whose name meant "Fine Servant") quipped, "Please don't try to make a free servant into a slave."

Eventually Liangjie came to study with Guishan Lingyou who, like Nanquan, was in Mazu's lineage. Liangjie was still concerned with the implications of the *Heart Sutra*, but he also wondered about a remark that had been made by the National Teacher, Nanyang Huizhong. When he first met Guishan, Liangjie spoke of the matter: "The National Teacher said that inanimate objects such as walls, tiles, and stones are continuously preaching the dharma. Who can hear such teaching?"

Guishan said, "There are sermons given by nonsentient beings, but few hear them."

"I don't understand," Liangjie admitted. "Please teach me."

Instead of speaking, Guishan simply held up his hossu, a ceremonial baton tufted at one end with horsehair.

"I still don't understand," Liangjie said.

"I can't tell you about this with the mouth given to me by my parents," the master told him.

At Guishan's suggestion, Liangjie sought out Yunyan. Once more he asked, "Who can hear the sermons of inanimate objects?"

"The inanimate hear them," Yunyan told him.

"Do you hear them?" Liangjie asked.

"If I heard them, you wouldn't be able to hear me."

"Why can't I hear them?" Liangjie persisted.

Yunyan did as Guishan had done and raised his hossu. "Do you hear it?" he asked.

"No."

"When you can't hear my preaching, how can you hope to hear the preaching of the inanimate?" Then Yunyan asked: "Do you know the sutra of the Amituo Buddha? [J: Amida Buddha: the Buddha whose name is chanted by practitioners of the Pure Land sect] It tells us: 'Streams, birds, trees and forests, all chant the name of Buddha.'"

Hearing this, Liangjie achieved his first awakening and wrote a poem to commemorate the event:

> How wonderful, how very wonderful!
> The preaching of the sentientless is inconceivable!
> Listening with the ear, it is difficult to understand,
> Hearing with the eye, then you know it.[14]

Liangjie realized, however, that his insight was still shallow and that he needed to deepen his understanding. He asked Yunyan if there were other teachings he should be aware of. Yunyan asked what his prior practices had been.

"I was not practicing the Four Noble Truths," Liangjie admitted.

"Did you find joy in this nonpractice?" Yunyan asked.

"It wasn't without joyful moments," Liangjie said. "It was like sweeping excrement into a mound, then rummaging through it to search for a precious jewel hidden within."

After remaining with Yunyan for a while, Liangjie set out on a pilgrimage to meet other Zen teachers in order to deepen his still shallow understanding. Prior to departing, he met a final time with Yunyan. The master asked him if he were returning home; Liangjie said he was not. Yunyan then asked, "Where are you going?"

"I'm not sure," Liangjie admitted

"When will you return?" Yunyan asked.

"When Your Reverence has a permanent dwelling, I'll return."

"Once you leave, it will be difficult for us to meet again.

"It will be difficult not to meet," Liangjie replied. He continued, "If, in some future time, someone were to ask me to describe your teaching, what should I say?"

"Say only this: 'Just *this* is it.'"

Liangjie did not know how to reply.

"In undertaking this matter you must investigate it minutely," Yunyan counseled.

During his travels, Liangjie met with several other Zen masters including Huizhao Zhanshi, who had been a student of Nanyue. Huizhao asked Liangjie the purpose of his visit.

"My mind still isn't at rest," Liangjie admitted, "and I have no control over it. That's why I've come to see you."

Huizhao nodded, then called out: "Liangjie!"

"Yes, sir," Liangjie responded immediately.

"What is that? Who responded?" Huizhao asked. When Liangjie could not answer, Huizhao remarked: "It's a fine Buddha, but it still doesn't emit any light."

Liangjie's great awakening finally occurred as he was crossing a stream. The man whose quest had begun by wondering about the assertions of the *Heart Sutra* happened to see his own reflection on the water and that was the cue he needed to understand Yunyan's parting instructions. He commemorated the event with a poem:

> Long seeking it through others,
> I was far from reaching it.
> Now I go by myself;
> I meet it everywhere.
> It is just I myself,
> And I am not itself.
> Understanding this way,
> I can be as I am.[15]

He eventually settled on Mount Dong (Dongshan), thus acquiring the name he is generally known by. Here he built a hermitage and dedicated himself to the practices of zazen and mindfulness in everyday activity, as counseled by the Buddha in the Eightfold Path. Mindfulness in daily activity became a hallmark of Dongshan's Zen. Slowly, he began to gather his own disciples and guided them both in meditation practice and in mindfulness. In so doing, he practiced a Zen that brought one into the present moment, experiencing events as they arose without judging them. As the poem of the Third Patriarch had expressed it:

The Perfect Way knows no difficulties
Except that it refuses to make preference.

A monk once complained to Dongshan about the discomforts of the monastery, which was too cold in winter and too warm in the summer. He asked the master how one could avoid these discomforts. Dongshan told him, "Go where there is neither cold nor heat."

"Where's that?"

"When cold, let the cold kill you; when hot, let the heat kill you."

On another occasion, a monk asked Dongshan who the Buddha was. Dongshan's often-quoted answer was "Three measures of flax!"

Dongshan was so wholly absorbed in each task with which he was involved that no trace of ego was present and he attained the emptiness described in the *Heart Sutra*. A folk tale relates that, because of this mindfulness, the guardian deity of his temple was unable to see Dongshan. Curious about the man who was now the temple's master, the guardian deity scattered some grain in the courtyard. Zen monasteries were noted for being kept scrupulously tidy, so when Dongshan saw the grain scattered carelessly, he wondered who had been responsible for it. The moment that thought arose, the guardian deity was finally able to see Dongshan.

When Dongshan held a memorial banquet on the anniversary of Yunyan's death, one of the monks asked him, "What was Master Yunyan's teaching?"

Dongshan told him, "Although I spent time with my master, I didn't receive any teaching from him."

"If you didn't receive any teaching, what's the meaning of this banquet? Doesn't it suggest that you agree with what your master taught you?"

"I agree with about half and reject half."

"Why can't you accept it all?" the monk persisted.

"If I accepted it all, I wouldn't be worthy of my master," Dongshan declared.

Dongshan was recognized not only as a Zen master but also as a celebrated poet, and he encapsulated the teachings he had received and sought to pass on in verse. One such teaching was a "secret transmission" that had come down from Yaoshan to Yunyan, and is now best known (in Japanese) as "Tozan's (Dongshan's) Five Ranks."

The Bent (the Relative) within the Straight (the Absolute):

> In the third watch of the night
> Before the moon appears,
> No wonder when we meet
> There is no recognition!
> Still cherished in my heart
> Is the beauty of earlier days.

The Straight (the Absolute) within the Bent (the Relative):

> A sleepy-eyed grandam
> Encounters herself in an old mirror.
> Clearly she sees a face,
> But it doesn't resemble hers at all.
> Too bad, with a muddled head,
> She tries to recognize her reflection!

The Coming from within the Straight (the Absolute):

> Within nothingness there is a path
> Leading away from the dusts of the world.
> Even if you observe the taboo
> On the present emperor's name,
> You will surpass that eloquent one of yore
> Who silenced every tongue.

The Arrival at the Middle of the Bent (the Relative):

> When two blades cross points,
> There's no need to withdraw.
> The master swordsman
> Is like the lotus blooming in the fire.
> Such a man has in and of himself
> A heaven-soaring spirit.

Unity Attained:

> Who dares to equal him
> Who falls into neither being nor non-being!
> All men want to leave
> The current of ordinary life,
> But he, after all, comes back
> To sit among the coals and ashes.[16]

## CAOSHAN BENJI

Dongshan's most important disciple was Caoshan Benji. At their first meeting, Dongshan asked, "What is your name?"

"Benji," the aspiring student replied.

"Say it again."

"I won't say anything."

"Why do you refuse to say anything?"

"Because I'm not named Benji."

Dongshan acknowledged that this was a good reply.

The young man studied with Dongshan until his own awakening was deep enough for him to go off on his on. As he prepared to leave the monastery, Dongshan came to see him and asked, "Where will you go?"

"I'm not going anywhere different," Benji told him.

"If you're not going to anywhere different, how can there be 'going'?"

"I'm going, but not to anywhere different."

During his time with Dongshan, Caoshan received the "Five Ranks," and these became the basis of his own teaching. The work he did in passing on this tradition eventually resulted in the establishment of the largest of contemporary Zen traditions, the *Caodong* school. Its name is taken from the "mountain" names of these two masters. In Japanese, where the teachers' names are Sozan Honjaku [Caoshan] and Tozan Ryokai [Dongshan], the school is known as Soto.

Caoshan composed the following commentary on the five ranks: "The absolute is not necessarily void. The relative is not necessarily actual. There is neither turning towards nor turning away. When mental activity dies down and both the material world and emptiness are forgotten, there is no concealment. The whole is revealed. This is the relative within the absolute. Mountains are mountains, rivers are rivers. No names; nothing can be compared. This is the absolute within the relative. Clean and naked, bare and free, the face in full majesty. Throughout heaven and earth, the only honored one. This is coming from the absolute. The ear does not enter sound. Sound does not block the ear. The moment you go within, there have never been any fixed names in the world. This is arriving in the middle. No mind, no objects; no phenomena, no principle. It has always been beyond name or description, beyond absolute and relative, beyond essence and appearance. This is unity attained."

A monk once approached Caoshan, complaining, "Master, I'm poor and destitute. Please assist me."

Caoshan called the monk's name, and he replied, "Yes, Master?"

"There!" Caoshan said. "You've had three cups of the finest wine and yet you ask for more."

On another occasion, Caoshan posed this question to a monk: "The Body of Buddha is vast emptiness. When a thing appears, it's like the moon reflected in water. How would you demonstrate this teaching?"

The monk replied, "It's like a donkey looking into a well and seeing its own reflection."

"Eighty percent," Caoshan remarked.

"What is your answer, Master?"

"It's like a well looking at the donkey."

Like many other masters of the Tang dynasty, Dongshan was credited with being able to predict his own death. The story is told that at the age of sixty-three he bathed ceremonially, had his head freshly shaved, and donned a new robe. Then he called his disciples together, bade them farewell, and appeared to pass away. The disciples burst into loud lamentation and, a moment later, Dongshan opened his eyes to remonstrate with them: "The hearts of those who enter the homeless life of the Buddha-way shouldn't form attachments. That's true practice. All things are subject to change and dissolution. What's the point of grieving?"

He remained with them for seven more days before finally dying.

*A Zen monk*

# THE HEIRS OF MAZU

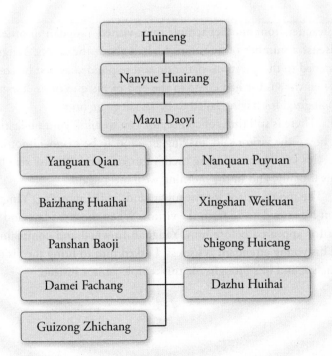

Mazu Daoyi is said to have had 139 heirs. Stories concerning him and his disciples continue to make up a large part of the koan collections still in use in both Japan and North America.

## YANGUAN QIAN

Some of these heirs are known for only a few notable events in their lives, such as Yanguan Qian, whose wonderful reply to the question "Who is Buddha?" was given in the preface to this volume. On another occasion, Yanguan asked his attendant to bring him a fan made of rhinoceros horn. When the attendant answered that the fan was broken, Yanguan directed him, "Then bring me the rhinoceros."

A teacher from another temple once visited Yanguan in order to discuss a number of questions he had about the sutras. Yanguan listened to the questions patiently and responded as best he could. When the visitor had come to the end of his questions, Yanguan apologized for having failed to be an adequate host.

"There is still time, of course, for you to fulfill your obligations as host," the visitor said, making an effort to be magnanimous.

"It's late now, and we're tired," Yanguan said. "Please stay here this evening, and in the morning we'll meet again."

The monk retired for the night, and, in the morning, Yanguan sent his attendant to fetch the visitor. When the attendant and the visitor appeared before him, Yanguan frowned and complained, "This young attendant is useless! I asked him to bring the visiting teacher, and he's brought me this temple janitor instead!"

## XINGSHAN WEIKUAN

Other descendants of Mazu, such as Nanquan Puyuan and Bai-zhang Huaihai, are the subject of many teaching stories and *mondo* (collections of conversations in the form of a series of questions and answers that demonstrate the participants' understanding of the dharma).

Several mondo focus on Xingshan Weikuan. For example, he was once asked the question that would later be addressed to Nanquan's disciple, Zhaozhou, with resounding consequences: "Does even a dog have Buddha-nature?"

Unlike Zhaozhou, Weikuan replied, "Yes."

"So all beings have Buddha-nature. Then you too have Buddha-nature?" the questioner continued.

"No, not me."

"But if all beings have Buddha-nature, why don't you have it?"

"I'm not one of 'all beings.'"

"Then what are you? The Buddha himself?"

"No. I'm not Buddha."

"What are you, then?"

"I'm not a 'what.'"

"Aren't you something that one can experience through the senses, through the mind?"

"No. What I am is beyond thought and comprehension. There-fore, it's called the unthinkable."

On another occasion, a monk asked Weikuan: "Where can I find Dao?"

"It's right before us."

"Then why don't I see it?"

"Because of your ego."

"If I am unable to see it because of my ego, can you see it?"

"As long as there is you or I, the Dao can't be seen."

"So when there's no you or I, can it be seen then?"

"If there's no you or I, who is there to see?"

A similar question was put to him by a third monk during a walk in the mountains. "What is the Dao?"

"What a fine mountain this is!" Weikuan remarked.

"I'm not asking about the mountain," the monk persisted. "I'm asking about the Dao."

"If you can't get beyond the mountain," Weikuan told him, "you'll never be able to attain Dao."

## DAZHU HUIHAI

Dazhu Huihai, another student of Mazu, is also featured in several mondo. One day an expert in the Vinaya (the rules governing the conduct of the members of the sangha) asked Dazhu, "When one seeks to follow the Dao, is there a particular manner in which he should behave?"

"There is," Dazhu said.

"Please tell me about it," the other requested.

"When one is hungry, one eats; when one is tired, one sleeps."

"But everyone does that," the Vinaya master complained. "Your behavior isn't different from that of commoners."

"They're not the same at all," Dazhu said.

"In what way are they different?"

"When most people eat, they don't just eat; their minds are preoccupied with a thousand different fantasies. When they sleep, they don't just sleep; their minds are filled with any number of idle thoughts."

Another monk asked, "What is nirvana?"—or the final release sought by Buddhists.

Dazhu answered: "Not to commit oneself to the consequences [karma] of birth-and-death, that's nirvana."

"So what is the karma of birth-and-death?" the monk asked.

"To desire nirvana is the karma of birth-and-death."

## GUIZONG ZHICHANG

The governor of Jiangzhou Province once visited another disciple of Mazu, Guizong Zhichang, in order to discuss a passage he had found in one of the Buddhist sutras regarding Mount Kunlun (Mount Sumeru, the mythical peak at the center of the world).

"It's said in the sutra," the governor said, "that there's a poppy seed within Mount Kunlun, and that within that poppy seed is Mount Kunlun. Now I can understand how there could be a poppy seed within the mountain, but it's nonsense to suggest a poppy seed could contain a mountain!"

Guizong said, "Governor, I'm told that you're a well-read man."

"I believe I am," the governor admitted.

"I've been told you've read as many as ten thousand books."

"That's very likely true."

"But your head is no bigger than a coconut, how could it possibly contain the contents of ten thousand books?"

The governor had no reply.

A student of the sutras once visited Guizong while he was working the soil in the garden with a hoe. Just as the student drew near, he saw Guizong use the hoe to cut a snake in half, killing it in violation of the Buddhist precept not to take any form of life.

"I'd heard that Guizong was a crude and ill-mannered man, but I didn't believe it until now," the student remarked.

"Is it you or I who's crude or refined?" Guizong asked.

"What do you mean by 'crude?'" the student asked.

Guizong held the hoe upright.

"And in that case, what do you mean by 'refined?'" the student asked.

Guizong made a motion as if cutting a snake in half.

"And yet," the student said, "if you had allowed it, it would have gone away on its own."

"If I'd allowed it to go away on its own, how would you have seen me chop the snake in two?"

The student did not know how to reply.

## Panshan Baoji

The experience of awakening does not necessarily come as a direct result of anything the student's teacher has said or done. Although Mazu was noted for the variety of techniques he employed to help his students attain awakening, it was the words of a butcher that provided his student, Panshan Baoji, the nudge he needed. Because of the precept against taking life, many Buddhists practiced vegetarianism and frowned upon butchery as a vocation. On this occasion, however, Panshan was walking through a market, and, as he passed the butcher's stall, he happened to overhear a woman speaking. "I must prepare a meal for a very special guest," she told the butcher. "Please show me the very best piece of meat you have for sale here."

"All the wares I have for sale here are the best," the butcher replied. "You can't find one piece that is not the best."

Hearing these words, Panshan came to awakening.

Later he would explain: "You can't seek it from others. No one can show it to you. You must look into it for yourself. Where can you find the mind? The original elements are all empty. So where does the Buddha abide? A tool such as a plow doesn't move; it doesn't say anything, and yet it reveals itself entirely. There's nothing else."

In one of his recorded sermons, Panshan said:

> When there are no affairs in the mind, the myriad things are not born. In the inconceivable mysterious function, where would a speck of dust alight? The Way [Dao] itself is form-less, but because of form, names are established. The Way itself is nameless but because of names, there is classification.
>
> If you say, "Mind is Buddha," then you still haven't en-tered the mystery. If you say, "No mind, no Buddha," then you're just pointing at the traces of the ultimate. Even a thousand saints can't transmit the higher road to others. You students are tormented by form. You're like apes grabbing at shadows.[17]

When Panshan was in his final illness, he asked if any of his students were able to "produce a likeness" of him. Several tried to sketch portraits, but he remained dissatisfied with them all. Finally one of his disciples announced, "I can produce a likeness." When Baoji challenged him to do so, the disciple turned a somersault and left the room.

## SHIGONG HUICANG

Hunters were held in even lower estimation than butchers. Shigong Huicang was a hunter and well aware of the opinion monks had of his trade; he reciprocated by despising them in turn. One day, as he was tracking deer, his path passed by Mazu's hermitage. The master was seated in front of the hut, enjoying the sun.

"Old man, did you see any deer pass by here?" Shigong demanded.

"Deer? Why are you asking me about deer? Who are you?"

"I'm a hunter," Shigong declared boldly.

"A hunter," Mazu mused. "I see you carry a bow and a quiver of arrows. Does that make you a hunter? Tell me, do you know how to shoot?"

"Of course I do."

"And how many birds can you shoot down with a single arrow?"

"With a single arrow? One."

"Well, then you don't know how to shoot after all, do you?"

"What would a monk know about it? Do you know how to shoot?"

"Oh yes. Most certainly."

"And how many can you shoot down with a single arrow?"

"An entire flock with one arrow."

"An entire flock! I thought you were a Buddhist. Aren't you supposed to respect all life? Why would you destroy the entire flock if all you needed is a single bird?"

"If you know that much, why don't you try shooting yourself?"

"Shooting myself? I wouldn't know how to proceed."

"Put a stop to all your past ignorance and passions."

This conversation was enough to inspire Shigong to lay aside his bow and become Mazu's student.

One day when Shigong had been training for a while, Mazu visited him while he was at work in the kitchen. "What are you doing?" the master asked.

"I am tending an ox," Shigong informed him.

"Are you now? How do you attend to this ox?"

"If it strays from the path, I pull it back by the nose without a moment's delay."

"That is certainly how to attend to it," Mazu admitted.

Eventually Mazu gave Shigong permission to teach, and the former hunter began to gather his own disciples. It is said that he kept his old bow, with an arrow notched in the string, by his side. When monks came with questions, he threatened them with the bow. One day the monk Sanping came before Shigong, who raised his bow as usual. "Watch out for the arrow," he warned.

Sanping pulled aside the top of his robe, revealing his chest, and said, "That's the arrow that kills. Show me the arrow that brings back to life."

Shigong plucked the bowstring like a musical instrument.

Sanping bowed.

Shigong laughed. "For thirty years, I've been using one bow and two arrows. Today at last I have shot down half of a wise man."

In another story, Shigong tested a monk's understanding by asking, "How do you take hold of empty space?"

The monk made a motion as if he were trying to grasp the air.

"That's not it at all!" Shigong snapped. Then he took hold of the monk's nose and gave it a sharp twist. "*That's* how you take hold of empty space."

And when yet another monk asked Shigong how he could escape the wheel of birth and death, Shigong's response was, "What's the use of escaping it?"

## DAMEI FACHANG

A monk named Fachang once asked Mazu, "What is the Buddha?"

Mazu told him, "The mind just as it is is the Buddha."

As is common in such brief records, the statement was sufficient to bring Fachang to awakening, although the implication is that he had had a period of extensive practice beforehand.

Fachang followed his master's example and secluded himself in a straw-roofed hermitage on Damei—or Plum—Mountain. Because of his residence, he was known as Damei Fachang. Legend has it that he survived on a diet of wild vegetation such as pine nuts and lotus leaves. To deepen his awakening, he spent his days practicing zazen.

When Damei had been living in the mountains for many years, Mazu was curious about how his practice was progressing. He sent a student to seek out Damei and ask him why he was living in isolation.

"My master, Mazu, told me that this very mind, just as it is, is Buddha. And for that reason I've made my dwelling here in these mountains."

"But our master no longer teaches that," the student said. "Now he says 'no mind, no Buddha.'"

"Mazu is a senile old dotard who enjoys bewildering others," Damei replied. "He can say whatever he wishes, but I still say this very mind is Buddha."

When the student returned to Mazu and reported Damei's disrespectful comment, Mazu was unoffended, noting, "The plum, indeed, is ripe."

Some time later, a disciple of Yanguan Qian was wandering about on the mountain and became lost. By happenstance he stumbled upon Damei's dwelling and was surprised to find a monk living in such isolation.

"Master," he asked, "how long have you been living in these mountains?"

"I've known the leaves on these mountains to turn from green to brown four separate times," Damei said.

After getting directions from Damei on how to find his way down the mountain, the monk returned to Yanguan and told him about the hermit he had met.

Yanguan said, "When I was still with my master, Mazu, I knew a monk like that. I wonder if this is the same person. Please go back to him and ask him to come visit me."

The young disciple did as he was told, but Damei refused the invitation. Yanguan then wrote a poem that he had the disciple take to the hermit:

The stump of the dead tree stands in the cold forest;
Even if it is exposed to the spring warmth, its heart is not moved.
Since no one takes notice of it, it being so stiff and hard,
Perhaps the carpenter will not want to use it.[18]

Damei wrote a reply, then moved his hermitage to a more isolated location. The reply read:

One cannot cut all the lotuses in the pond;
One cannot eat all the pine seeds.
Since the world has discovered my dwelling so easily,
I shall move my hermitage deeper into the mountains.[19]

Mazu's two most important disciples were Nanquan Puyuan, who would be the teacher of Zhaozhou Congshen, and Baizhang Huai-hai, from whom the Rinzai school of Zen would descend.

*Shide and Hanshan*

CHAPTER TEN

# THE POETS

From the time of the Third Patriarch (Jianzhi Sengcan, who wrote the *Xinxin Ming*), the Zen tradition in China was associated with poetry. Adepts wrote poems to commemorate their enlightenment experiences; Zen masters wrote poems prior to their deaths as last testaments; and, as had Sengcan, they sought to express their understanding of Zen in verse.

Verse—which makes use of imagery rather than reasoned argument to evoke a response —may be a more appropriate vehicle to attempt to express the Zen experience than is prose. In *The Song of the Jewel Mirror Samadhi*, Dongshan Liangjie warns that "the meaning is not in the words," and goes on to say: "Just to depict it in literary form" is to defile it. He then continues, however, for another sixty lines,

The historian Will Durant refers to the Tang dynasty (618–907) as the Age of Poets. As with the Elizabethan age in England, it was a period when works were composed that would later become part of the national heritage. It is also considered the golden age of Chinese Zen.

Poetry was one of the traditional forms all educated Chinese were expected to master; one's skill as a poet was tested in civil service exams. Even emperors prided themselves on their ability to compose verse. When, a thousand years later, scholars in the Qing dynasty sought to compile an anthology of Tang poetry, the result was thirty volumes containing 48,900 poems by 2,300 individual poets.

All poetry necesarily suffers from translation, but perhaps Chinese poetry even more so, according to Durant:

> Certain subtle qualities of [Chinese poetry] are hidden from us in translation: we do not see the picturesque written characters, each a monosyllable, and yet expressing a complex idea; we do not see the lines, running from top to bottom and from right to left; we do not catch the meter and the rhyme, which

adhere with proud rigidity to ancient precedents and laws; we do not hear the tones—the flats and sharps—that give a beat to Chinese verse; at least half the art of the Far Eastern poet is lost when he is read by what we should call a "foreigner." In the original a Chinese poem at its best is a form as polished and precious as a hawthorn vase; to us it is only a bit of deceptively "free" or "imagist" verse, half caught and weakly rendered by some earnest but alien mind.[20]

The late Tang was a time of epic events. The reigning emperor, Xuanzong, was himself a poet. When he began his reign, he proved to be one of the ablest rulers China had. He governed from 713 to 756. Mazu Daoyi and Shitou Xiqian were among his subjects. He was noted for reorganizing the vast Chinese bureaucracy, ridding it of corrupt officials, and establishing a system of examinations to help select people of merit to serve in government. He received tribute from as far away as Persia and Turkey.

He was not, however, a supporter of Buddhism, believing that the many temples and monasteries, which were exempt from taxes, were a drain on the national economy. He forbade the copying of sutras and the bronze-casting of Buddhist statues; government officials were prohibited from having contact with Buddhist monks.

The emperor's decline began with the death of his favorite concubine, Consort Wu, in 737. To try to cheer the grieving emperor, who was then sixty years of age, one of his eunuchs arranged for him to meet the famous beauty, Yang Yuhuan. The emperor was immediately smitten, but the woman was already married to one of his sons. The emperor overcame this impediment by arranging for Yang to become a Daoist nun, thus dissolving her marital status. Later she was able to become the emperor's consort and was given a new title, Yang Guifei. The emperor was so enamored by his new concubine that he withdrew from active involvement in his government in order to focus his attention on her, eventually raising her to the rank of empress. To please her, he found government positions for several of her family members and appointed her incompetent brother, Yang Guozhong, Prime Minister.

A provincial governor, An Lushan—himself an admirer of Yang Guifei—had China's most powerful army garrisons under his control, and, responding to growing popular discontent with Yang Guozhong, he rebelled in 755, declaring himself emperor. An Lushan's troops took over the capital city with relative ease. Xuanzong's armies blamed the emperor's infatuation for their defeat, and, in retaliation, they killed both Yang Guifei and her brother. A civil war then raged for eight years, claiming a staggering thirty-six million deaths. Eventually, An Lushan was murdered by his own son. That son was in turn assassinated, and, in 762, Xuanzong returned to his capital city. But the glories of the Tang dynasty had waned.

Because Zen temples were located in mountainous regions, they were not as affected by the events taking place as were the cities and towns. The temples even became places of refuge for people seeking to escape the chaos of civil conflict. One of those temples was Guoqing at Tientai, which became associated with the legendary poets Hanshan and Shide.

These two became favorite subjects of both Chinese and Japanese painting, and, in Japan, Hanshan would later be revered as a reincarnation of the Bodhisattva Manjusri. Although the details of their lives were sketchy, they came to be representative of freedom from convention and rebellion against established structures, characteristics that were popularly associated with Zen Buddhism by the early North American Zen enthusiasts in the 1950s.

The stories told of these poets may be based on the lives of actual persons, but the details are largely fictional—as is the authorship of the poems attributed to them. The poems credited to Hanshan were written over a period longer than the span of a single man's life. In paintings, they are portrayed wearing ragged clothes and hats made of birch bark. They are shown with wide grins, reflecting their humorous attitude towards life.

# HANSHAN

Hanshan was the more significant figure. Unlike Shide, he was not officially associated with the Zen tradition, and the poems attributed to him reflect a Daoist as much as a Buddhist perspective. He was described as living apart from society in the wilderness. Perhaps he was in hiding because of his involvement in the An Lushan rebellion, or perhaps the Daoist vision inspired him to live as close to nature and natural processes as possible.

One biographer asserts that Hanshan had been born to a noble family, where he received the training and education appropriate to his class. However, he sustained an injury to his foot as a result of a riding accident that left him slightly disabled. This physical impediment prevented him from advancing in the Chinese civil service, and he was unable to rise beyond the lowly position of clerk.

As a result, he became disenchanted with the established traditions of his day, which may have led him to be a supporter of the rebel forces. Whether that was the case or not, he gave up his office, left his wife and child, and went into obscurity. He is said to have gone to the mountains, where he found shelter in caves and makeshift huts. As with the Zen masters of his day, he adopted a new name based on his dwelling place—Hanshan means "Cold Mountain."

His retreat was near the monastery at Guoqing, which he visited from time to time, scrounging scraps left by the monks at mealtime. It is said that he would walk the halls of the temple talking to himself during the monks' periods of meditation. When his behavior was felt to be too disruptive and he was asked to leave, he would clap his hands and laugh as he made his way back to his cave.

## SHIDE

Shide's name means "picked up." He had been an abandoned orphan, found in the forest by a monk named Fenggan, who heard him crying. Fenggan brought the infant back to the Guoqing Temple, where he was raised by the monks and given work in the kitchen and doing general cleaning. Once, when he was told to clean the meditation hall, the monks found him seated companionably in front of the statue of the Buddha, helping himself to the fruit that had been left on the altar as an offering, as if sharing a snack with a friend.

When Hanshan visited the monastery, the two met and became friends. Shide would save leftovers and set them aside in a hidden place for Hanshan to pick up.

D. T. Suzuki tells the following story about the two of them:

> While [Shide] was sweeping the monastery court, the master asked, "You are known here as 'the Picked-up' because [Fenggan] came back with you, saying you were picked-up on his way home. But, really, what is your family name? and where do you come from?" Thus asked, [Shide] threw up the broom and stood with his hands crossed before his chest. The master did not know what to make of it. [Hanshan] happened to pass by. Striking his own breast, he cried, "Oh! Oh!" [Shide] said, "What is the matter with you, O Brother?" [Hanshan] remarked, "Don't you know the saying, 'When a next-door neighbor is in mourning, we all share the sorrow?" They then both danced, and went away crying and laughing.[21]

The two friends traveled about the region, drinking wine without inhibition, sticking their tongues out at passers-by, and composing poems. Lay people became fond of them and would leave food for them in the forests, in exchange for which the poets left their verses inscribed on rocks or bits of bark. In the essay quoted above, Suzuki provides this example attributed to Hanshan:

> I think of the past twenty years,
> When I used to walk home quietly from the [Guoqing];
> All the people living in the [Guoqing] monastery—
> They say, "[Hanshan] is an idiot."
> "Am I really an idiot?" I reflect.
> But my reflections fail to solve the question:
> For I myself do not know who the self is,
> And how can others know who I am?
> I just hang down my head—no more asking is needed;
> For of what service can the asking be?
> Let them come then and jeer at me all they like,
> I know most distinctly what they mean;
> But I am not to respond to their sneer,
> For that suits my life admirably.[22]

Hanshan and Shide inscribed their poems on the limbs of trees, rock faces, and walls. Later a collector named Xu Lingfu copied them from these sources and preserved them.

Fewer poems are attributed to Shide than to Hanshan, and they differ both stylistically and in terms of content. Hanshan was not a member of the Buddhist sangha, and some of his poems are critical of both Buddhists and Daoists. Shide's poetry, on the other hand, has a more distinctly Buddhist flavor.

This example of Shide's work is translated by Red Pine (Bill Porter):

> Up high the trail turns steep
> the towering pass stands sheer
> Stone Bridge is slick with moss
> clouds keep flying past
> a cascade hangs like silk

the moon shines in the pool below
I'm climbing Lotus Peak again
to wait for that lone crane once more.[23]

The following poems attributed to Hanshan are rendered into English by Gary Snyder, a Zen practioner and poet who was the model for the character Japhy Ryder in Jack Kerouac's 1958 novel, *The Dharma Bums*.

In the mountains it's cold.
Always been cold, not just this year.
Jagged scarps forever snowed in
Woods in the dark ravines spitting mist.
Grass is still sprouting at the end of June,
Leaves begin to fall in early August.
And here I am, high on mountains,
Peering and peering, but I can't even see the sky.

I settled at Cold Mountain long ago,
Already it seems like years and years.
Freely drifting, I prowl the woods and streams
And linger watching things themselves.
Men don't get this far into the mountains,
White clouds gather and billow.
Thin grass does for a mattress,
The blue sky makes a good quilt.
Happy with a stone under head
Let heaven and earth go about their changes.

I've lived at Cold Mountain—how many autumns.
Alone, I hum a song—utterly without regret.
Hungry, I eat one grain of Immortal medicine
Mind solid and sharp; leaning on a stone.

When men see Hanshan
They all say he's crazy
And not much to look at—
Dressed in rags and hides.
They don't get what I say
And I don't talk their language.
All I can say to those I meet:
"Try and make it to Cold Mountain."[24]

A final example is quoted in Kenneth Kraft's *Zen: Tradition and Transition*:

My father and mother left me a good living,
I needn't envy the fields of other men.
Clack-clack—my wife works her loom;
jabber jabber goes my son at play.
I clap hands, urging on the swirling petals;
chin in hand, I listen to singing birds.
Who comes to commend me on my way of life?
A woodcutter sometimes passes by. [25]

*The* Ox Herding Pictures, *sometimes called the* Ten Bulls, *are a series of ten pictures portraying the stages of growth in Zen. The first pictures in the series is entitled* Searching for the Ox.

# CHAPTER ELEVEN

# NANQUAN PUYUAN AND BAIZHANG HUAIHAI

## NANQUAN PUYUAN

The most famous story told of Nanquan Puyuan is recorded in a koan found in both the *Wumenguan* (J: *Mumonkan*) and the *Blue Cliff Record*.

The monks at Nanquan's monastery were divided into two "halls," referred to as the Eastern and Western Halls respectively. One hall was set aside for the monks who spent their time in meditation. Monks who were engaged in the general maintenance and operations of the monastery resided in the other hall. During the course of their training, monks would move from one hall to the other several times.

One day Nanquan found the monks of the Eastern and Western Halls quarrelling over a cat. In order to avoid the consequences of breaking the Buddhist principle that forbad the taking of life, people from the neighboring villages would leave unwanted kittens and other animals at monasteries. Perhaps that is how the cat came to be at the temple.

Nanquan obviously thought the monks were engaged in trivialities and were neglecting their practice. He grabbed up the cat and said, "If one of you can say a word, the cat will live. Otherwise, I'm going to kill it."

The monks were so surprised that their master would even talk about breaking the precept that they were stunned into silence. As it was, none did say a word, and the koan recounts that Nanquan cut the cat in two. This was so out of keeping with Buddhist principles that some commentators try to mitigate the event by saying he only mimed cutting the cat in half. But the koan is clear; the cat died.

Nanquan's chief disciple, the famous Zhaozhou Congshen, had been absent when these events took place. He returned to find his fellow monks bewildered by their teacher's behavior, and, when Zhaozhou went to see his master, Nanquan related what had occurred. Without saying a word, Zhaozhou took off one of his sandals, placed it on his head, and left the room.

"If you'd been there," Nanquan Puyuan called after him, "that cat would have lived!"

Puyuan was born in the Zheng Province. His family name was Wang. At the age of nine, his head was ceremonially shaved, signaling his entrance into the Buddhist community. As a young man he studied in various schools before he finally came to the temple of Mazu. Until he met Mazu, Puyuan's understanding of Buddhism had only been theoretical. Under Mazu's instruction he came to experience awakening, and it is said that he forgot all he had previously been taught.

After Mazu's death, Puyuan retired to Mount Nanquan, where he became known as Nanquan Puyuan or at times, less formally, simply as "Old Man Wang." He built himself a small hut and intended to live there as a hermit, but it so happened that the governor of the district, a man named Lugeng Tafu, had an interest in Zen. When he learned that one of Mazu's disciples was nearby, he sought the Zen master out. After that, Nanquan's fame spread, and a number of students gathered around him.

Several stories are told of Nanquan and Lugeng. Once, for example, Lugeng asked Nanquan, "In my house there's a stone. Sometimes it sits. Sometimes it lies down. Now I'm trying to carve it into a Buddha. Is it possible?"

"Possible," Nanquan said.

"So, it's not impossible?" the governor persisted.

"Impossible, impossible," Nanquan told him.

On another occasion, Lugeng told Nanquan this story: "Long ago, there was a man who hatched a goose egg and raised the gosling in a bottle. But as the bird grew larger, it was unable to get out of the bottle. The man wanted to rescue the goose, but he didn't want to break the bottle. What would you have done in his place?"

Nanquan called, "Governor!"

"Yes, master?"

"There! It's out!"

Lugeng was once at the monastery when Nanquan took his place in front of the monks assembled in the Dharma Hall. The governor invited the teacher to "expound the dharma for the sake of all sentient beings."

"What would you like me to say?" Nanquan asked.

"How can one enter the Way?"

"What's lacking?"

"Why are there so many realms of being and so many manners of birth?" Lugeng persisted.

"I don't bother with all that," Nanquan said.

After the governor had gained some understanding of Zen, he and Nanquan were walking in the temple garden one day. Lugeng remarked, "Thanks to your teaching, your disciple has at last acquired a little understanding of Buddhism."

Nanquan asked, "How do you demonstrate this understanding throughout the day?" Lugeng quoted a common Zen saying, "He goes about without even a shred of clothing." The remark was intended to demonstrate one free of all worldly attachments.

Nanquan scoffed. "Such a fellow is still outside the hall. He still hasn't realized Dao. A virtuous ruler doesn't make use of clever retainers."

Lugeng acknowledged his error. "Heaven-and-Earth and I both have the same source," he remarked. "The ten thousand things and

I both have the same body. Isn't that extraordinary?"

Nanquan replied by pointing to a flower and saying, "These days, people see this flower as though in a dream."

At that moment, Lugeng came to full awakening.

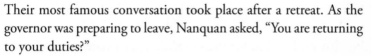

Their most famous conversation took place after a retreat. As the governor was preparing to leave, Nanquan asked, "You are returning to your duties?"

"I am."

"How do you plan to govern the people?"

"With wisdom and compassion," Lugeng said.

"In that case, every one of them will suffer."

Several other dialogues of Nanquan have been preserved as koans. In one, a monk asked, "Is there a teaching that hasn't yet been preached to the people?"

"There is," Nanquan admitted.

"What is this truth that hasn't been taught?"

"It isn't mind. It isn't Buddha. It isn't things."

Another monk traveled a long distance to see Nanquan. He came upon the teacher while he was cutting grass with a sickle, but the monk did not recognize him. He called to the grass cutter and asked, "What's the way to Nanquan?"

The master stood and held up his sickle. "I bought this sickle for thirty small coins."

The monk thought the grass cutter was a fool and said, "I didn't ask you about your sickle; I asked the way to Nanquan." In Chinese, the expression can also mean "Nanquan's way."

"I still use it with both pleasure and profit," Nanquan said.

A folktale tells of a time when Nanquan and an attendant were traveling far from their mountain temple. The master of a manor house in the region had a dream in which one of the gods that were worshipped locally appeared to him and told him that a distinguished guest would arrive the next day. The dream was so convincing that the lord had his servants make appropriate preparations.

When Nanquan arrived he was surprised that the lord and his servants seemed to be expecting him. He asked how they knew he was coming.

"The god who looks over our lands and fields informed me that you would arrive today," the lord explained.

"Poor old Wang," Nanquan said, referring to himself. "He has so little power that even the gods and demons can spy upon him."

The attendant objected, "No, master. You're such a good teacher, why shouldn't the gods and demons spy upon you?"

Nanquan waved off his attendant's words and told him, "Before we leave, put out an offering for the God of the Fields."

When Nanquan was in his final illness, his disciples crowded about his bed. The head monk asked, "Master, after your death, a hundred years from now, where will you be?"

"I'll be a water buffalo and work for the people," Nanquan told him.

"And will I still be your disciple?" the head monk asked.

"If you want to be my disciple, you'll need to chew grass."

On January 27, 835, at the age of eighty-seven, Nanquan told his students, "The star has been fading and the lamp growing dim for a long while. Don't say that I came or went." Those were his last words.

## BAIZHANG HUAIHAI

Baizhang Huaihai studied with Mazu at roughly the same time as Nanquan. One day, Baizhang and Mazu were walking together as a flock of geese flew overhead.

"What are those?" asked Mazu.

"Wild geese," Baizhang told him.

"Where are they going?"

"They've already flown away."

Mazu grabbed Baizhang's nose and twisted it sharply. "You can say they've flown away, but all the same they've been here from the beginning. How could they ever have flown away?"

At that moment, Baizhang's mind was opened.

He returned to his quarters, where one of the other monks found him weeping. The monk asked if Baizhang was feeling homesick.

"Not at all," Baizhang replied.

"Are you ill then?"

"No."

"So why are you weeping?"

"The master twisted my nose, and the pain was unbearable."

"He twisted your nose! What offense had you committed to justify him treating you in such a manner?"

"Go ask him."

The monk sought out Mazu and said, "Monk Huaihai is weeping in his quarters and tells me you twisted his nose. What offense did he commit?"

"He knows," Mazu told the monk. "Go ask him."

The monk return to Baizhang's room, saying, "The master says you know what offense you committed and that I should ask you about it."

At that, Baizhang laughed loudly.

"What is this?" the monk said. "One moment you're weeping and the next you're laughing!"

"My weeping of a moment ago is the same as my laughing now," Baizhang told him.

The next day, Mazu's disciples gathered in the meditation hall to listen to a dharma talk. A mat was spread on the floor before the image of the Buddha, where the master would perform ceremonial bows before speaking. Just as Mazu came into the room, Baizhang stepped forward and rolled up the mat, signaling the end of the talk.

Mazu returned to his room without comment. However, a little later he called Baizhang to explain himself.

"Yesterday you twisted my nose," Baizhang told him. "It was very painful."

"And today?"

"It's no longer painful."

When it was time for Baizhang to set out on his own, he went to pay his respects to his teacher before leaving the monastery. Mazu was holding a hossu at the time. Referring to the hossu, Baizhang asked, "Are you in the use of it or apart from the use of it?"

Mazu answered by hanging the hossu from a hook by his seat. He then asked Baizhang, "So you're setting out now. Tell me how you'll make use of those lips of yours for the sake of others."

Baizhang reached over, took up the hossu, and held it upright.

"Ah," Mazu remarked. "So are you in the use of it or apart from the use of it?"

Baizhang returned the hossu to its hook, and just as he did so, Mazu gave a great shout: "*Ho!*"

Baizhang would later claim that Mazu's shout left him deaf for three days. It also deepened his awakening.

Baizhang was a reformer whose restructuring of Zen monasteries helped the tradition survive the persecution of Buddhism that occurred just thirty years after his death. There were several reasons members of the ruling classes continued to object to Buddhism. It was viewed by native Confucianists as a foreign religion whose egalitarian sentiments were a threat to the existing social order. They objected to the fact that some of the monasteries had amassed great wealth at the expense of the country and believed they were refuges for individuals seeking to avoid military service or payment of taxes. The monasteries depended upon the donations of the Buddhist faithful for their maintenance, and in many cases the monks supported by those donations had become drones who neither promoted the dharma nor contributed to society.

Baizhang understood that Zen temples were not immune to these abuses, although because the Zen centers tended to be located in remote regions they did not draw the same attention as the monasteries of other Buddhist sects. Baizhang believed that Zen monks should be self-sufficient and insisted that they produce their own food rather than depend upon the donations or labors of others. Since some Buddhist sects forbade their monks from any activity, including farming, that might even inadvertently take the life of any creature, no matter how small, Baizhang's reforms were revolutionary.

Baizhang formalized what had previously been traditional guidelines into a formal rule. The structure of his monasteries included both physical labor and meditation. Both were part of the practice, and one was not to be considered superior to the other. On one occasion, when his disciples had asked him to speak to them about the dharma, he told them: "First prepare the fields for planting. After that I'll talk to you about the great principle of Zen." After the monks completed their work, they washed up and presented themselves in the Dharma Hall. Baizhang took his place before them and extended his arms wordlessly.

In his own activity, he provided an example of the life he expected his disciples to lead. Well into his eighties, he continued to work in the fields every day. As he became frailer with age, however, some of his disciples decided he should refrain from such exertions and they hid his gardening tools. When Baizhang could not find his tools, he went back to his room and, at meal time, remained there. He did not eat that day or the next. The disciples discussed this and wondered if he were angered by the missing tools, so they put them back in their usual place. Baizhang returned to his work in the fields and resumed his meals as well. He told his disciples, "A day of no work is a day of no food."

Many of the conversations he had with his followers took place as they were working together. When asked what the secret of Zen was, he told one disciple, "When hungry, eat; when tired, sleep." Another asked about the proper way to practice, and Baizhang said, "Don't cling; don't seek."

On one famous occasion, the monks at Baizhang's temple gathered to hear one of the master's dharma talks, but he entered the dharma hall brandishing his staff like a weapon and chased them all out the door. As they scrambled away from him, he called to them, and, when they turned to face him, he demanded, "What is it!?"

A pilgrim who had explored various sects of Buddhism came to see Baizhang and admitted that his studies had so far been unsatisfying. "I've been seeking the Buddha but still don't know how to proceed."

"It's very much like looking for an ox while riding one," Baizhang told him.

"What should a man do after finding him?"

"It's like going home on the back of an ox."

"So how should I proceed?" the monk asked.

"It's like a cowherd who, while looking after his cattle, uses his staff to keep them from wandering into another's pasture."

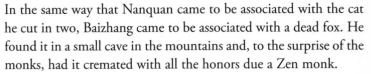

In the same way that Nanquan came to be associated with the cat he cut in two, Baizhang came to be associated with a dead fox. He found it in a small cave in the mountains and, to the surprise of the monks, had it cremated with all the honors due a Zen monk.

That evening, he explained to the monks that the fox was not actually a fox at all.

"One day after my dharma talk to you," he told them, "I noticed an old man in the hall. When everyone else had left, I approached him and asked who he was. He told me, 'I'm not a human being, although I once was. In fact, at one time I was the head monk of a monastery located on this very mountain. This was during the lifetime of the Kashyapa Buddha [the Buddha prior to Gautama Shakyamuni Buddha]. One day a monk came to me and asked, "Is the enlightened man subject to causation or not?" I said, "He is not." And for that I have been condemned to spend five hundred lifetimes reborn as a fox. Now I come to you hoping to find release. So, please tell me, is the enlightened man subject to causation or not?'

"I told him that the enlightened man does not ignore causation.

"The old man bowed to me with gratitude and told me he was now freed from his rebirths as a fox. Then he said he would remain on this mountain and informed me where to find his body, asking me to have it treated as the body of a monk. This we've now done."

One of Baizhang's most illustrious disciples was Huangbo Xiyun. He was seven feet tall and had a commanding presence. After he heard his master's story about the fox, he stood and said: "So the old man was doomed to be reborn five hundred times as a fox because he gave the wrong answer. Tell us, what would have happened if he'd given the right answer?"

"Come up here," Baizhang told him, "and I'll tell you."

Huangbo strode up to Baizhang but, before the master could do anything, Huangbo slapped him on the face. Baizhang laughed happily and clapped his hands. "I had thought the barbarian [Bodhidharma] had a red beard," he exclaimed. "But now I see before me the red-bearded barbarian himself!"

*The second of the* Ox Herding Pictures,
Finding the Footprints of the Ox

# CHAPTER TWELVE

# ZHAOZHOU CONGSHEN

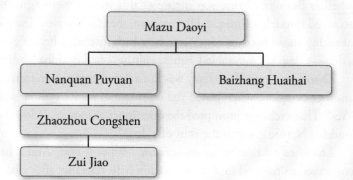

## ZHAOZHOU CONGSHEN

In the Rinzai tradition, the koan most commonly given to beginning Zen students is called, in Japanese, "Joshu's Mu." It originated with Zhaozhou Congshen, the man who could have saved Nanquan's cat had he been there. The koan is very short. A monk asks Zhaozhou if even a dog has Buddha Nature, and Zhaozhou answers, "Wu! [J: Mu!]," which means "No!" or "Nothing!"

The story is more complex than it may appear. The monk who put the question would have known that Buddhist teaching affirms that all creatures have Buddha Nature, not only dogs but even mosquitoes and worms. What the monk was looking for was reassurance. Although he knew in theory that he had Buddha Nature, he still had not realized it himself. He may have begun to wonder whether Buddha Nature was innate or if it were something to be acquired through technique. His question, therefore, was sly. Instead of asking about his own condition, he asked, instead, whether even a dog—a despised animal in Chinese culture—had Buddha Nature.

Zhaozhou's immediate reply was not a literal negative. In fact, on another occasion, when posed the same question, Zhaozhou said, "Yes!" That exchange prompted the questioner to inquire, "How did Buddha Nature get into the skin of a dog?"

The koan asks, in its Japanese form, "What is *mu*?" And it has continued to resound in Zen meditation halls centuries after Zhaozhou responded to that initial inquirer.

Zhaozhou came to study with Nanquan Puyuan when he was eighteen years old. At the time, Nanquan was ill, and he was lying in bed when he received the new pupil. He asked Zhaozhou which previous temples he had visited, and Zhaozhou told him that he had recently been at Ruixiang, which means "Auspicious Image."

"And did you see the Auspicious Image?" Nanquan asked.

"No, I didn't," Zhaozhou admitted. Then he added, cheekily, "But I've seen a reclining Buddha."

Shortly after beginning to study with Nanquan, Zhaozhou asked the master, "What is the Way [Dao]?"

Nanquan's frequently quoted reply was: "Everyday mind is the Way."

"How do I find it?" Zhaozhou asked.

"By seeking it, you only separate yourself from it."

"But if I don't seek it, how will I find it?"

"The Way is not a matter of finding or not finding, of knowing or not knowing. Knowing is delusion; not knowing is confusion. When you have really reached the true Way, you'll find it is as vast and boundless as the sky."

These words brought Zhaozhou to awakening. He described the experience by saying he felt "suddenly ruined and homeless." He had found the Way that was as vast, boundless, and empty as the sky.

To deepen his experience, he studied with other teachers for a while, then returned to his master and stayed with Nanquan until the older man's death in 835.

One day Zhaozhou challenged Nanquan, "Say a word that goes beyond the four statements and one hundred negations of Nagarjuna [statements about the nature of being]."

Without saying a word, Nanquan returned to his room.

"The old master is ready enough to talk except when he's asked to," Zhaozhou remarked.

When Nanquan's attendant reprimanded Zhaozhou for being disrespectful, Zhaozhou slapped him. At that, Nanquan came back into the courtyard. He locked the gate of the monastery and said,

"If any of you can say a word of Zen, the gate will be opened. Otherwise it remains locked."

A number of monks gave their views of the dharma, all of which Nanquan rejected. Finally, Zhaozhou said, "Oh, for goodness sake!"

Nanquan opened the gate.

After Nanquan's death, Zhaozhou, then in his late fifties, went on a pilgrimage to visit the other Zen masters of his day. Before setting out, he declared, "If I find a child of seven whose understanding is greater than mine, I'll ask him to instruct me; if I meet a man of one hundred years whose understanding is less than mine, I'll instruct him." It was a bold statement to make in China at a time when Confucianists were decrying the way in which Buddhism threatened the social order, which insisted upon strict proprieties between the generations.

While on pilgrimage, Zhaozhou would enter into dharma combat with other Zen practitioners. These feisty dialogues took the form of asking and answering questions. They differed from mondo, in which the dialogue was between master and student. Dharma combat was a means for two masters to test one another's depth of understanding. When, for example, Zhaozhou visited Daitzu, he asked: "What is the body of Prajna [wisdom]?" In so doing, he was not asking for information; he was issuing a challenge.

Daitzu simply repeated the question back to him: "What is the body of Prajna?"

In reply, Zhaozhou laughed heartily and went his way.

A little later, Daitzu came upon Zhaozhou sweeping the ground. This time Daitzu put the question first, "What is the body of Prajna?"

Zhaozhou threw down his broom and, once more with a hearty laugh, went his way.

On another occasion, Zhaozhou went to visit Touzi Dadong, who lived in a straw hut. Zhaozhou encountered Touzi on the path leading to the other's hut, and he asked, "Aren't you Touzi?"

Instead of replying to the question, Touzi demanded: "Give me some money to buy oil." Then he continued on his way into town.

Zhaozhou proceeded down the road and reached the hut before its owner had completed his errands. There he waited. When Touzi returned, he was carrying a pitcher of oil.

"I'd heard so much about Master Touzi," Zhaozhou remarked. "But all I see before me is an old peddler of oil."

"You see the peddler but not Touzi," the other replied.

"Where then is Touzi?" Zhaozhou asked.

"Oil for sale! Oil for sale!" Touzi called out.

When Zhaozhou visited the temple of Huangbo Xiyun, the dharma heir of Baizhang Huaihai, he went to pay his respects to the teacher. Huangbo saw him approaching and closed the door to his rooms. Undeterred, Zhaozhou grabbed up a flaming log from a brazier and walked about the Dharma Hall shouting, "Fire! Fire!"

Huangbo came from his rooms and grabbed Zhaozhou by the collar of his robe, shouting, "Speak! Speak!"

"It's only after the thief has run off that you've drawn your bow," Zhaozhou remarked.

In his travels, Zhaozhou came upon a monk who was known for his devotion to the sutras. He asked the monk how many sutras he read in a day.

"Seven or eight, at times even ten."

"Ah," Zhaozhou muttered. "Then you don't know how to read the sutras after all."

"I don't? And how many sutras do you read in a day?"

"In a day, I read only a single word."

Zhaozhou did not gather his own disciples until he was eighty years old, at which time he was invited to take command of a temple named for Guanyin, the Bodhisattva of Compassion, in the city of Zhaozhou.

Zhaozhou was not as physical in his presentation of Zen as some of his predecessors had been. His teaching was verbal, and it was said that his "lips flashed light." He was so confident of his method, however, that he is recorded to have said: "A metal Buddha will melt in the forge. A wooden Buddha will burn in fire. A clay Buddha will dissolve in water. None of these are the real Buddha; the real Buddha resides within you. Mind is not born; the ten thousand things are without flaw. Sit for twenty or thirty years, and if you still don't understand, then you may cut off my head and use it as a chamber pot!

"Your true nature existed before this world appeared. When this world ends, your true nature will not. From the moment I discovered my true nature, there hasn't been anyone else. There's just the one in charge. What is there to be sought elsewhere? At this moment, you already have it. But if you think about it, it's lost."

His verbal instructions have been preserved in several koan that often remain opaque to those who first encounter them. His skill was in knowing precisely what to say to individuals in specific circumstances in order to bring them to awareness. For example, the story has already been recounted that on one occasion a new monk presented himself to Zhaozhou, saying, "I've just arrived at this temple, and I've come to ask you to accept me as a disciple."

"Have you eaten?" Zhaozhou asked.

"Yes, sir. I have."

"In that case, wash your bowl." It is said that this instruction was all it took to bring the new monk to realization.

Zhaozhou, commenting on the *Xinxin Ming* of Sengcan, remarked, "The Way is not difficult to attain. Just avoid choice and attachment. As soon as there are words, there is choice and understanding. So, is understanding a thing for you to uphold or sustain?"

One of his monks asked, "If the Way isn't found in understanding, what is there to be upheld?"

"I don't know," Zhaozhou told him.

"If you don't know," the monk went on, "then how can you say it's not found in understanding?"

"You've put your question and received an answer," Zhaozhou chided him. "After that, all that remains is to bow and withdraw."

A monk said: "You frequently quote the Third Patriarch's saying, 'The real Way is not difficult except that it refuses to show preference, abhorring choice and attachment.' Isn't that your attachment?"

"Someone asked me the same question once before," Zhaozhou answered, "and five years later I still don't find any justification for it."

Another monk said, "You say 'The real Way is not difficult except that it refuses to show preference, abhorring choice and attachment.' What are non-choice and non-attachment?"

Zhaozhou replied by quoting the Buddha, "Throughout heaven and earth, I alone am the holy one."

"That's still choice and attachment."

"You dolt! Where are choice and attachment?"

A third monk said, "The real Way isn't difficult except that it refuses to show preference, abhorring choice and attachment. But if you say anything, there's choice and attachment. How then can one help another?"

Zhaozhou said, "Complete the quotation."

The monk admitted: "I only know this much."

"Well, you know," Zhaozhou told him, "the real Way isn't difficult except that it refuses to show preference, abhorring choice and attachment."

A monk asked, "If we come upon a person living in poverty, what should we give him?"

"He doesn't lack anything," Zhaozhou asserted.

The city of Zhaozhou, from which the master took his name, was famed for a stone bridge that may have been little more than a ford crossing the river. One day a monk, who had traveled some distance to meet Zhaozhou, presented himself, saying, "The stone bridge of Zhaozhou is famed throughout the region, but all I see here is a rough set of stepping-stones." The statement was a challenge, in effect saying, "I've heard a great deal about this famous teacher, but all I see here is a miserable old man."

Zhaozhou echoed the words of Touzi, "You see only the stepping-stones and don't see the stone bridge."

"What's this stone bridge?"

"It allows horses and donkeys to pass over."

A monk asked Zhaozhou, "In one of the sutras it's said that all things return to the One. To what does this One return?"

Zhaozhou said, "When I was in the province of Tsing I had a hemp robe that was seven units of weight."

Another monk posed this somber question: "After the body has died and has been reduced to its constituent elements and scattered, is there anything that remains, eternal, non-material?"

"The wind is brisk today," Zhaozhou replied.

In a relationship reminiscent of that between Nanquan and Governor Lugeng, the governor Wang Rong became a disciple of Zhaozhou. Their first meeting, however, did not begin according to protocol. Instead of coming to the temple gate to meet the governor, Zhaozhou remained seated in the meditation hall. The governor ignored this apparent discourtesy and went in to pay his respects to the Zen master. Some time later, a lesser state official came to the temple and Zhaozhou rushed to meet him at the gate. Zhaozhou's disciples were confused by their master's apparent misplaced priorities and asked him about them. He replied, "It's my habit to receive eminent guests in the meditation hall; for those not as eminent, I'll descend from my place to greet them; it is only the least that I'll receive at the temple gate."

When the remark was reported to Wang Rong, he was impressed by it, and after that a close relationship developed between the two men.

Guanyin Temple was an old building in need of extensive repairs, and the governor offered to pay for these. But Zhaozhou declined the assistance. When repairs were required, he had the monks use scrap materials. It is said that when a leg of his stool broke off, Zhaozhou replaced it with a piece of partially burnt firewood.

The temple was located near Mount Tai, one of the five sacred mountains of China. It was a popular destination for pilgrims, and an elderly woman operated a tea shop on the road leading to the mountain. On occasion, travelers looking for Zhaozhou would stop at the shop and ask the old woman the way to the mountain. She would tell them, "It's straight ahead." But when the monk proceeded on his way, the old woman would remark, just loud enough for him to hear, "He might look like a good monk, but he goes off just like the others."

One of these traveling monks described his encounter with the old woman to Zhaozhou, complaining about her lack of respect. Zhaozhou told the monk that he would look into the matter. Zhaozhou made his way to the old woman's tea shop and asked her the same question his disciples had, "What's the way to Mount Tai?"

"Straight ahead," the old woman replied.

Zhaozhou thanked her and went his way. As he left the shop, he heard her sneer, "He might look like a good monk, but he goes just like the others."

When Zhaozhou returned to the temple, he reported to his disciples, "I've looked into the matter of the old woman."

A monk asked Zhaozhou, "Who is the Buddha?"

Zhaozhou said, "He's in the shrine."

"All that's in the shrine is a statue made of clay," the monk complained.

"That's it."

"But who's the Buddha?"

"The one in the shrine."

"That Buddha has form. What is the Buddha without form?" the monk persisted.

"Mind," Zhaozhou replied.

"Mind is subjective. I still want to know: Who is the Buddha?"

"No-mind [*wuxin*]."

"May one discriminate between mind and no-mind?"

"You've already done so. What more do you want me to say?"

A new monk presented himself at Guanyin Temple, and Zhaozhou asked him, "Have you been here before?"

"Yes, I have," the monk said.

"Please have some tea before you leave."

On another occasion, Zhaozhou asked a different monk, "Have you been here before?"

"No, sir, I haven't."

"Please have some tea before you leave."

One of Zhaozhou's disciples inquired, "Why did you say 'Please have some tea before you leave' to both the monk who'd been here before and the one who hadn't?"

Zhaozhou called the disciple's name. "Yes?" the disciple replied.

"Please have some tea before you leave," Zhaozhou told him.

When a monk asked Zhaozhou, "Why did Bodhidharma come from the west?" Zhaozhou said, "The cypress tree in the garden."

"Don't talk to me of things of the external world," the monk complained.

"I didn't," Zhaozhou told him.

"Then tell me, why did Bodhidharma come east?"

"The cypress tree in the garden."

## Zui Jiao

Zui Jiao was a disciple of Zhaozhou. After his master's death, Zui visited the Zen teacher Fayan Wenyi. Fayan commented, "Your teacher was a remarkable man. I understand that once a cypress tree was the subject of his talk. Is that so?"

"There was no such talk," Zui asserted.

"There wasn't? That's odd. All of the monks I've met who studied with Zhaozhou speak of his reference to a cypress tree in answer to the question, 'Why did Bodhidharma come from west?' How can you claim otherwise?"

Zui roared, "My master said no such thing! Please don't disrespect him by saying so!"

Fayan nodded his head in admiration and said, "You're certainly the lion's son."

*The third of the* Ox Herding Pictures,
Glimpsing the Ox

# CHAPTER THIRTEEN

# ZHAOZHOU'S CONTEMPORARIES

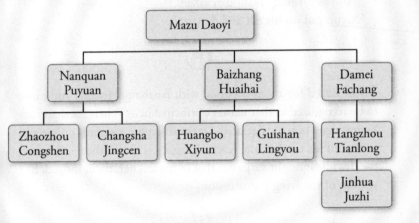

## HUANGBO XIYUN

Huangbo Xiyun received his Buddhist name (Xiyun) when he took the precepts at Mount Huangbo in Fujien Province. After that, he studied with several Buddhist teachers of the day, including both of Mazu's most important heirs, Nanquan Puyuan and Baizhang Huaihai.

He was with Nanquan first and must have made an impression on him, because when Xiyun left Nanquan, the master accompanied him to the monastery gate. There he held up the younger man's hat and commented: "You're fairly large, but your hat isn't too big for you, is it?"

Xiyun accepted the hat, saying, "That's so, but the entire universe is covered beneath it."

"And as for me?" Nanquan asked.

Xiyun put on his hat and departed.

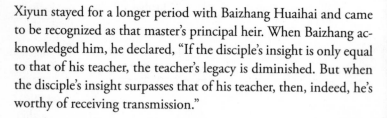

Xiyun stayed for a longer period with Baizhang Huaihai and came to be recognized as that master's principal heir. When Baizhang acknowledged him, he declared, "If the disciple's insight is only equal to that of his teacher, the teacher's legacy is diminished. But when the disciple's insight surpasses that of his teacher, then, indeed, he's worthy of receiving transmission."

Xiyun's own disciples included Linji Yixuan (J: Rinzai Gigen), from whom the Rinzai school of Zen takes its name, and Governor Pei of the local prefecture. The governor was wealthy enough to be able to finance a temple for his teacher. The mountain where the temple was built was renamed Mount Huangbo, after the mountain where Xiyun had first accepted the precepts. The temple came to be known as Huangbo Temple, and Xiyun to be known as Huangbo Xiyun.

He remained a man of great humility even as a teacher, and it is recorded that he acquired a red mark on his forehead from the vigor with which he performed prostrations before the image of the Buddha. At one time, the heir-apparent to the emperor was placed at the temple as a novice, and he questioned Huangbo about these prostrations: "One isn't supposed to look for the Buddha, the dharma, or the sangha outside of oneself. So what is the master seeking when he bows?"

"Not seeking Buddha, dharma, or sangha, one simply bows," Huangbo said.

"If you're not seeking anything, why bow?"

In spite of the extensive protocols protecting royal persons, that question earned the future emperor a slap from the Zen master. When the young man protested, Huangbo struck him again, remarking: "Consider where we are! Is this a place for idle chatter?"

Huangbo was dismissive of the pretensions of others. The story is told of a journey he undertook during which he fell into the company of another monk traveling in the same direction. They enjoyed one another's companionship and so proceeded together, walking and chatting in a friendly manner. However, when they came to a river, the other monk strode across the waters without breaking stride. Huangbo waited for the ferry and was heard to remark, "Had I known he was that kind of fellow, I would have broken his legs before he came to the water."

When Governor Pei wanted to have his understanding of Zen tested, he wrote his ideas on a sheet of paper that he presented to the master. Without looking at the writing, Huangbo laid it aside. The governor and Huangbo both remained silent for a period, then Huangbo asked, "Do you understand?"

The governor admitted he did not.

"If it can be expressed in this manner," Huangbo told him, indicating the paper, "then it's not true teaching. The essence of our school can't be captured by brush and ink."

Zen tales were becoming more common, and on occasion aspirants imitated the spontaneity of the great masters without necessarily having any real understanding. So it was with a member of a group of young men who applied to be accepted as novices. Huangbo received them in the Dharma Hall. All but one of the applicants bowed as the master approached. The exception picked up his cushion and circled it in the air above his head.

Huangbo said to the young man, "I've heard that it's against the precepts to keep a hunting dog."

The young man responded with, "I'm following after the sound of the wild sheep."

"The sheep make no sound. There's nothing for you to follow."

"Then I'll follow their tracks."

"There aren't any tracks to follow."

"Then the sheep are dead," the applicant said.

Huangbo accepted the young men as novices, but the next day, during the assembly, he asked, "Where's the monk who claimed to be following after wild sheep?"

The novice came forward.

"The matter we were discussing yesterday hasn't been concluded," Huangbo said. "After we finished speaking, what did you think?"

The novice didn't know how to reply.

"I thought that you might've been a student of the true way," Huangbo admitted, "but now I see that you're nothing more than a dialectician."

The central issue for Huangbo, as for most Zen teachers, was "mind" (*xin*), and he pointed out that just as the eye cannot see the eye, so mind cannot be found by mind. All beings, he held, are the One Mind, outside of which nothing exists. It was natural that the disciples who came to him often believed that it was incumbent upon them to seek their true natures, but Huangbo insisted there was nothing to attain or to do because, like all other sentient beings, these disciples already were Buddha. "There's no distinction between Buddha and sentient beings," he taught. "Both are the One Mind. To awaken to the realization that your Mind, just as it is, is the Buddha; to realize that there's nothing to be attained, nothing to be done, this is the Dao." To seek what one already was or already had was to misunderstand the situation. Therefore the act of seeking put realization at a distance.

Because realization is not something that can be found outside oneself, nor something one can acquire from another, Huangbo declared to his disciples that throughout all of China there were no teachers of Zen.

One of the monks objected, "How can you say that? Aren't we all here students of Zen?"

"I didn't say there was no Zen," Huangbo told him, "I only pointed out that there were no teachers of Zen."

## CHANGSHA JINGCEN

Changsha Jingcen was one of Nanquan's heirs. After he received transmission, Jingcen established his own temple at Tanzhou. Later he moved to Lake Dongting in the Changsha district.

After Nanquan's death, Sansheng Huiran sent a messenger to Changsha. The messenger asked Changsha, "Now that he's dead, where has your late master, Nanquan, gone?"

"When Shitou Xiqian was still a novice, he attended upon the Sixth Patriarch," Changsha told him.

"I wasn't asking about Shitou's novitiate," the messenger persisted. "I asked where Nanquan went after he died."

"Hmm," Changsha mused. "It makes one think, doesn't it?"

The messenger said, "You're like an ancient pine a thousand feet high that can withstand the winter cold. But there's nothing of the bamboo-shoot, which can break its way through rock, about you."

Changsha did not bother to say anything in reply.

The messenger waited a moment, then he bowed and said, "I thank you for your reply."

Changsha continued silent.

Afterwards the messenger returned to Sansheng and reported his interview with Changsha. Sansheng expressed admiration. "It seems Master Changsha has gone even further than my own teacher, Linji. I must visit him myself in order to test how deep his understanding is."

Sansheng presented himself to Changsha and said, "I heard of your conversation with my messenger regarding where Nanquan went after death. Your answer was one of the most remarkable and illuminating I'm aware of in the history of Zen."

Changsha still remained silent.

On other occasions, Changsha was noted for the aggressiveness with which he demonstrated the dharma. For example, Yangshan Huiji, a disciple of Guishan Lingyou, spent some time with Changsha. One evening, the two were observing the full moon. Yangshan remarked, "All men without exception have this but can't use it."

Changsha nodded his agreement but then challenged Yangshan, "What about your use of it?"

"How do you use it?" Yangshan responded.

Changsha grabbed Yangshan by the lapels of his robe, shook him, and threw him to the ground.

Gathering himself together, Yangshan remarked, "You're like a tiger!" After this incident, Changsha acquired the nickname "Tiger."

When Changsha was asked, "What is the Dao?," his answer was, "It doesn't exclude you."

"Who then is the teacher of all the Buddhas and bodhisattvas?"

"Who has concealed him?"

In their book, *Zen Dust*, Isshu Miura and Ruth Sasaki provide this sample from one of his sermons:

> The entire universe is your eye; the entire universe is your complete body; the entire universe is your own luminance; the entire universe is within your own luminance. In the entire universe there is no one who is not your own self. I repeat what I am continually saying to you: All the Buddhas of the Three Worlds (past, present, and future) and all the sentient beings in the Dharmadhatu, these are the light of Great Intrinsic Wisdom.[26]

One of Changsha Jingcen's disciples once paid a visit to a priest who had been a student of Nanquan. The disciple asked the priest, "What was it like after you met Nanquan."

The priest said nothing.

"In that case, what was it like *before* you met Nanquan?"

"The same as after I'd met him," the priest said.

The disciple reported this conversation to Changsha, who composed this poem in reply:

> Atop a hundred-foot pole, an unmoving person,
> Although he's gained entry, he hasn't reached the truth.

He must step forth from the top of the pole,
Then the world in ten directions is the complete body.[27]

"How does one advance one more step from the top of a hundred foot pole?" the amazed disciple asked.

"In this province there are mountains; in that province there are rivers."

"I don't understand," the disciple admitted.

"The four seas and the five lakes are within them."

A monk asked Changsha, "Can one become a Buddha or not?"

Changsha replied, "Does the emperor work in the rice fields?"

"I still don't understand. Who becomes a Buddha?"

"You do."

The monk did not know how to reply.

"Do you understand?" Changsha asked him.

"No, I don't."

"If one trips and falls on the ground, it's the ground they use to push themselves back up again. Does the ground have anything to say about it?"

## HANGZHOU TIANLONG

Hangzhou Tianlong was the dharma heir of Damei Fachang. He is remembered for introducing his own disciple, Juzhi, to his "one-finger Zen." Other than that there are only a few recorded stories regarding him. In one encounter, he was asked by a monk, "How does one escape the three realms [the realm of desire, the realm of the end of desire while remaining in form, and the realm beyond form]?"

Hangzhou's response was to ask the inquirer, "Where are you right now?"

# JINHUA JUZHI

Jinhua Juzhi was a devout Buddhist who lived as a hermit in an old temple in the mountains, where he spent his time in sutra-chanting and practicing a form of meditation. It was the habit of such hermits to offer lodging to the many Zen pilgrims who traveled from place to place to deepen their insight. But some of these pilgrims were selective about where they would lodge.

One day the nun Shiji came into the temple while Juzhi was meditating. She did not remove her traveler's hat or lay down her staff but rather walked in a circle around Juzhi's cushion three times. Then she declared, "Say a word of Zen and I'll take off my hat."

Juzhi did not know how to reply. She put her demand a second time, and Juzhi remained silent. When she started to leave, he said, "It's late and getting dark. You should stay here tonight."

"Say a word of Zen, and I will. Otherwise I'll leave."

Juzhi still did not know what to say, and Shiji departed. When the nun was gone, Juzhi felt ashamed that he should have spent so much time in meditation and yet still could not say a single word of Zen when called upon to do so. He determined he would set out the next day to seek a teacher to help him achieve awakening. That night, however, he had a dream in which such a teacher came to his temple, so he resolved to remain where he was.

Somewhat later, Hangzhou Tianlong came to the hermitage. Juzhi recognized him as an accomplished Zen teacher, and he told him the story of his encounter with the nun, Shiji. "Then I dreamt that a master who could help me would visit this temple," he continued. "I'm certain that dream presaged your arrival. Please teach me."

All Tianlong did in reply was raise a single finger. That gesture was enough to bring Juzhi to awakening.

Once he received transmission and began to work with his own students, his response to all questions he was asked was simply to raise a single finger.

As Juzhi became older, he needed the services of an attendant. It happened that the attendant took to imitating his master; when someone would ask about Juzhi's teaching, the attendant also just raised a finger. When Juzhi caught him in this mimicry, he grabbed the attendant's hand and, using a knife, cut off the offending finger. The attendant screamed in pain and tried to rush from the room. Before he reached the door however, Juzhi called his name. The attendant turned to look at the master, and Juzhi raised a single finger. The attendant came to awakening.

When his death approached, Juzhi called his disciples together and told them: "I received my one-finger Zen from my master, Hangzhou Tianlong, and throughout my entire life I have not yet been able to exhaust it." After saying this, he passed away.

## GUISHAN LINGYOU

Guishan Lingyou became a Buddhist monk at the age of fifteen and studied with a variety of teachers who lectured on the meaning of the sutras until, at the age of twenty-two, he finally came to Baizhang and asked to be allowed to undertake the practice of Zen.

One evening, the two were sitting up late, the younger in attendance on the older beside a fireplace that appeared to have gone cold. Suddenly Baizhang asked, "Who are you?"

"Lingyou," the younger man answered.

"Lingyou, rake the ashes in the fireplace and find an ember."

Lingyou poked among the ashes with a pair of tongs then announced, "I can't find any embers."

Baizhang took the tongs from him and, searching deeper in the ashes, brought out a small ember still burning. He showed the ember to Guishan, saying, "Just this! Do you see?"

This event was enough to bring Lingyou to awakening, and he bowed to Baizhang in gratitude.

Baizhang told him, "In the sutra we read, 'To be aware of Buddha-nature, one needs to be aware of time and causation.' When the time is appropriate, one realizes it as if remembering something one had previously known but had forgotten. It isn't obtained from another. And when one is enlightened, it's no different from before one was enlightened. If one makes no discrimination between enlightened and unenlightened, one's original self will become manifest. You've attained it; now you must cultivate it with mindfulness."

Lingyou stayed with Baizhang for twenty years, during which time he was given the post of head cook, an honored position within the Zen community because it was believed that the state of mind of the cook affected the meals he prepared.

One day a man named Sima Toutuo came to see Baizhang. Sima was a student of Daoism and was famed for his understanding of Chinese medicine and his ability to judge a person's character simply by observing his comportment. Sima had found a mountain in the south, Mount Gui, which he believed would make a good site for a new monastery. He asked Baizhang to recommend someone suitable for the task of establishing it.

Baizhang gave the request some thought, then said, "I myself would be willing to travel there."

"With all due respect, that wouldn't be appropriate," Sima said. "The character of the man and the place must be in accord. You have an ectomorphic personality, like a lone wolf, thin and bony— a man of strict character who remains aloof from others. You wouldn't be at home in such a rich and fertile place. If one of your personality presided over the new monastery, the monks gathered there wouldn't exceed a thousand. But if one of a more endomorphic personality presided, the number would be greater."

"In that case," Baizhang said, "I recommend my chief monk, Hualin."

Sima asked Baizhang to call Hualin into the room so he could observe him. When Hualin presented himself, Sima asked him to clear his throat, then walk across the floor. Once Hualin retired, Sima told Baizhang, "This man still isn't appropriate for Gui Mountain."

"There is one other I could recommend," Baizhang said, and he sent for Lingyou.

Sima needed only a brief look before declaring, "This is the very man for the position!"

An announcement was made to the community that the cook was being sent to establish the new monastery. When Hualin heard of this, he sought an interview with Baizhang and complained, "I'm your head monk. Why then have you passed me over for this honor and bestowed it on Lingyou?"

Baizhang understood Hualin's grievance so he agreed to call the members of the monastery together and put a test to both the contenders for the position. When the assembly was gathered, Baizhang placed a pitcher on the ground in front of him and addressed Hualin and Lingyou. "Tell me what this is without naming it."

"You can't call it a block of wood," Hualin proffered.

Baizhang shook his head.

Then Lingyou stepped forward and pushed the pitcher over with his foot, after which he left the room.

"The cook has triumphed," Baizhang announced.

Lingyou was sent to the mountain and took the name Guishan as a result. The region was still wilderness, and, in spite of Sima's predictions, for many years Guishan dwelt by himself. During that period, his only companions were the monkeys of the region and his only food were the chestnuts they ate. He remained on the mountain, however, and eventually had 1,500 disciples and would acknowledge forty-one of these as dharma heirs. The most important was Yangshan Huiji. The Guiyang School, the first of the Five Houses of Zen, takes its name from the combination of the two names, Guishan and Yangshan.

*The fourth of the* Ox Herding Pictures,
Catching the Ox

# CHAPTER FOURTEEN

# GUISHAN'S DESCENDANTS

"The Five Houses of Zen" refers to separate teaching lines that evolved from the traditions associated with specific masters. Three of these traditions, the Caodong (J: Soto), Yunmen, and Fayan, descended from the transmission line traced back to Qingyuan Xingshi and Shitou Xiqian. The other two, the Linji (J: Rinzai) and Guiyang, proceeded from Mazu Daoyi and Baizhang Huaihai. The Linji House later produced two offshoots, the Yangqi and Huanglong. When these last two are added to the Five Houses, together they are referred to as the Seven Schools of Zen.

Each school had a different approach to the Zen process. The two schools that remain active today can be compared as an example. They are best known by their Japanese names, Soto and Rinzai. While the goal of both is to guide practitioners to awakening, their approaches differ both in custom and focus. A basic difference in custom is that in the Rinzai tradition, meditators sit facing into the room, while meditators in the Soto tradition sit facing a wall, following the example of Bodhidharma. A difference in focus can be found in the preferred mode of meditation. For the Rinzai, students working with a teacher are generally given a series of koans to meditate upon. The Soto student, on the other hand, is usually taught a subjectless meditation, known in Japanese as *shikan-taza* or "just sitting." In shikan-taza, one is aware of one's breath without specifically following it or counting the breaths, as is done in preparatory exercises. The Soto School, however, does make occasional use of koans, and Rinzai students can be advised to practice shikan-taza.

The most significant characteristic of the Guiyang School was demonstrated in the way in which Guishan responded to Baizhang's challenge to tell him what the pitcher was without naming it. Hualin's answer had been verbal: "You cannot call it a block of wood." Guishan eschewed language and tipped the pitcher over with his foot.

All Zen schools recognize that students cannot be brought to awakening solely by verbal instruction. Awakening is not a matter of coming to an intellectual understanding; rather, it is an experience. The difference is similar to that between knowing fire is hot and actually feeling the heat. The Guiyang School, therefore, focused on action and silence rather than on lecture or analysis.

## YANGSHAN HUIJI

When Yangshan Huiji was a child, he asked permission of his parents to become a monk. They refused his request and reminded him of his familial duties. To demonstrate the depth of his desire to take up the religious life, Yangshan cut off two of his fingers and presented them to his parents, telling them that he could best fulfill his family obligations by seeking the dharma. Recognizing his resolve, his parents gave their permission, and Yangshan began his journey.

Before becoming the disciple of Guishan, Yangshan studied with several other masters, including Baizhang and Danyuan Yingzhen, the heir of Huizhong Guoshi (the National Teacher). While with Baizhang, Yangshan had a reputation for verbosity. It was said that he needed ten words to reply to each of Baizhang's, which prompted the master to say that Yangshan would eventually meet a teacher who would serve him better.

Yangshan next served as attendant to Shishuang Qingzhu. In that capacity he was with the master on an occasion when a traveling monk presented himself at the monastery and put the traditional question, "What was the reason the First Patriarch came from the west?" Shishuang replied, "Imagine a man at the bottom of a well one thousand units of measure deep. Show me how you'd get him out without using a rope, and I'll tell you the significance of the First Patriarch's visit."

Instead of responding to Shishuang's challenge, the monk remarked, "Yes. There's another teacher at the monastery in Hunan who also speaks like this."

Shishuang dismissed the visitor, telling young Yangshan to "Show this lifeless fellow out."

The question perplexed Yangshan, and when he came to study with Danyuan Yingzhen, he related the story to his new teacher and asked, "How can one get the man out without a rope?"

"What a fool!" Danyuan said. "Who's in the well?"

After Danyuan's death, Yangshan came at last to study with Guishan. When he first presented himself to the master, Guishan noted, "I've been told that while you were with Baizhang you had ten words to his one. Is that so?"

Yangshan admitted it was.

"Very well," Guishan said. "Tell me, what do you have to say about the ultimate truth of Buddhism?"

But as Yangshan opened his mouth and before he could utter a sound, Guishan shouted: "Ho!"

Again, Guishan asked, "About the ultimate meaning of Buddhism?"

And again, before Yangshan could reply, Guishan shouted, "Ho!" Guishan put the question a third time, and a third time shouted before Yangshan could reply.

Finally the young man bowed his head and, with tears in his eyes, said, "My late master, Baizhang, said that I'd meet a teacher who would be better suited to me, and now I've found him."

When he was accepted by Guishan as a disciple, Yangshan also told him Shishuang's story of the man in the well and asked how he could be got out with using a rope.

"Huiji!" Guishan called.

"Yes, sir?"

"There! He's out!"

Later Yangshan would say, "From Yingzhen I got the name. From Guishan, I got the substance."

Under Guishan's direction, Yangshan dedicated himself to zazen. After three years, Guishan came upon him as he was seated in meditation beneath a tree. The master prodded the student's back with his staff. Yangshan turned to him, and Guishan asked, "Do you have anything to say?"

"Not a word," Huiji said. "Nor would I borrow one from anyone else."

Once Yangshan was recognized as Guishan's heir, he worked with his master to develop the school that would later be named after both of them. They continued to test each other's understanding throughout their time together. Once Guishan's assembly of monks was harvesting tea. As they worked, Guishan suddenly called to Yangshan: "All day long I've heard your voice, but I haven't seen you. Show me your original body."

Yangshan shook a tea plant.

"You have the function," Guishan told him, "but not the substance." [This referred to a distinction made in classical Chinese thought between an object and its use.]

"And what would you say?" Yangshan demanded.

Guishan kept silent.

"You have the substance but not the function," Yangshan told him.

"I spare you twenty blows," Guishan said, ending the discussion.

On another occasion, Guishan saw Yangshan coming in the compound gates with a mattock on his shoulder.

"Where are you coming from?" he asked.

"From the fields," Yangshan told him.

"And how many people are there?

Yangshan swung the mattock and drove it into the ground, then stood still.

"There are too many people on the mountain cutting grass," Guishan remarked.

Yangshan pulled his mattock free and continued on his way.

During an assembly, Guishan told his disciples, "When I die, I'll be reborn as a water buffalo in the village at the foot of the mountain. On the side of the buffalo, you'll find these words written: 'This is the monk Guishan.' If you call it Guishan, it's actually a buffalo. But if you call it a buffalo, it's actually Guishan. What, then, will you call it?"

A number of suggestions were put forward that Guishan rejected. Then Yangshan stepped forward, bowed, and left the assembly.

## XIANGYAN ZHIXIAN

Xiangyan Zhixian's enlightenment story is one of the most frequently recounted in books on Zen.

He is recognized as one of Guishan's heirs, but he began, as did Guishan, as a disciple of Baizhang. Before coming to Baizhang, Xiangyan had devoted himself to the study of the Chinese classics as well as the traditional Buddhist scriptures, and he acquired a reputation for scholarship. He kept copious notes on his studies and was known to have a ready answer to every question he was asked.

After Baizhang died, Xiangyan presented himself to Guishan, who had been declared the master's dharma successor, and, even though they were probably about the same age, Xiangyan asked to be accepted as a disciple. Guishan, however, was reluctant to grant the request.

"When we were both disciples of our late master," Guishan said, "you were said to be able to give ten answers to a single question. This, however, isn't the way of Zen. Such intellectual attainments only result in an abstract or analytical comprehension, which really isn't of much use. Still, perhaps you do have some insight into the truth of Zen. So tell me: what is your true self, your self before your mother gave birth to you, before you came to know east from west?"

Xiangyan was unsure how to reply to this question but ventured a number of attempts, each of which Guishan dismissed. Finally Xiangyan said, "Please, then, teach me. Show me this original self."

"I've nothing to give you," Guishan told him. "Even if I tried to instruct you, that would only provide you an opportunity to ridicule me later on. After all, whatever I have is my own and can never be yours. How can that be of any help to you?"

Xiangyan retired to his quarters, where he searched through the books and notes he had collected over the years, but nothing he found in them helped him understand what Guishan was asking for.

"A picture of rice cakes will never satisfy hunger," he admitted to himself. Then he gathered all of his papers together, took them outside, and set fire to them. "What's the use of studying Buddhism, so difficult to comprehend and too subtle to receive instruction from another?" he said to himself. "I'll become a simple monk, abiding by the precepts, with no desire to try to master things too deep for thought."

He left Baizhang's temple that day and traveled for many weeks, eventually coming to Mount Baiya in Nanyang, where the remains of the National Teacher, Nanyang Huizhong, were buried. Xiangyan found the tomb in a state of deterioration. So he built a grass hut nearby and took upon himself the responsibilities of caretaker.

He carried out his tasks as mindfully as he could, and one day, as he was sweeping the grounds with a broom, a stone he cleared away struck a bamboo stalk. The sound, sharp and hollow, was clear in his attention, and the moment he heard it he came to a deep awakening. He was speechless for a moment, then broke out laughing.

He went into the ruined temple, lit incense in gratitude, and bowed in the direction of Guishan's temple. Then he traveled to see the man who had refused to teach him. "Your kindness to me was greater than even that of my parents," Xiangyan told Guishan. "Had you tried to explain this truth to me in words, I would never be where I am now."

He wrote the following poem to commemorate his enlightenment:

> With one stroke, all previous knowledge is forgotten.
> No cultivation is needed for this.
> This occurrence reveals the ancient way
> And is free from the track of quiescence.
> No trace is left anywhere.
> Whatever I hear and see does not conform to rules.
> All those who are enlightened
> Proclaim this to be the greatest action.[28]

When Yangshan Huiji heard this verse, he criticized it for being derivative. This prompted Xiangyan to write a second poem:

> My poverty of last year was not real poverty.
> This year it is want indeed.
> In last year's poverty there was room for a piercing gimlet.
> In this year's poverty even the gimlet is no more.[29]

Yangshan still remained critical, saying, "You may have grasped the Zen of the Buddha, but not even in your dreams have you comprehended the Zen of the patriarchs."

Xiangyan immediately responded with a third verse:

> I have my secret
> And look at you with twinkling eye.
> If you do not understand this
> Do not call yourself a monk.[30]

Hearing these words, Yangshan finally congratulated his brother monk for the depth of his understanding.

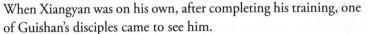

When Xiangyan was on his own, after completing his training, one of Guishan's disciples came to see him.

"Tell me what Guishan is teaching these days," Xiangyan asked the monk.

"Well, if someone asks him why Bodhidharma came from the west, he just holds up his hossu."

"And how do you and your fellow monks understand that?" Xiangyan asked.

"We believe that the master's intention is to reveal Mind by means of Form."

"Your understanding is too abstract," Xiangyan objected.

"How then do you understand the matter?" the traveler asked.

Xiangyan raised his hossu.

Xiangyan once posed this situation to his own disciples as a koan:

"Imagine that a man has climbed high into a tree then falls. Before he hits the ground, he is able to grab a branch between his teeth. There he hangs, his hands unable to grasp anything, his feet dangling. A sincere inquirer comes by and asks him, 'Why did the First Patriarch come east?' If he speaks, he'll fall and die. If he doesn't speak, he fails in compassion by not responding to the question. If you were in his circumstances, what would you do?"

One of the monks replied, "Let's not bother with the tree. Tell us about before climbing it."

Xiangyan laughed.

## Chanqing Daan

Another monk who began his studies with Baizhang and then came to study with Guishan was Chanqing Daan. His early studies had been in the Vinaya. Although he did not find that route satisfying, he had been unsure how to proceed until he chanced to meet an old man who advised him to seek out the Zen master Baizhang.

In his first encounter with the teacher, Chanqing asked, "How can I come to know the Buddha?"

"That's much like looking for an ox while riding one," Baizhang told him.

"And after finding the ox, what then?"

"It's much like riding home on the ox."

"And how does one attain this?"

"Like an oxherd who keeps watch over his charge, not allowing it to stray by eating the grass of others."

Chanqing once gave the following sermon to his followers:

"What are you looking for by coming to me? Are you seeking to become a Buddha? Then you should know that you already are Buddha. Why run from place to place, like a deer chasing the mirage of water? Your mind, just as it is, with its thoughts and imaginings, just this is Buddha-mind. Where else will you find it?

"I lived with Guishan for more than thirty years. I ate Guishan's food. I shat Guishan's shit. But I didn't study Guishan's Zen. All I did was to look after an ox. If the ox strayed from the path, I brought him back. If he trampled the grain in another's field, I disciplined him. For a long time it was a pitiful beast. Now he has become a magnificent white animal always in front of my face. All day long, he reveals himself clearly. Even though I let him roam as he will, he doesn't stray.

"Each of you has a treasure beyond price. It's the light of your eye that illuminates the mountains and rivers. It's the power of your ears that allows you to hear pleasant and foul sounds. So it is with all your six senses, although you're unable to comprehend it."

*The fifth of the* Ox Herding Pictures,
Taming the Ox

# CHAPTER FIFTEEN

# LINJI YIXUAN

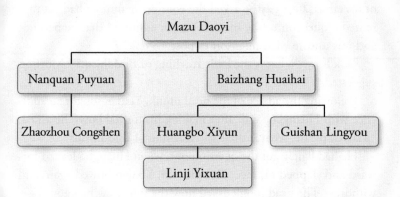

Linji Yixuan followed the pattern common to many of the great Tang dynasty Zen masters, beginning his studies in the traditional Buddhist schools that focused on the precepts and those Indian sutras that had been translated into Chinese. But he, too, found the intellectual study of Buddhism ultimately unsatisfying, and, while still in his twenties, he sought a teacher who would be able to help him understand the teaching that was beyond words. This search brought him to the monastery of Huangbo Xiyun.

As a novice, Yixuan had almost no contact with the master. He was taught how to meditate and was given a work assignment, and so three years passed. Muzhou Daozong, the head monk of the monastery, observed Yixuan's practice and recognized the sincerity of his effort. One day he asked the younger man if he had yet presented a question to the master. Yixuan admitted that he had not and was unsure what question to pose.

"Ask him, 'What is the basic teaching of Buddhism?'" Muzhou suggested.

Following the advice of the head monk, Yixuan sought an audience with Huangbo, and, after making his formal bows, he asked, "Master, please, what is the basic teaching of Buddhism?"

He had barely got the question out, when Huangbo leaned forward and slapped his face. Nonplussed, Yixuan bowed again and withdrew. The head monk asked how the interview had gone.

"I'd hardly put my question when the master struck me!" Yixuan complained.

"Very well. Ask him again."

So twice more, Yixuan asked Huangbo about the basic teaching of Buddhism, and both times Huangbo replied with a blow.

Yixuan decided that he had either offended the master or had failed him in some manner, so he told Muzhou, "I thank you for your efforts on my behalf, but whenever I speak to our master, his only response is to strike me. Apparently I have some karmic obstruction that prevents me from understanding the matter of Zen. So I've determined to leave the monastery."

"That's for you to decide," the head monk admitted. "But if you're leaving the monastery, it is customary for you to formally take leave of the master first."

Yixuan promised to do so.

Before Yixuan arranged for his final meeting with Huangbo, Muzhou went to the master and told him, "The young monk who's been to see you three times is a sincere seeker of the truth. When he presents himself again, please treat him appropriately. Provided he receives proper training, he'll become a great teacher and become a large tree under which many will be able to take shelter."

When Yixuan came before Huangbo to announce his departure, the old master told him: "If you must leave, you should go from here to see Master Dayu. He alone can answer your questions."

Yixuan was still hopeful that if he found the appropriate teacher he would be able to understand Zen, so he sought out Dayu's riverside temple and presented himself to the master. Dayu asked him where he had come from.

"I've spent the last three years at the temple of Master Huangbo."

"And what is the teaching of Huangbo?" Dayu asked.

"I don't know," Yixuan admitted. "Three times I've asked him to explain the basic teaching of Buddhism, and each time he's struck me. I don't know what my fault was."

"Such ingratitude!" Dayu exclaimed. "Huangbo has exhausted himself with grandmotherly kindness on your behalf, and you wonder what your fault was!"

As soon as he heard these words, Yixuan came to enlightenment. "Ah! There's not so much to Huangbo's Buddhism after all!" he exclaimed spontaneously.

Dayu grabbed Yixuan's shoulders and shook him: "You bedwetting infant! First you wonder what your fault was; now you say there isn't so much to Huangbo's Buddhism after all. What is it that you see? Speak! Speak!"

Yixuan jabbed Dayu in the ribs three times.

Dayu pushed the younger monk away and said, "Huangbo's your teacher. It's none of my business."

Yixuan traveled back to Huangbo's temple. The master, who was standing by the gate at the time, happened to see him approaching. "Here's that fellow again!" Huangbo called out. "Coming and going. Going and coming. When will it ever end?"

"It's the result of your grandmotherly kindness," Yixuan said. He bowed formally, then stood waiting.

"Who's gone and who's returned?" Huangbo asked.

"You were kind enough to send me to Dayu."

"And what did he have to say?"

Yixuan described his meeting with Dayu. After listening, Huangbo remarked, "That scoundrel! The next time I see him, I'll give him twenty blows."

"Why wait?" said Linji. "Have them now!" And with that he slapped Huangbo.

"What arrogance! What impudence!" Huangbo exclaimed.

Yixuan replied by shouting, "*Ho!*"

"Where's my attendant?" Huangbo called. "Take this madman away and house him in the monks' quarters."

Although Huangbo appeared to be angry with Yixuan, he was, in fact, proud of the younger man's attainment. The give and take between master and student continued through the remainder of Yixuan's time with his teacher.

On one occasion, Huangbo was working in the fields with a hoe when Yixuan walked by.

"Why don't you have a hoe?" the teacher demanded.

"Someone's taken it," Yixuan shot back.

Huangbo raised his own hoe and said, "Only this, but the whole world is unable to hold it up."

Yixuan took the hoe away from Huangbo and asked, "So how is it that it's in my hands?"

"Here's a man doing a great work today!" Huangbo remarked.

On another occasion, Huangbo saw Yixuan standing in the field, resting and leaning on his hoe.

"Are you tired?" he asked.

"I haven't even lifted the hoe. Why should I be tired?"

Huangbo raised his stick to strike Yixuan, but the younger man grabbed the stick away and pushed the master down.

Huangbo called his attendant to help him get up, and the attendant said, "Why do you allow this madman to take such liberties?"

Once he was on his feet again, Huangbo struck the attendant. Yixuan began to work the soil with the hoe, commenting, "In some places they cremate you. Here, they bury you alive."

After completing his studies with Huangbo and receiving transmission, Yixuan undertook the traditional pilgrimage to visit other Zen masters throughout China. Before setting out, he went to see Huangbo a last time. Huangbo presented Yixuan with the backrest that had been used by his master, Baizhang. Yixuan responded by passing the backrest to Huangbo's attendant and telling him to throw it into the fire.

"That's all right," Huangbo said. "Take it with you anyway. In the future you'll cut off the tongue of every man on earth."

There are several stories about Yixuan's encounters with Zen masters he met during his travels. In one, he came to the temple overseen by Jinniu, one of Mazu's heirs. As Yixuan approached him, Jinniu took his staff and held it in front of his body. Yixuan came up to him and struck the staff three times with his hand. Then he walked into the meditation hall and took the first seat. Jinniu followed him and remarked, "There are certain formalities to be adhered to when one arrives as a guest. Tell me where you come from and what right you have to be so discourteous."

"What are you talking about, old man?" Yixuan said. Then before Jinniu could reply, Yixuan struck him. Jinniu pretended to fall down. Yixuan struck him again.

"Things aren't going my way today," Jinniu laughed.

During his travels, Yixuan visited Bodhidharma's memorial stupa. The temple caretaker welcomed him, asking, "Do you wish to pay your respects to the Buddha first or to the Patriarch?"

"I don't pay respect to either Buddhas or patriarchs," Yixuan declared.

The caretaker was taken aback and asked, "What did the Buddha or patriarchs do to offend you that you should be so disrespectful?"

Yixuan just swung the sleeves of his robes and left the temple.

When he had completed his pilgrimage, he settled in a small temple on the banks of the Hutuo River. The temple was known as Linji-yuan (J: Rinzai-in), the "Temple Overlooking the Ford." Yixuan now acquired the name Linji by which he and the school that descended from him are best known. Although he received disciples at the temple, their numbers were never large. The tradition they established, however, proved to be enduring. He was famous for the freedom with which he used his stick and for shouting "Ho!" in response to questions.

Near Linji's temple, on Mount Wutai, there was a shrine to the Bodhisattva Manjusri. Occasionally pilgrims traveling to this shrine spent a short time with Linji as well. One of those visitors was Zhaozhou Congshen. Linji was washing his feet in a basin of water as Zhaozhou approached the monastery. The visitor called out, "Why did the First Patriarch come east?"

Linji appeared to ignore his visitor and continued washing his feet. Zhaozhou came up to him, saying, "I asked you, 'Why did the First Patriarch come east?'"

When Linji still didn't reply, Zhaozhou leaned forward and cupped his ear as if straining to hear the other's answer.

Linji poured the dirty water onto the ground.

Although it is assumed he was not referring to the accomplished Zhaozhou, Linji had this to say about the people who came to visit Manjusri's shrine: "The pilgrim who comes to Mount Wutai seeking the Bodhisattva is already lost, because the Bodhisattva isn't to be found on the mountain. If you wish to find him, he's right before your eyes at this very moment. There's nothing else. Don't doubt! This is the living Bodhisattva!"

On another occasion, he told his students, "Do you want to know the Buddha or the Patriarch? He's none other than you yourself, just as you are now, standing and listening to my speech. It's only because you lack faith in yourselves that you seek for the Buddha or the Patriarch outside of yourselves. Even if you find something through your searching, whatever you find will be nothing more than words and you'll fail to attain the mind of the living Buddha or Patriarch."

Linji acquired a reputation for the rough treatment he dealt out to his followers, but it was also recognized that his methods were effective. Two stories are told about the treatment meted out to a disciple named Dingzhou Shizang.

One day Linji told his disciples: "Over a mass of reddish flesh there sits a true man of no rank." [In Chinese society, the idea of a man without rank was difficult to comprehend; each person was expected to know his place within the Confucian hierarchy of responsibilities and obligations.] "This true man of no rank comes in and goes out of your face all of the time. If you haven't identified him yet, do so now. Look!"

Dingzhou stood and asked, "Who is this man of no rank?"

Linji, true to form, stood up, took hold of the monk's robes, and shook him. "Speak! Speak!" he demanded.

Dingzhou, not knowing how to reply, remained silent.

"What a piece of dried shit this true man of no rank is!" Linji said, releasing the monk.

During an assembly, Dingzhou asked, "What is the purpose of Buddhism?"

This time, Linji slapped his face.

Dingzhou was as confused as Linji had been when he had first been struck by Huangbo. Not knowing what to do, he stood where he was. A fellow monk leaned towards him and whispered, "Why don't you bow?"

And just as Dingzhou started to bow, he came to awakening.

"Your body is composed of the four elements—earth, water, fire, and air," Linji told his disciples. "None of these can hear or understand my preaching. Your stomach, your liver, they can't understand this preaching. Nor can empty space understand it. So who, then, is hearing? Who understands?"

He made a similar point when he demanded of his assembled monks, "Just at this moment, right before your eyes, who's the one listening to this lecture?"

Linji's methodology was not limited to physical demonstrations. If the circumstances were appropriate, as when he described the true man of no rank, he was willing to use language. A monk asked him about the meaning of the First Patriarch's trip east, and Linji said, "If there were any meaning in it, no one would be able to save himself."

The monk persisted, "If there's no meaning, what was it that the Second Patriarch attained from the First Patriarch?"

"What you call 'attained,' is really something 'not attained.'"

"Then what's meant by 'not attained'?"

"Because your mind pursues every object that comes before it without restraint, the patriarchs describe you as one who foolishly seeks a second head over the one you already have. If, instead of seeking something outside yourself, you were to turn your attention within, as you've been instructed, you'd realize that your mind isn't different from that of the Buddhas and patriarchs. When you come to this state of doing nothing, then you'll have attained the truth."

In his *Essays in Zen Buddhism, First Series*, D. T. Suzuki provides this example of Linji's sermons:

O you, followers of Truth, if you wish to obtain an orthodox understanding [of Zen], do not be deceived by others. Inwardly or outwardly, if you encounter any obstacles, lay them low right away. If you encounter the Buddha, slay him; if you encounter the Patriarch, slay him; if you encounter the Arhat [an enlightened monk] or the parent or the relative, slay them all without hesitation: for this is the only way to deliverance. Do not get yourselves entangled with any object, but stand above, pass on, and be free. As I see those so-called followers of Truth all over the country, there are none who come to me free and independent of objects. In dealing with them, I strike them down any way they come. If they rely on the strength of their arms, I cut them right off; if they rely on their eloquence, I make them shut themselves up; if they rely on the sharpness of their eyes, I will hit them blind. There are indeed so far none who have presented themselves before me all alone, all free, all unique. They are invariably found caught by the idle tricks of the old masters. I have really nothing to give you; all that I can do is to cure you of the diseases and deliver you from bondage.

O you, followers of Truth, show yourselves here independent of all objects, I want to weigh the matter with you. For the last five or ten years I have waited in vain for such, and there are no such yet. They are all ghostly existences, ignominious gnomes haunting the woods or bamboo groves, they are elfish spirits of the wilderness. They are madly biting into all heaps of filth. O you, mole-eyed, why are you wasting all the pious donations of the devout [alms given to begging monks]! Do you think you deserve the name of a monk, when you are still entertaining such a mistaken idea [of Zen]? I tell you, no Buddhas, no holy teachings, no disciplining, no testifying! What do you seek in a neighbor's house? O you, mole-eyed! You are putting another head over your own! What do you lack in yourselves? O you, followers of Truth, what you are making use of at this very moment is none other than what makes a Patriarch or a Buddha. But you do not believe me, and seek it outwardly. Do not commit yourselves to an error. There are no realities outside, nor is there anything inside you may lay your hands on. You stick to the literal meaning of what I speak to you, but how far better it is to have all your hankerings stopped, and be doing nothing whatever![31]

While on one occasion, Linji asserted, "As far as I can see, my awakening and insight into truth isn't any different from that of the Buddha himself," on another he warned his disciples not to treat the Buddha with too much veneration: "I think of him as being much like the hole in a privy."

When asked how one should go about seeking awakening, Linji said: "All one has to do is to attend to the circumstances of his life. Rise in the morning and put on your clothes, then go to work. When hungry, eat; when tired, rest. Don't have a desire to attain Buddhahood. Don't have even the least thought of it. A wise man of old warned, if you strive for Buddhahood by any conscious deed, this will only lead to constant rebirth."

After ten years, Linji left the temple on the river and retired to a smaller one at Weifu. A small number of disciples accompanied him in his retirement, including Sansheng Huiran.

The story is told that as he felt his death approaching, Linji called these remaining disciples together and asked, "After my death, how will you ensure that my teaching [my 'True Dharma Eye'] doesn't disappear? If someone were to ask you what I taught, how would you respond?"

Sansheng came forward and shouted, "*Ho!*"

"Who would have thought that my True Dharma Eye would disappear when it reached this blind ass?" Having said this, Linji sat in meditation posture and passed away.

*The sixth of the* Ox Herding Pictures,
Riding the Ox Home

# CHAPTER SIXTEEN

# DESHAN XUANJIAN AND HIS STUDENTS

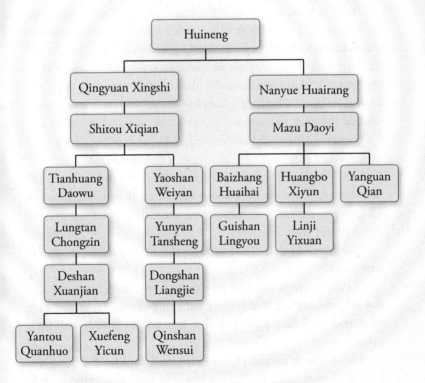

## DESHAN XUANJIAN

Deshan Xuanjian was a contemporary of Zhaozhou. He began his career in Buddhism as an academic; the particular focus of his scholarly studies was the *Diamond Sutra*. He was familiar with all of the commentaries on this sutra and had written one himself of which he was quite proud. When he learned about a school of Buddhism in the south that proclaimed it was a special transmission outside the scriptures and without dependence on words or letters, he considered the claim heretical. He decided to investigate the Zen teachers for himself and perhaps show their followers the errors of their masters' teachings. At that time, Lungtan Chongzin was a well-respected Zen teacher, so Deshan determined to visit and challenge him.

Travel in those times was difficult and long, and rest houses were set up along the most frequently traveled routes to provide travelers places to relax, have a cup of tea, and get something to eat. As Deshan drew close to Lungtan's monastery, he stopped at one of these rest houses and ordered tea and a plate of cakes that were popularly known as "mind refreshers." The old woman who ran the rest house noticed the pack Deshan was carrying and asked what was in it.

"Nothing you would understand," Deshan told her. "It's a commentary I've written on the illustrious *Diamond Sutra*."

"The *Diamond Sutra*—very impressive," the old woman said. "Let me ask you a question about that sutra. If you can answer it, I'll give you the cakes for free. If you can't, then you must go your way without them."

"Ask away," Deshan said, confident that he would have no trouble answering.

"In that sutra, it says that past-mind is no more; future-mind is not yet; and present mind is beyond comprehension. In that case, Reverend Sir, which mind is it that you seek to refresh with these cakes?"

The question caught Deshan off guard, and he did not know how to answer, so he left the tea house without the "mind refreshers." Disturbed by his failure to be able to deal with the old woman of the rest house, he wondered how he would fare when he met Lungtan; he had been warned that, for all their heresy, Zen teachers were very clever.

Lungtan Chongzin, as was common, had derived his name from the monastery where he taught. "Lungtan" referred specifically to a body of water known as the "Dragon's Pool." At his first meeting with Lungtan, Deshan immediately took the offensive: "I've heard people speak about the famous dragon pool (Lungtan), but I see neither dragon nor pool."

The Zen master replied, "You are in the midst of Lungtan."

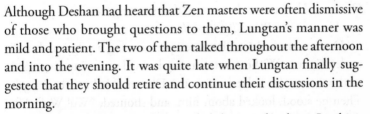

Although Deshan had heard that Zen masters were often dismissive of those who brought questions to them, Lungtan's manner was mild and patient. The two of them talked throughout the afternoon and into the evening. It was quite late when Lungtan finally suggested that they should retire and continue their discussions in the morning.

Deshan bowed respectfully and slid open the door. Looking outside, he remarked, "It's very dark."

Lungtan lit a candle and handed it to his guest, saying, "Take this to light the way."

Deshan reached to take the candle, but, before he could grasp it, Lungtan blew it out. That act and the sudden darkness were enough to bring Deshan to awakening.

"What have you seen?" Lungtan asked.

"From this time on," Deshan said, "I won't doubt what the teachers of Zen proclaim."

The next morning, Deshan woke and felt a great embarrassment about his former pride in his intellectual achievements. He built a fire in the temple courtyard and burned all the papers he had been carrying in his pack, the commentaries (including the one he had written) as well as his copies of the sutras. He told Lungtan, "I now know that no matter how deep and profound the writings are, in comparison with awakening they're like a single hair compared to infinite space or like a drop of water compared to the vast ocean."

In that morning's assembly, Lungtan declared, "There's one new to our community among you today. His fangs are like swords, and his mouth like a bowl of blood. Strike him, and he won't bother to turn to look at you. One day he'll climb the highest peak and establish the Dao there."

Deshan remained with Lungtan until it was time for him to make the traditional pilgrimage to test his understanding with other teachers. One of the masters he visited during those travels was Guishan. The bizarre elements of that meeting have been preserved as a koan in the *Blue Cliff Record*.

Deshan entered Guishan's temple carrying a pilgrim's bundle under his arm. Without introducing himself or paying his respects to the master, he walked across the Dharma Hall and back again. Then he stood, looked about him, and shouted, "Wu! Wu!" After that he left. Coming to the temple gate, he said to himself, "Perhaps I shouldn't be so hasty."

He donned his ceremonial robes and presented himself before Guishan. Holding up a kneeling cushion, Deshan said, "Master!"

Guishan reached for his hossu.

Deshan shouted, "Ho!" Then he stood, shook out the sleeves of his robe, and left the interview room.

That evening, Guishan asked his assistant where the recently arrived monk had gone.

"He put on his sandals and went away," the assistant told him.

"Someday that fellow will establish a hermitage from which he'll abuse all the Buddhas and patriarchs."

In spite of, or perhaps because of, his own career as an academic, Deshan had little patience with students who came to him seeking an intellectual understanding of Buddhism. When one inquirer asked him, "Who is the Buddha?" he responded, "An old monk from India." Another asked about *bodhi* (wisdom), and Deshan said, "No shitting here!" When yet another monk asked him to explain Zen, Deshan shouted at him, "I have nothing to give you!"

On another occasion, a monk asked, "Where have all the Buddhas and patriarchs gone?"

"What's your question?" Deshan asked in turn.

"I called for a fine racehorse to spring forward, but all that responded was a lame tortoise," the monk commented.

Deshan did not deign to respond to the remark.

Like Linji, Deshan used his stick freely, and several stories told of him are variations on a theme. Once he exclaimed, "If you speak, thirty blows! If you keep silent, thirty blows! What? What?"

During an assembly, a monk stood to ask a question. Before he could complete his bows, Deshan struck him.

"What have I done to deserve being struck?" the monk complained. "I haven't even posed my question."

"Where did you come from?" Deshan demanded. "What's your home village?"

The monk named a community on the other side of the water.

"Even before you got into the boat to come here," Deshan told him, "you merited thirty blows."

When another monk complained that Deshan struck him before he had had a chance to speak, Deshan's reply was, "What use was there in waiting for you to open your mouth?"

Linji heard of Deshan's behaviour and sent one of his own disciples, a monk named Luopu, to investigate and report back to him whether Deshan's teaching was genuine or merely imitative. "Ask him why it is he says 'If you speak, thirty blows! If you remain silent, thirty blows!'" Linji instructed the disciple. "Then, when Deshan moves to strike you—as no doubt he will—grab his stick and use it on him. Let's see how he behaves in those circumstances."

Luopu went to Deshan and did as Linji instructed. When Deshan was struck with his own stick, he said nothing but quietly retired to his quarters. Luopu described what had occurred to Linji. Linji remarked, "I'd had some doubt about him until now but no longer. How do you understand him, Luopu?"

When Luopu was unable to respond immediately, Linji struck him.

In *Zen's Chinese Heritage,* Andy Ferguson provides an example of Deshan's dharma talks:

> I don't hold to some views about the ancestors. Here, there are no ancestors and no buddhas. Bodhidharma is an old stinking foreigner. Shakyamuni is a dried piece of excrement. Manjushri and Samantabhadra [another bodhisattva] are dung carriers. What is known as "realizing the mystery" is nothing but breaking through to grab an ordinary person's life. "Bodhi" and "nirvana" are a donkey's tethering post. The twelve divisions of scriptural canon are devils' texts; just paper for wiping infected skin boils. The four fruitions and the three virtuous stages, original mind and the ten stages, these are just graveyard-guarding ghosts. They'll never save you.[32]

# Yantou Quanhuo
# Xuefeng Yicun
# Qinshan Wensui

Deshan's two principle disciples were Yantou Quanhuo and Xuefeng Yicun. Xuefeng was the head monk at the monastery where Deshan was master. The head monk was charged with the management of temple affairs, leaving the master free to teach. In a famous story, Deshan brought his bowls into the dining area one day, but the meal was late, and Xuefeng said, "The bell hasn't rung. What're you doing here, old man?"

Deshan nodded his head, then turned and went back to his room.

Xuefeng mentioned the event to Yantou, who remarked, "Our master may be a great man, but he fails to understand the final word."

Deshan learned of Yantou's comment and sent for him. "Have you a criticism to make of me?" he asked.

Yantou bent forward and whispered something to Deshan.

Deshan said nothing, but the next day when he stood to address the assembled disciples, his manner was forceful. Yantou clapped his hands and laughed aloud, saying, "Indeed our master does have the final word! No one in the country can best him!"

Yantou and Xuefeng along with a third companion, Qinshan Wensui, began their pursuit of Zen together. They studied with Yanguan Qian and Dongshan Liangjie before coming to Deshan's monastery. Qinshan had difficulty with Deshan's manner and eventually returned to Dongshan, whose disciple he is considered to be.

Several stories are recorded of the three companions before their paths separated. For example, they were walking together in the courtyard one evening and came upon a pail of water. Qinshan commented, "When the water is still, the moon comes out."

Xuefeng countered, "When the water is still, the moon doesn't come out."

Yantou pushed the pail over with his foot and continued walking.

Once when they were still with Dongshan, the companions were practicing zazen. The master brought in tea for them. Qinshan's eyes were closed, and he didn't notice that tea was being served. Dongshan asked him, "Where are you?"

"I've entered samadhi," Qinshan replied.

"Samadhi has no gate, so how can you have entered it?" Dongshan asked.

Before he left Deshan, Qinshan once asked the master his opinion about a remark reported to have been made by Tianhuang Daowu.

"Why don't you ask Tianhuang ?" Deshan said.

Qinshan started to object that Tianhuang was dead, but, as soon as he opened his mouth, Deshan struck him.

Qinshan later complained to Yantou that he felt the treatment he had received was undeserved. Yantou told him, "If you speak like this, you'll never see Deshan."

Yantou and Xuefeng remained with Deshan after Qinshan returned to work with Dongshan. Eventually the time came for both of them to leave as well, although Xuefeng still had not come to full understanding. On the day they were to depart, the master went with them to the monastery gate and asked, "Where will you go?"

"We're leaving the mountain for a while," Yantou said.

"And later?"

"We won't forget."

"What do you mean by that?"

"Didn't Baizhang say that only one whose understanding surpasses that of his teacher is worthy to teach? One whose understanding only equals that of his teacher is only half as worthy as his teacher."

Deshan smiled and said, "That's so."

Yantou and Xuefeng bowed and went their way.

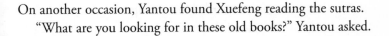

Although Xuefeng Yicun was older than Yantou, he came to awakening later than Yantou and was humble enough to seek the guidance of the younger man, whom he addressed by the honorific, "Elder Brother."

A blizzard arose as they traveled through a mountain pass one winter, and they were unable to proceed for several days. They found an inn where they took refuge and waited for the storm to pass. Xuefeng spent his time at the inn seated in zazen, but Yantou just lay in bed and slept. After a few days, Xuefeng shook Yantou's arm and said, "Elder Brother, let's not waste our time. Get up."

Yantou complained about being wakened from his nap, but Xuefeng persisted, "It's said that when monks are on pilgrimage, they must make profound knowledge their companion and be ever vigilant. And yet you spend all day sleeping."

"And you spend the day sitting cross-legged like a clay statue found in some peasant's hut."

"I practice with such diligence because my doubts still haven't been resolved."

"Do as Master Linji suggested. Eat when hungry; sleep when tired," Yantou advised him. "If you sit all day like that, you'll just frighten the simple-minded."

On another occasion, Yantou found Xuefeng reading the sutras.

"What are you looking for in these old books?" Yantou asked.

"I still haven't attained peace of mind," Xuefeng said. "So I'm reading what the Buddhas and patriarchs have to say about the matter."

"I thought you'd already resolved this issue," Yantou said. "But since you say it isn't the case, let me ask you: What do you think you can learn from the sutras and commentaries? It's what you discover within the depths of your own mind that moves heaven and earth."

At hearing those words, Xuefeng finally came to full awakening.

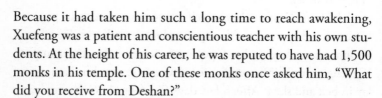

Because it had taken him such a long time to reach awakening, Xuefeng was a patient and conscientious teacher with his own students. At the height of his career, he was reputed to have had 1,500 monks in his temple. One of these monks once asked him, "What did you receive from Deshan?"

"I came to Master Deshan with empty hands, and I left with empty hands."

Another monk asked, "It's been said that if one were to meet the First Patriarch on the road, one should speak to him without words. How does one do this?"

Xuefeng replied, "Please have some tea."

Even after they became masters of separate communities, Xuefeng and Yantou remained friends.

Two traveling monks once paid Xuefeng a visit. He noticed them coming down the path towards him. He opened the gate before they arrived but then stood there, blocking the way. As they came nearer, he asked, "What is this?"

The monks, who must have had some experience of this form of dharma combat, replied with the same words, "What is this?"

Xuefeng closed the gate on them and returned to his quarters.

The monks continued their journey and came to Yantou's monastery.

"Where have you come from?" Yantou asked.

The monks told him of the other teachers they had visited and included a description of their encounter with Xuefeng. "But he blocked our way and demanded, 'What is this?' We replied immediately, 'What is this?' and he closed the gate on us."

"Ah," Yantou sighed. "I'm sorry I hadn't shared the last word with him when we were companions. Had I done so, no one in the whole world would have been able to claim to surpass him."

The monks remained for a while at Yantou's temple. Then they sought an audience with him and reminded him of their meeting with Xuefeng and Yantou's comment about the last word. "Now we've come to ask you for instruction," they told him.

"Why didn't you do so earlier?" Yantou asked.

"We've been struggling with this matter and admit we don't know how to proceed."

"Xuefeng came to life in the same way that I did, but he doesn't die in the same way. If you want to know the last word, I'll tell you, simply—*this!*"

During an assembly, Xuefeng told his disciples: "This whole world, if I were to pick it up with my fingertips, is like a grain of rice. I throw it in front of your face, but you don't see it. Beat the drum. Call the monks to come out and search for it!"

One day in the year 887, Yantou's temple was attacked by bandits. All the monks, except Yantou, fled; he remained seated in zazen.

When the bandits searched through the temple and found nothing worth stealing, they took their anger out on the meditating monk and stabbed him with their swords. As he died, Yantou let out a scream that could be heard for miles around.

Eight hundred years later, in Japan, Yantou's scream became a matter of great difficulty for Hakuin Ekaku, who would eventually become one of the great masters of Zen in that country. As a young man, he believed Zen masters should retain equanimity in all situations. He wondered, then, why a master like Yantou would scream at the moment of his death and whether that cast doubt on the legitimacy of Zen teaching. When Hakuin finally achieved awakening, however, he declared that he himself was Yantou.

Xuefeng survived his friend by twenty-one years. In 908 he became ill, and the governor of the province arranged for a doctor to visit him. Xuefeng dismissed the doctor, saying, "I'm not sick, and there's no need for medicine."

A few weeks later, he took a long walk in the countryside, then returned to his quarters and bathed. Afterwards, he lay down on his bed and, that evening, died in his sleep.

*The seventh of the* Ox Herding Pictures,
Ox Forgotten

# CHAPTER SEVENTEEN

# THE LINJI LINE

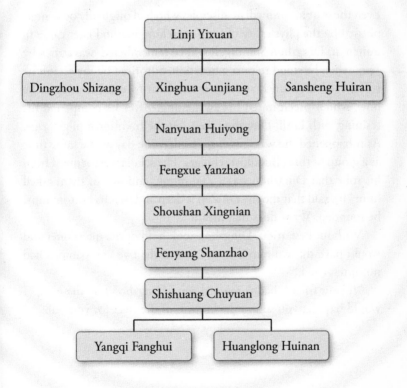

Linji Yixuan had been one of the great personalities of Tang dynasty Zen. His descendants over the next several generations, however, were not as well known, in part because, rather than developing their own styles, they dedicated themselves to carrying on the traditions associated with their teacher. The distinctive characteristics of the school—including the liberal use of the stick and shouting "Ho!"—were techniques copied from Linji.

## DINGZHOU SHIZANG

Even those of his immediate disciples who had originally been nonplussed by the physicality of Linji's teaching method later came to imitate it. Dingzhou Shizang, it will be remembered, was struck by Linji when he stood to pose a question. Surprised by the assault he stood speechless until another monk bent forward to suggest he bow, which precipitated his awakening. After he completed his training with Linji, Dingzhou went on the traditional pilgrimage. As it happened, he was crossing a bridge one day at the same time as a group of three Buddhist scholars. The scholars recognized from his robe that Dingzhou was a Zen monk, and one of them asked him: "It's said that the river of Zen is deep and that its bottom must be sounded. What does that mean?"

Without hesitation, Dingzhou took hold of the questioner and would have thrown him into the river if the two companions had not intervened.

"If your friends hadn't rescued you," Dingzhou told the man, "I would have let you sound the bottom of the river for yourself."

## SANSHENG HUIRAN

Sansheng Huiran, another of Linji's disciples, was the compiler of the *Linjilu*, a collection of talks given by the master. During Sansheng's pilgrimage, he paid a visit to Xiangyan Zhixian, the heir of Guishan. Xiangyan asked Sansheng where he had come from.

"Linji," Sansheng replied, simultaneously referring to the teacher and to the temple on the river bank.

"Is that so? Did you bring Linji's sword with you?" Xiangyan asked him.

In a flash, Sansheng grabbed up a meditation cushion and struck Xiangyan with it.

Xiangyan smiled.

Sansheng visited Deshan's monastery and was setting out his few belongings in the monk's quarters when Deshan came in and told him, "Don't bother to unpack your bowls; there's no rice here."

Sansheng continued unpacking, commenting, "It's here for all although it can't be shown."

Deshan raised his staff to strike Sansheng, but the younger monk grabbed it from him and pushed the master away. Deshan laughed. Sansheng shouted "Ho!" and left the room.

Sansheng also attended one of Xuefeng's dharma talks. The teacher said, "Without exception all have an ancient mirror."

Sansheng stood to object: "From time beyond memory, it's been nameless. Why do you call it an ancient mirror?"

"Because of defective existence."

"I don't know how you came up with this stuff."

"My apologies. I've so many duties I have to attend to as abbot," Xuefeng said.

## XINGHUA CUNJIANG

The most important line descending from Linji was that of Xinghua Cunjiang. There are not many stories recorded about him. However, he is remembered for warning his followers of the danger of merely aping the mannerisms of his late master. "All day long I hear monks shouting 'Ho!' in the corridors and in the halls. But you must beware of shouting for its own sake. Even if you were to shout so loudly that it took my breath away, when my breath returned I'd tell you, 'Still not it!' I haven't been passing out gift-wrapped gems to you. What's all this shouting about?"

## NANYUAN HUIYONG

Xinghua's successor, Nanyuan Huiyong, was known for the strictness of his manner and the frequency with which he used his staff. On one occasion Nanyuan asked a newly arrived monk his reason for coming to the monastery.

"I've come to pay my respects to Master Nanyuan," the monk said.

"He isn't here."

The monk shouted, "Ho!"

"I said Nanyuan isn't here. What's the use in shouting?"

The monk shouted again, and Nanyuan struck him, after which the monk bowed in response.

"Actually," Nanyuan remarked, "it was you who struck me. I merely struck back."

Nanyuan assigned his students passages to meditate upon from the recorded talks of Linji and earlier Zen masters. What he sought from them was not a verbal explanation of these passages but rather an active demonstration of their understanding. The demonstration gave evidence that the students had more than a conceptual grasp of the passage. Because of his use of this technique, Nanyuan is credited with beginning the koan tradition so closely associated with the Linji (Rinzai) school of Zen.

## FENGXUE YANZHAO

Nanyuan had only one transmitted heir, Fengxue Yanzhao. Like many other Chinese masters, Fengxue came to the Zen tradition after first studying in other schools. He began as a member of the Tiantai (J: Tendai) sect. This school's name is derived from the mountain where its main temple was located. It was considered the first wholly Chinese school of Buddhism and over time became both popular and wealthy. The sect had many richly decorated and furnished temples, millions of lay devotees, as well as a large number of monks who had withdrawn from the world to dedicate themselves to meditation and the study of the sutras and their commentaries.

The school had evolved as a result of a confusion that had arisen in the history of Chinese Buddhism long before Bodhidharma's voyage from the west. For many years, Chinese travelers had brought back Buddhist documents from India even though they could not read them, because it was believed that the scrolls were inherently sacred. Often these documents were stored for many years before scholars arose who were able to translate them. The translators then discovered that some of the documents were only fragments and others had missing passages. More problematic was the fact that the documents reflected a wide range of perspectives within the long history of Indian Buddhism, both of the Hinayana and Mahayana traditions. The teachings proclaimed in one document might be difficult to reconcile with those in other documents, although they both purported to reflect the instructions of the Buddha. The founders of the Tiantai School set themselves the task of trying to determine which of these apparently contradictory teachings were those of the historical Buddha. They finally based their exposition of Buddhist doctrine on the *Lotus Sutra*, which they believed to be the least corrupt of the documents they had to work with.

Although meditation was practiced in the Tiantai tradition, the majority of Tiantai adherents were satisfied with understanding it as a doctrinal system that was intellectually coherent and able to meet the devotional needs of ordinary people. However, occasionally individuals like Fengxue found the teaching too abstract and sought to share the actual awakening experience that had brought the Buddha to enlightenment. Since this was what the Zen tradition claimed to be able to do, it was natural for those dissatisfied with Tiantai to seek a Zen teacher. The fundamental difference between the Zen School and the other schools of Buddhism was the emphasis it put on practice as opposed to study.

Fengxue visited a number of contemporary masters before he became the disciple of Nanyuan. Nanyuan introduced Fengxue to the *Linjilu*, which had become a standard text for the teachers of this lineage. It had evolved into a heftier document than Sansheng's original manuscript and now included commentaries and other additions that had been appended by various teachers. Nanyuan's use of the *Linjilu* differed from the Tiantai study of the *Lotus Sutra* in that the student was expected less to come to an intellectual understanding of the writings than to come to the concrete experience of awakening.

Fengxue stayed with Nanyuan until that master's death. Then he went off on his own to seek a hermitage where he could continue to practice in private. He found a deserted Vinaya temple on Mount Fengxue. The rafters of the old building had collapsed, and the walls were falling in. All that remained of the previous temple furnishings was a statue of the Buddha, a drum, and a bell. Fengxue took up residence here, begging for food in the mountain villages by day, and meditating at night by the light of a pine-resin torch. He lived like this for ten years before the first students sought him out. When the regional prefect became his disciple, further students came as well, and through them the Linji (Rinzai) tradition was continued.

One of the techniques used in the emerging tradition was that of the mondo. The speed with which students responded to a question put by their master was a demonstration of the completeness of their understanding. The quick reply of a teacher to a student's question led the student away from the conceptual and back to the concrete.

Several of Fengxue's mondo have been preserved.

A monk brought this problem to him: "Neither speaking nor silence will do. How, then, can we be free from error?"

Fengxue replied with a quote from a popular verse:

I always remember Konan in the spring,
The partridges crying and flowers spilled their fragrance.[33]

On another occasion, a monk asked: "Why is it that those who don't understand at all still aren't plagued by doubt?"

"When a tortoise crosses the mud, he can't avoid leaving traces," Fengxue replied.

Just before he died, at the age of seventy-eight, Fengxue called his disciples together and recited this verse:

Truth, availing itself of the flow of time,
Must of necessity save all beings.

Remote from it though they who long for it may be,
Step by step they will approach it.
In years to come, should there be an old man
Whose feelings resemble mine,
Day after day the incense smoke will rise,
Night after night the lighted lamp will burn.[34]

## SHOUSHAN XINGNIAN

Shoushan Xingnian succeeded Fengxue. Like his master, Shoushan began in the Tiantai school. He was so fond of chanting the *Lotus Sutra* that he acquired the nickname of "Lotus chanter."

Shoushan lived after the fall of the Tang dynasty, during the period known as the Five Dynasties and Ten Kingdoms (907–960). It was an unstable period during which Buddhism was once more politically suspect, and Shoushan had to maintain the Linji tradition in secret.

One of the challenges he made to his assembly of monks after becoming a teacher of Zen is retained as a koan in the *Mumonkan*. He held up his staff and said: "If you call this a staff, you overlook its reality. If you deny it's a staff, you ignore the facts. So tell me, apart from affirming and denying, what can you call it? Say something now!"

A monk asked Shoushan to explain Linji's use of shouting and the stick. Shoushan asked the monk to demonstrate his understanding. The monk shouted "*Ho!*"

"Blind," Shoushan commented.

The monk tried shouting again.

"Why is this blind fellow shouting like this?" Shoushan asked.

The monk bowed. Shoushan struck him.

When a man asked to be taken on as a student, Shoushan told him, "I don't have time for that type of thing."

The supplicant asked, "How can one who is a master behave like this?"

"I said I haven't any time. If you wish to practice, practice! If you wish to sit zazen, sit zazen!"

## FENYANG SHANZHAO

In spite of his claim not to have time to teach, Shoushan had several heirs, the most important of whom was Fenyang Shanzhao.

It is said that Fenyang visited seventy-one teachers, many in the Caodong (J: Soto) tradition, before becoming Shoushan's disciple. He was the first teacher in the Linji lineage also to make use of elements from the Caodong School.

A monk once asked him, "What is Dao?"

"Emptiness unobstructed. One wanders as one desires."

The monk bowed his thanks, and Fenyang asked, "How do you understand Dao?"

The monk stood silent.

"You might be able to mount the tiger," Fenyang said, "but you don't know how to get off."

The local governor was an admirer of Fenyang and hoped that the master would take command of a temple that was under his sponsorship. He sent a messenger to present this request to Fenyang, who courteously but adamantly refused. The governor was angered by the refusal and punished the messenger for failing to carry out the task assigned to him. Then he ordered the man to go back to Fenyang and put the request a second time. Again Fenyang declined the invitation. Once more the governor took his anger out on the messenger. The messenger was sent a third time to see Fenyang, this time adding that an "invitation" extended by one of the governor's rank should not be ignored. Nonetheless, the same results followed.

Finally, on a fourth attempt, the messenger told Fenyang how he had been beaten every time he returned from their meetings. "If you refuse a fourth time, I'm sure I'll be beaten to death!"

"I apologize for having been the cause of this injustice," Fenyang said. "It's because of my old age and ill health that I haven't been able to accept the governor's invitation. If I'm to go to the city, however, I would like to be able to determine the appropriate time to do so."

"If you'd only agree," the messenger assured him, "I'm certain that you would be free to decide when."

Fenyang asked the messenger to wait another day. The next day he invited his disciples to attend a farewell feast. He came in dressed in his travel clothes.

"I'm going ahead," he told the assembly. "Is there any of you able to come with me?"

Several monks volunteered to accompany him. When he asked them how far they could travel in a day, one said fifty *li*—[a single *li* is approximately a quarter-mile.

"That's not enough," Fenyang said.

Another boasted he could go seventy.

"Neither of you can follow me," Fenyang told them.

His attendant then said, "I'll go wherever you go."

"You can follow me."

Then Fenyang turned to the messenger and said, "Please let the governor know that I'm going to go ahead." With those words, he put down his chopsticks and passed away.

## SHISHUANG CHUYUAN

After Fenyang's death, the Linji tradition was continued by Shishuang Chuyuan.

As a young man, Chuyuan had been encouraged to seek out Fenyang and ask to be accepted as his disciple. It is said that on their first meeting, Fenyang recognized the young man's potential, but that did not make Chuyuan's training easier. For two years, the new monk was expected to follow the rules of the monastery and be diligent in his practice of zazen. However, every time he presented himself at the entrance to Fenyang's quarters for personal instruction, the master simply sent him away with a curse.

Finally, one evening, Chuyuan refused to leave and complained that he was being treated unjustly. Fenyang took up his staff and started to beat the young man. When Chuyuan cried out, Fenyang clapped his hand over his mouth. At that moment, Chuyuan achieved awakening.

He stayed on with Fenyang to continue his training and is reputed to have used an awl to stab himself in the leg during prolonged periods of zazen to keep from falling asleep.

After receiving transmission from Fenyang, Chuyuan went on the traditional pilgrimage to test his understanding of Zen before establishing a temple on Mount Shishuang. His dharma talks were renowned, and he soon attracted a large number of disciples.

An example of these talks is provided by D. T. Suzuki in his *Essays in Zen Buddhism, First Series*:

> As soon as one particle of dust is raised, the great earth manifests itself there in its entirety. In one lion are revealed millions of lions, and in millions of lions is revealed one lion. Thousands and thousands of them are indeed, but know ye just one, one only.[35]

Then he raised his staff, saying, "Here's my staff. So now, tell me, where's the one lion?"

When the assembly didn't know how to reply, he shouted "Ho!" Then he set the staff down and left the pulpit.

## YANGQI FANGHUI
## HUANGLONG HUINAN

Shishuang Chuyuan died at the fairly young age of fifty-four, but he left over fifty heirs. The two most important of these were Yangqi Fanghui and Huanglong Huinan. These two began the schools named for them. (In Japanese, the Yangqi School is called the Yogi School and the Huanglong the Oryo School.) These two schools and the original Five Houses comprise the Seven Schools of the Chinese Zen tradition.

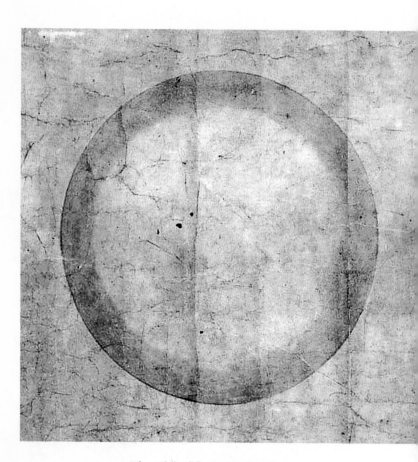

*The eighth of the* Ox Herding Pictures,
Ox and Self Forgotten

# CHAPTER EIGHTEEN

# THE FAYAN HOUSE

Deshan Xuanjian

Xuefeng Yicun

Xuansha Shibei

Luohan Chichen

Fayan Wenyi

Tiantai Deshao

Yongming Yanshou

Daoyun

## XUANSHA SHIBEI

Xuansha Shibei was the dharma heir of Xuefeng Yicun. Several stories concerning him are still quoted. One describes an occasion when Xuansha was serving tea to an important general. As they sipped the tea, the general asked, "What's meant by the statement that 'people don't know it even when they're making use of it'?"

Xuansha offered the general a rice cake. The general accepted it, ate it, and then, after a while, put his question a second time.

"Just that we make use of it everyday and yet we fail to recognize it," Xuansha replied.

Another story tells of a monk who, in spite of his practice, was unable to grasp the significance of Zen. Perhaps concerned that his problem might be due to his use of an inadequate technique, he approached Xuansha and asked, "How does one enter the Way?"

They were seated by a brook at the time, and Xuansha asked, "Can you hear the sound of the water flowing by?"

" Of course."

"Then there's the way to enter."

On one occasion, Xuansha took his place before the assembly that had gathered to listen to his dharma talk, but, instead of speaking, he remained silent for such a long time that eventually the monks, one by one, stood up and withdrew. As the last of them departed, Xuansha remarked, "They're all the same. They watch my lips, looking for meaning in words, but when I bring it forth, they fail to recognize it."

# LUOHAN CHICHEN
# FAYAN WENYI

Xuansha's heir was Luohan Chichen, who, in turn, was the teacher of Fayan Wenyi. Fayan's lineage, although it did not last as long as the Linji or Caodong lines, made up one of the Five Houses of Zen.

At an early age, Fayan was recognized for having a good grasp of the philosophy of the Huayen (J: Kegon) School of Buddhism. This school was also known as the "Consciousness Only" School because it posited that all things were contained within one's consciousness. After completing his formal studies in the Huayen School, Fayan did a tour of the major centers of Buddhism then current in China. He had not intended to visit Zen master Luohan, but, as it happened, a rainstorm drove him to seek shelter at Luohan's temple. Not much comfort would have been found in the old temple, which Fayan later described as having been in such poor repair that the rain and wind came unimpeded through the walls and rafters.

Luohan made his guest as welcome as possible under the circumstances, then asked him, "Where are you going to in this weather?"

Fayan was wandering from place to place with no particular itinerary. So he answered truthfully, "I don't know."

"Not knowing is the better way," Luohan said.

Fayan was unsure what the teacher meant by that remark, and he decided to stay with Luohan for a while. During the formal meetings between teacher and student, Fayan would often reply to Luohan's questions with quotations from the *Avatamsaka Sutra* on which the Huayen School was based. Luohan dismissed these replies, telling Fayan, "That isn't the teaching of the Buddha."

Eventually, Fayan had exhausted all that he had thought he had learned, and, in despair, he told Luohan, "I've nothing left, neither words nor concepts."

It was at that point that his Zen training began. What Luohan taught him went beyond the Huayen teaching. "In the true Buddhist understanding," Luohan told him, "all things present themselves."

Luohan rejected the abstract understanding promoted by a literal interpretation of the Huayen doctrines and sought to bring Fayan back to the world of practicality. Years later, Fayan made the same point to a group of four travelers who sought shelter with him at the hermitage he had established. As the travelers ate their evening meal, Fayan overheard them discussing the issue of objectivity and subjectivity. Fayan interrupted the discussion by pointing to a large stone and asking them, "In your understanding, is that stone inside or outside your mind?"

"In our study of Buddhism we've come to understand that all things are the product of mind," one of the travelers told him. "So I'll say that the stone is in my mind."

"Your head must be very heavy if you're carrying a stone as big as that about in it," Fayan remarked. (In a variation of this tale, it was Luohan who asked the question and Fayan who replied.)

Fayan's style was gentler than that employed by the followers of the Linji tradition. One of his basic methods was to repeat, without comment, the question or statement put to him. Once a monk introduced himself before putting his question: "My name is Echo. Tell me, what is Buddha?"

Fayan's famous reply was, "You are Echo."

On another occasion, Fayan asked Shaoxiu, "It's said, 'The smallest difference separates heaven and earth.' How do you understand this?"

"The smallest difference separates heaven and earth," Shaoxiu replied without hesitation.

"How can this interpretation be verified?"

"What's your answer then?" Shaoxiu asked.

"The smallest difference separates heaven and earth."

A new student named Hsuanze took part in the daily life of the monastery but never made use of the opportunity for private interviews with the teacher that is a standard tool used to hone the understanding of Zen students. One day, Fayan asked Hsuanze why he had not sought to take part in these interviews.

"When studying with my previous teacher," Hsuanze explained, "it was my good fortune to have my mind's eye opened somewhat, and I believe I've acquired some insight into this matter of Zen."

"Is that so," Fayan said. "So, tell me about this insight."

"When I asked my master who the Buddha was, he told me, 'Bingting comes for fire.'"

"That's a fine reply," Fayan said with admiration. "However, I'm afraid that you might have misunderstood what your master was saying. Tell me, in your own words, what do you think he meant?"

"Well," the student replied, "Bingting is the god of fire, and so, of course, his nature is fire. It's clearly ridiculous to suggest that one whose nature is fire should have to come for fire. In the same way, the nature of human beings is Buddha-nature; so it's just as ridiculous for one whose nature is already Buddha-awareness to ask another who the Buddha was."

"Uh-huh!" said Fayan, nodding his head. "It's as I expected. You didn't understand."

"I didn't?" the student said with surprise. "In that case, please instruct me. What would you say?"

"Very well, ask me your question."

"All right: Who is the Buddha?"

"Bingting comes for fire," Fayan replied.

When a monk asked Fayan what the primary teaching of the Buddha was, Fayan's reply was: "You have it as well!"

Another monk asked about the best path for those seeking to understand Buddhism, and Fayan told him, "It doesn't pass by here."

While his teaching style was not as harsh as that of the Linji line, Fayan still stressed the importance of traditional zazen practice. On one occasion, a monk asked: "What is Buddha?

Fayan's response was, "First, I ask you to practice. Second, I ask you to practice."

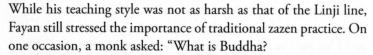

He did, however, also include elements of the Huayen tradition in the training of his students. As a result he may have made more use of the sutras and commentaries than previous Zen masters had.

A debate had been raging for some time about the relationship between the "Buddhism of the sutras" (the Buddhism taught by schools such as the Huayen and Tientai) and the "Buddhism of the patriarchs" (the Zen line). When Fayan's contemporary, Baling Haojian was asked if there were any difference between them, his reply was: "When the weather turns cold, wild fowl fly up into the trees and ducks go down to the water." Fayan heard of Baling's remark and commented, "Baling only has half the truth. I say that when water is scooped up in the hands, the moon is reflected therein, and when flowers are handled, their scent perfumes one's robe."

With the passing of time, Zen communities and monasteries had become more mainstream, and larger numbers of people came to seek training. However, these new students did not always have the same zeal or commitment their predecessors had had. Many students were unwilling to accept the hardships earlier Zen seekers had taken for granted. The story is told, for example, that one day a group of Fayan's students came to him and complained about the poor condition of the monastery buildings and their lack of amenities. In response, he told them of the austerities he had endured while studying with Luohan. "In winter, the wind blew into the meditation hall, and venerable old monks had to brush snow off their heads. The younger monks argued that they couldn't do zazen in these conditions and demanded that my master build a new temple. But the old master told them, 'The Lord Buddha taught us about the impermanence of all things. Even mountains wear down and valleys fill up. All things are as fleeting and empty as thoughts. This is also the case with this old temple where we gather. How can it be otherwise? The patriarchs didn't have temples. They practiced on the ground beneath trees or in caves. If we compare our practice with theirs, we see how weak our efforts are. How little time we have for practice!—forty or fifty years, no more. When do we have time to construct a new building?'

"And that's how it is with us. Make do with what we have now and concentrate on your practice."

One of the reasons students might not have been as willing to accept the austerities of the past was that in some cases they had come to the monasteries not so much to pursue awakening as to escape the political turmoil common throughout China during this time.

Luohan Chichen and Fayan Wenyi lived in the late Tang dynasty, during the sustained period of unrest after the An Lushan Rebellion (755–763). Conditions in many parts of the land were harsh. Local gangs arose in the areas most affected by poverty. One of these was headed by a man named Huang Chao, who was involved in the illegal salt trade (as in India during the Raj, salt production in China was controlled by the government). When conditions deteriorated even further because of a drought, Huang Chao presented himself as a rebel leader. His followers were augmented by peasants angered by the inability of the government to respond to their needs. Huang Chao fought a guerilla war against the formal military forces of the government and had some early victories.

Although the ensuing rebellion came to be named after Huang Chao, his was not the only rebel band in the country. In order to prevent the spread of these gangs, the imperial government ceded more authority to local military governors. The local authorities proved to be more efficient in responding to the uprisings, and Huang Chao and other rebel leaders were eventually brought under control. (Huang Chao committed suicide in order to avoid capture.) However, the rebellion also marked the beginning of the end of the once mighty Tang dynasty. China became fragmented as regional governors established their own fiefs, and, from 907 to 960, China was divided into what came to be known as the Five Dynasties in the North and the Ten Kingdoms in the south. In such uncertain times, the isolated Buddhist monasteries hidden away in the mountains provided refuge to those fleeing the chaos. As a consequence a wide range of commitment to the actual practice of Zen was now found within those communities.

This may have been one of the factors behind a story told of Fayan that later was included as a koan in the *Mumonkan*:

The assembly was called together to attend one of Fayan's formal lectures. Two monks came forward to roll up the bamboo blinds. Although they both rolled up the blinds in exactly the same manner, Fayan commented afterwards, "One has it. The other doesn't."

Fayan devised teaching techniques very different from those used by other Zen teachers. One of these was the contemplation of a circle within which the "Six Attributes of Being" were written. These were: *totality and differentiation, sameness and difference, becoming and passing away.* The six attributes are a way of coming to terms with a basic Buddhist problem—if all things are essentially One, how is multiplicity explained? The six attributes are neither identical nor different.

Fayan explained it this way:

> The meaning of the six attributes . . . is that within sameness there is difference. For difference to be different from sameness is in no way the intention of all the Buddhas. The intention of all the Buddhas is both totality and differentiation. How can there be both sameness and difference? When a male body enters *samadhi*, a female body is indifferent to it. When there is indifference, terms are transcended. When the ten thousand appearances are utterly bright, there is neither reality nor appearance.[36]

The practice of meditating on the circle was used to assist the student to come to an experience, rather than simply an understanding, of Oneness.

# TIANTAI DESHAO
# YONGMING YANSHOU

Fayan's dharma heir was Deshao, who, after the master's death, became an adherent of the Tiantai tradition; for this reason, he is known as Tiantai Deshao. Deshao, in turn, was succeeded by Yongming Yanshou, who sought to bring together the various schools of Buddhism then current in China.

Yongming helped popularize the Pure Land sect, which was much more accessible to the general population than Zen. Attaining awakening, as taught in the Zen tradition, was a long and difficult process that was generally only pursued by monks. In contrast, the Pure Land sect taught that the Buddha Amituo had promised that those who chanted his name with devotion would be rewarded by being reborn in the Pure Land of Bliss. This was a devotional practice anyone could undertake, and soon the Pure Land School became the most popular form of Buddhism practiced in China.

## DAOYUN

Deshao's other heir, Daoyun, was much more important to the Zen tradition. He was the author of the collection of biographies that make up the *Jingde Chuandenglu*, or *The Transmission of the Lamp*. It is a record of the lives of the Zen masters in China and their lines of transmissions. His intention in compiling these stories was to demonstrate that there was an uninterrupted teaching lineage proceeding from Bodhidharma down to the present. This collection would become a major source of material for later Zen writers, including the compilers of the great koan collections.

*The ninth of the* Ox Herding Pictures,
Returning to the Source

# CHAPTER NINETEEN

# YUNMEN WENYAN

## YUNMEN WENYAN
## MUZHOU DAOZONG
## XUEFENG YICUN

Yunmen Wenyan came from a very poor family. Because they could not afford to pay for a secular education, his parents placed their son at the local Buddhist school, where he studied the Vinaya. As he matured, however, he realized that knowledge of the rules of behavior alone would not fulfill his desire to come to awakening. So he sought out the Zen teacher Muzhou Daozong, who was a dharma heir of Huangbo.

There are a couple of interesting stories about Muzhou that give some indication of what his personality was like. In the first, a monk asked him, "How can we escape from the constant repetitive need to get dressed and eat every day?"

"We get dressed and we eat." Muzhou told him.

"I don't understand."

"In that case, get dressed and get something to eat."

On another occasion, a monk challenged Muzhou: "What is the teaching that goes beyond that of the Buddhas and patriarchs?"

Muzhou held up his stick and said, "I call this a staff. What do you call it?"

The monk, suspicious that there was a trap here, remained silent.

"You asked for a teaching that goes beyond that of the Buddhas and patriarchs, didn't you?" Muzhou asked.

When young Wenyan went to see Muzhou, the master was an old man and something of a recluse. Muzhou saw the youth coming down the path, and he shut the gate to his compound in Wenyan's face. Wenyan knocked to seek admittance. After a long while, and probably after Wenyan had knocked a few times more, a voice called out: "Who is it?"

"My name is Wenyan. I've been a student of the Vinaya and I now come seeking to discover the ground of my own being."

Muzhou opened the gate just wide enough to peek out. He took one look at the supplicant standing there then shut the gate tight. Wenyan was uncertain how to proceed, but he came back again the next day. Once more he knocked at the gate. Muzhou peeked through it as before, then slammed it shut again. Wenyan decided that Muzhou was testing his perseverance, so on the third day when Muzhou cracked the gate, Wenyan forced his way through the opening. Muzhou grabbed him by the robe and shook him. "Speak! Speak!" Muzhou demanded. But Wenyan did not know what to say. "What a worthless fellow!" Muzhou sneered. He pushed Wenyan back through the gate and slammed it shut. Wenyan's leg was still in the opening, and when the gate was forced home, his foot was broken. Wenyan cried out in pain and at that moment came to awakening. His foot remained crippled for the rest of his life, but he considered himself adequately repaid.

Muzhou felt that he was too old to take on a new disciple, and he advised Wenyan to continue his study of Zen with Xuefeng Yicun. When Wenyan came to the village not far from Xuefeng's monastery, he met one of its monks there. Wenyan asked if the monk were returning to the monastery, and he admitted he was.

"Will you do me a favor?" Wenyan asked. "When the assembly is gathered together, tell the master, 'This monk's head is trapped in iron stocks. Will you please remove them?'"

The monk agreed to this unusual request, and, at the appropriate time, spoke as Wenyan had asked him to. Xuefeng told him, "Those aren't your words. Whose are they?"

"A monk in the village asked me to speak in this fashion," the monk admitted.

Xuefeng then told the assembly, "All of you, prepare to welcome this new brother who will become the teacher of hundreds of students."

The following day, Wenyan presented himself at the monastery gate. Xuefeng said, "This isn't an easy place to reach, especially for a cripple. Why have you come here?"

Wenyan bowed, and it is said that teacher and student recognized one another at that moment.

It was from Xuefeng that Wenyan received transmission, and Wenyan is considered his disciple. After completing his training with Xuefeng, Wenyan made a pilgrimage to visit Shaoguan, where the mummified corpse of Huineng was kept. Along the way, he paid a visit to one of Muzhou's disciples, the layman Chen Zunsu. The layman had a reputation for being able to disconcert visiting monks. When Wenyan met him, Chen Zunsu said, "I've no interest in your understanding of the sutras. But let me ask you this: Why is it you journey about speaking with teachers of Zen?"

"How many others have you put this question to?" Wenyan inquired.

"I'm asking you now."

"Very well. Let me ask you, then: what's the teaching of the Buddha?"

Chen Zunsu quoted a popular saying, "One has no words to describe it. The mind is stymied when one tries to think about it."

"This saying comes from using words," Wenyan countered. "The mind is stymied because of delusive thinking. So tell me, what's the teaching of the Buddha?"

Chen Zunsu admitted he was beaten.

"It doesn't matter. The masters of Zen give up all things worldly as well as all learning. For ten and twenty years, they give undivided attention to this matter in zazen. And still they can't say. What made you think you could solve it?"

"It was my mistake," Chen Zunsu admitted.

When Wenyan came at last to Shaoguan, he presented himself at the gate of Lingshu, a monastery headed by Rumin Zhanshi, who was in the lineage of Nanyue Huairang.

An odd story is told of the relationship between Wenyan and Rumin. For many years before Wenyan came to the monastery, Rumin had refrained from appointing a head monk for his assembly. Occasionally monks, who possibly considered themselves worthy candidates for the post, would ask if it was not time for such an appointment to be made. But each time the question was raised, Rumin would say something like, "My head monk hasn't become a novice yet"; or "My head monk has just taken the precepts"; or "My head monk has just attained awakening."

Finally, one day, he announced to his assembled disciples that his head monk had completed his training and was beginning his pilgrimage. Shortly after this, he told the monks, "My head monk will arrive today. Send a delegation to meet him." The monks, perhaps somewhat skeptically, went to the monastery gate, where they saw Wenyan coming down the road.

They brought Wenyan in and presented him to Rumin. Rumin told the traveler, "I've been expecting you."

"How can you have been expecting me," Wenyan asked, "when I had no particular intention to visit this temple?"

"We two have a karmic relationship that goes back many generations, to the lifetime of the Buddha Sakyamuni himself. We were both his disciples and developed our powers of samadhi under his instruction. However, because of your worthiness, you were reborn into a royal family, where unfortunately you grew up to lead a self-indulgent, worldly life. So it was that you lost the spiritual strengths you had previously displayed. In my subsequent lives, on the other hand, I continued to return to the sangha, disciplining myself in zazen. Now I have capacities that have allowed me to follow your progress during this lifetime, and so I knew when you would arrive at this monastery."

Wenyan remained with Rumin, and, when that master died, he assumed the post of teacher. Later in life, he founded a temple on Mount Yunmen and acquired the name he is best known by.

His powers as a teacher were renowned even during his lifetime, and no other Zen teacher, except Zhaozhou, is as frequently cited in the traditional koan and mondo collections. One of the most frequently quoted anecdotes is his reply to a monk who asked, "What is Buddha?" This was a formal question, but it should be assumed that the monk put it in all seriousness, which makes Yunmen's reply all the more shocking: "A dried shit-stick." [Sticks were used, instead of paper, for personal hygiene.]

In another case, the inquiring monk begins by quoting a literary source: "The brilliance of the Buddha quietly illuminates the whole universe. . . ."

Before the monk could go any further, Yunmen interrupted him and said, "Aren't those the words of Zhangzhuo Xiucai?"

The monk admitted they were.

"You've misspoken," Yunmen told him.

He challenged his monks not to follow monastic rules unthinkingly. "The world is vast and broad. So why is it that you put on your robes at the sound of the bell?"

A monk asked, "What is moment by moment samadhi?"

Yunmen said, "Rice in the bowl, water in the pail."

A new monk came to the monastery, and Yunmen asked him where he had come from. The monk named the teacher with whom he had been studying.

"What words has he offered lately?" Yunmen asked.

The monk stretched out his hands. Yunmen struck him.

The monk said, "I've something to tell you."

Yunmen stretched out his own hands. The monk remained silent. Yunmen struck him again.

Addressing his assembly of monks, Yunmen declared: "In our school there is absolute freedom; sometimes it negates; sometimes it affirms. At times it kills; at times it brings to life."

"How does it kill?" a monk asked.

"After winter comes spring," Yunmen told him.

"And what after spring arrives?"

"One takes one's staff and rambles about the fields in whichever direction one pleases, beating the stumps of fallen trees to one's heart's content."

On another occasion, he took his place before the seated assembly and told them, "In our school words are not needed. So, then, tell me: what is the essence of our teaching?"

When no one spoke, Yunmen thrust out his arms, then retired to his quarters.

When asked, "What is the supreme teaching that transcends the Buddha and patriarchs?," Yunmen replied, "A sesame bun."

When asked, "What is the Dao?," he replied, "Walk on!"

When asked, "What is the pure body of the teaching?," he replied, "The flowering hedge by the privy."

Yunmen was just as earthy in his sermons:

Why are you all aimlessly coming here looking for something? I only know how to eat and shit. What use is there in explaining anything else?

You've taken pilgrimages everywhere, studying Zen and inquiring about Dao. But I ask you, what have you all learned in those places? Let's see it and check it out! In the midst of all this, what's the master of your own house attained? You've trailed around behind some old fellows, grabbing something they have already chewed on and spit out, and then calling it your own. Then you say, "I understand Zen!" or "I understand Dao!" Even if you can recite the whole Buddhist canon, what will you do with it?

The ancients didn't know when enough was enough. They saw you scurrying around, and when they said "bodhi" and "nirvana" they covered you up and staked you down. Then when they saw you didn't understand they said "no bodhi" and "no nirvana." It should have been made clear from the start that this just goes around and around! Now you just keep looking for commentaries and explanations!

You who act like this destroy our school. You've been going on like this endlessly, and where has it brought you to today?

Back when I was making pilgrimages there was a group of people who gave me explanations. They were well intentioned. But one day I saw through what they were saying. They are a bunch of laughingstocks. If I live a few more years I'll break the legs of those people who destroy our school! Nowadays there're plenty of things to get mixed up with. Why don't you go do them? What piece of dried shit are you looking for here?[37]

Then he chased all the monks from the dharma hall.

## DONGSHAN SHOUCHU

Yunmen's disciple, Dongshan Shouchu needs to be distinguished from Dongshan Liangjie, who was the disciple of Yunyan and from whom the Caodong (J: Soto) House descended. Both of them are known as Tozan in Japanese, and stories about the two can be confused.

Shouchu was born and raised in northern China. When he decided to seek his true nature, he made the long and difficult journey south to seek a Zen teacher. After practicing for a while at a lakeside monastery, he continued his travels, eventually coming to Yunmen's temple. There he presented himself and asked to be accepted as a student.

Yunmen began the interview by asking the young man where he had come from. Shouchu named his home province.

"And where did you spend the summer?" Yunmen asked.

Shouchu named the monastery beside the lake.

"When did you leave the monastery?"

"On the twenty-fifth of August."

"I spare you thirty blows."

In spite of that odd statement, Yunmen accepted Shouchu as a student, and he was allowed to take his place among the other monks. However, he spent the night reflecting on Yunmen's remark. It disturbed him so much that in the morning he sought another audience with the master.

"Yesterday you said I was spared thirty blows. Please, tell me what I'd done that deserved that punishment?"

"You worthless rice bag!" Yunmen scolded him. "Is this how you travel about? Coming from the north, staying by the lake?"

The remark was enough to bring Shouchu to awakening.

"Now that I understand," he said, "I'll retire to a hermitage where I won't store a single grain of rice nor plant a single stalk of rice. As monks pass by who go from one master to another to develop their supposed understanding, I'll make them discard their traveling hats and soiled robes. Then they'll be free with nothing to obstruct them, nothing to dim their sight. Won't that be perfect joy?"

"Hmph!" Yunmen grunted. "Your head is no larger than a co-conut but your mouth is pretty big!"

Once a monk asked Shouchu, "Who is the Buddha?"

Shouchu's famous reply was "Three weights of hemp."

## BALING HAOJIAN

Baling Haojian was also a disciple of Yunmen. Yunmen told him, "One day my master Xuefeng ordered me to open the gate because Bodhidharma was coming. What do you make of that?"

"He hit you on the nose," Baling replied.

"And when your nose is broken, what then?"

Baling remained silent.

"Hmph!" Yunmen grunted. "I see that your Zen is no more than lip-Zen."

When he finally attained awakening, Baling presented Yunmen with what are now known as the "Three Pivotal Words." Yunmen was so pleased with them that he told Baling, "After I've died, when the anniversary of my death comes around, you won't need to carry out the traditional ceremonies. Just recite these three words and that will be sufficient to repay my tutelage."

The Three Pivotal Words were Baling's reply to three questions:

A monk asked [Baling], "What is the [Zen] Sect?"
"Filling a silver bowl with snow," [Baling] replied.
"What is the Blown Hair Sword?" [the sword so sharp that
   hair is cut just from being blown onto it]
"The tip of each branch of coral supports the moon."
"What is Dao?"
"A bright-eyed man falls into a well."[38]

## XIANGLIN CHENGYUAN

Yunmen's disciple Xianglin Chengyuan began his study of Zen at the age of nineteen. He spent eighteen years meditating on the question, "What is it?" Finally he went to Yunmen and declared, "Now I understand."

"Very well," Yunmen said. "Don't tell me. *Demonstrate* your understanding."

So Xianglin spent another three years practicing zazen and finally came to full awakening. He would later declare, "It wasn't until I was forty that I was of one piece."

He became a teacher in his own right and is noted for once responding to the traditional question, "Why did the first patriarch come east?" by saying, "It's not good for one's health to sit too long."

On another occasion, however, he was asked, "What is the wellspring of Xianglin?"

"Mindfulness without interruption."

"And what of one who drinks from this spring?"

"He ladles it out according to his ability."

Another monk asked him, "What is your teaching?" (Literally, "What medicine do you prescribe?")

"It's none other than the ten thousand things," Xianglin answered.

"What effect does this medicine have?"

"Take some and see."

When Yunmen was eighty-five, he gave a farewell sermon to his assembly, then forced the foot that had been crippled since Muzhou broke it into formal full-lotus posture. Seated thus, he passed away.

The school his disciples founded after his death flourished for over two hundred years.

*The tenth of the* Ox Herding Pictures,
Going Among the People in the Markplace

# CHAPTER TWENTY

# THE SONG DYNASTY

The majority of the classic Chinese Zen tales come from the Tang dynasty, which was a period of growth and innovation in the meditation school. After the collapse of the Tang, China was subjected to the cultural chaos of five dynasties that succeeded one another in the fifty-three-year period between 907 and 960. In 960 the reigning emperor died, to be succeeded by his infant son. This provided an opportunity for General Zhao Kuangyin to declare himself emperor and, with the support of the army, begin the Song dynasty. He was able to unify the country under a central government, although the national territories no longer extended as far as they had during the Tang. After his death, he was given the posthumous title *Taizu*, or "Great Ancestor." An orderly succession of emperors followed Taizu, who was himself succeeded by his half-brother.

When, in 1127, the South lost dominion over the northern provinces to the Jin, the Song leadership simply moved their capital south and continued to govern a smaller but more stable country.

The social stability brought about during the Song era allowed for a cultural flowering that has been called a Chinese Renaissance—a Renaissance that anticipated that in Europe by four centuries. Will Durant, who referred to the Tang as the Age of Poets, called the Song the Age of Artists. There were advances in landscape painting, calligraphy, bronze casting, lacquerware, and ceramics. The Chinese had been using print since at least 868 (the date of a copy of the *Diamond Sutra* considered to be the world's first printed volume), and during the Song dynasty it became a more sophisticated process, including the use of moveable type. The world's first bank notes were released in Song dynasty China. There were technological advances as well, including the development of gunpowder. There was a great interest in literature, writing, and scholarship. Dictionaries and even encyclopedias were composed. It was an intellectually fertile period during which the first histories of the Chinese Zen tradition were composed, such as the work in which the story of the Flower Sermon and Mahakasyapa is first recorded.

Following a suppression of Buddhism in the mid ninth century, the two sects that fared best afterwards were the Pure Land and Zen.

These were the dominant schools of Buddhism when the Song dynasty started. During the Five Dynasties, the houses of Guiyang and Fayan had both faded away. Of the remaining houses of Zen, the one that came to dominance was the Linji lineage. Its monasteries spread throughout the land, attracting numerous adherents. As the number of monks increased, the monasteries had to find ways of accommodating and dealing with larger numbers and with persons of varying aptitude. Consequently, while the monasteries thrived, they also became more formalized. One result of this was that the innovative techniques of the teachers of the Tang dynasty, who often worked with only a few close disciples, were replaced by the developing koan system.

A number of outstanding teachers, however, still deserve mention.

## HUITANG ZUXIN

During the Song period, Confucianism re-established its primacy in Chinese society. Candidates for positions within the government bureaucracy were examined both on their familiarity with the classic works of this school and their understanding of how Confucian principles could be applied to current situations. Although this "Neo-Confucianism" had been strongly influenced by both Buddhism and Daoism, the more conservative Confucianists still looked upon Buddhism as a foreign teaching, inappropriate for the Chinese people.

The story is told of a statesman and poet who visited the Zen master Huitang Zuxin. The statesman, who was an orthodox Confucianist, asked Huitang to explain the matter of Zen to him.

"There's a passage in the writings of your master, Confucius, which explains Zen very well. Are you familiar with these lines: 'My disciples, do you think I've withheld anything from you? Be assured, I haven't held back anything at all.'"

The statesman started to reply, and Huitang cut him off, shouting, "No!"

The statesman was left confused by the encounter. Sometime later, however, he and Huitang were walking in the mountains. It was spring, and the flowering trees were in blossom. Huitang said, "Can you smell them?"

"Yes. Of course."

"As I said, I've kept nothing back."

And the statesman came to awakening.

There is a codicil to this story, however, which suggests that the statesman's original awakening was fairly shallow. A few months later, Huitang asked him, "When you and I are both dead and our bodies reduced to two heaps of ash, where and when shall we meet again?"

The statesman did not have an answer, and he pondered the question for several days. Then, one afternoon, he woke from a nap, and, as soon as he returned to consciousness, he understood Huitang's meaning.

One day Huitang entered the meditation chamber while the monks were engaged in zazen. Striking the platform on which the monks sat, he said, "When a single speck of dust arises, the whole world arises. A single sound fills the ears of all beings. If it's as swift as a bird of prey, then all's well, but if the waters are stagnant and the fish somnolent, then there are no ripples on the water."

When monks came to Huitang for private interviews, he would raise his hand and form it into a fist. "What do you call this?" he demanded. "If you say it's a fist, I'll hit you with it. But if you don't call it a fist, you're being evasive. So! Tell me! What is it?"

# WUZU FAYAN

Wuzu Fayan was a contemporary of Huitang. He began his studies in the Yogacara tradition, a speculative school based on the study of original Indian Buddhist texts. One day Fayan was reading an argument between adherents of the Yogacara tradition and their opponents on the nature of knowing. He could not tell from their reasoning which side was correct. Then he came upon a commentary on the argument made by the Chinese collector and translator of Indian texts, Hsuan Zhuang, who quoted General Ming's statement to Huineng: "It is like drinking water. One knows for oneself whether it is cool or warm." This passage made Fayan realize that what he hungered for was an actual, rather than intellectual, understanding of the teachings of Buddhism.

Coming to believe that he would not be able satisfy this desire in the Yogacara community, he sought a teacher who would be able to help him. The first Zen teacher he met was Yuanjien Fayuan, who, somewhat enigmatically, told him, "Sakyamuni Buddha had a secret word that he passed onto Mahakasyapa, but Kasyapa couldn't keep it hidden."

Fayan meditated on this statement for a year. Then Yuanjien, who was quite elderly at the time, told him he needed to work with a younger teacher who would be able to dedicate more attention to him. Yuanjien suggested that Fayan go to Boyun Shoutuan.

Boyun presented Fayan with Joshu's *Mu* as a koan. It was while working with Mu that Fayan eventually came to awakening. The poem he wrote to commemorate the event reads:

> A piece of land in front of the hill,
> Which I asked the old man, my teacher, about;
> And I sold and bought it many a time.
> Now, how I enjoy the cool breeze that blows through
> The pines and bamboo that I've carefully tended.[39]

Fayan received transmission from Boyun and became his principal dharma heir. He took up residence on Mount Dong, which was popularly known as the Fifth Patriarch's Mountain (Wuzu Shan), and it was from this that he derived his dharma name.

Wuzu had a gentle, humorous, and self-effacing manner. He referred to himself as "that fellow who lives somewhere-or-other at the foot of the East Mountain." D. T. Suzuki, in his first volume of Zen essays, provides this example of Wuzu's dharma talks:

> Yesterday I came across one topic which I thought I might communicate to you, my pupils, today. But an old man such as I am is apt to forget, and the topic has gone off altogether from my mind. I cannot just recall it." So saying, [Wuzu] remained quiet for some little time, but at last he exclaimed, "I forget, I forget, I cannot remember!" He resumed, however: "I know there is a mantram in one of the Sutras known as *The King of Good Memory*. Those who are forgetful may recite it, and the thing forgotten will come again. Well, I must try." He then recited the mantram, "Om o-lo-lok-kei svaha!" Clapping his hands and laughing heartily, he said: "I remember, I remember; this it was: When you seek the Buddha, you cannot see him: when you look for the patriarch, you cannot see him. The muskmelon is sweet even to the stems, the bitter gourd is bitter even to the roots.[40]

He then came down from the pulpit without further remark.

Asked to describe Zen training, Wuzu used this analogy: "When I'm asked about Zen, I tell people it's like learning the art of burglary. There was a young boy who was the son of a very successful burglar, but he noticed that his father was getting older and wasn't as spry as he'd once been. This worried the boy. 'What will our family do when my father isn't able to pursue his craft any longer?' he wondered. 'How will we avoid poverty and starvation?' After dwelling on this for some time, the boy made up his mind to ask his father to teach him the family trade.

"The father was pleased that his son had taken this initiative, and, that evening, he took the boy with him. They came to a large house occupied by a wealthy family, and the father showed the son how to break through the fence and enter the house without being heard. Then he brought him into one of the bedrooms, where the family was sleeping. He indicated the large chests where clothes for various seasons were stored. 'Go over to that chest and gather its contents for us to take.' But when the son bent over the chest, his father pushed him into it, closed the lid, and latched it. The father then crept out of the room and, once safely outside, shouted as loud as he could: 'Thieves! Thieves!'

"His cries woke the household. The family could see that the house had been broken into, but it appeared that the burglar had escaped. The boy in the chest, however, was very angry about what his father had done to him. As he thought about how to escape, it occurred to him to make a sound like that of a mouse caught in the chest. The household servant, holding a lantern, went over to the chest to investigate the noise. As soon as she lifted the lid, the boy jumped out, blew out the lantern, pushed the startled woman aside, and rushed through a window.

"As he ran away, the members of the household chased after him. He could hear them gaining on him as he passed an old well. Looking about, he found a large stone that he threw into the well making a loud splash. He left one of his sandals by the well and continued on his way. The household members gathered around the well and peered into it but couldn't see anything. Deciding that the burglar must have drowned, they went back home.

"The boy came to his own house, still very angry with his father. But his father told him to calm himself and describe what had happened. When the boy completed his tale, the father embraced him and said, 'Well done! You've learned the family art.'"

Four of Wuzu's statements are included as koans in the *Mumonkan*. On one occasion, he posed this question: "A water buffalo comes through the window. His head, horns, and four legs all go through easily. Why can't his tail pass?"

He declared, "Both Gautama Buddha and Maitreya Buddha [the Buddha to come in the future] are the servants of another. Who is it?"

He challenged his disciples with this question: "If you encounter a man of the Dao on the way (Dao/path), do not greet him with words or silence. Tell me, then, how are you going to greet him?"

One of Wuzu's most obscure koans, preserved in the *Wumenguan*, is based on a popular Chinese ghost story. According to the story, there were two children Qian and her cousin, Zhau, raised together in a small fishing village. Zhau was an orphan and grew up in his uncle's household. The two children were together constantly and got along so well that people often commented that they seemed made for each other and would, no doubt, one day be married. Qian and Zhau heard this type of remark so often that they came to believe it themselves and took it for granted that one day they would be wed.

However, Qian matured into a great beauty, and, when she neared the age of marriage, a rich merchant approached her father and offered him a substantial bride price. Qian's father was unable to resist it, and, according to the customs of the time, he arranged for his daughter to marry the merchant.

Qian and Zhau were devastated. Zhau was so distraught that he determined to leave the village, telling his cousin that the pain of seeing her as another's bride would be too much to bear. The next morning, while the fog was still thick, he put his boat into the river and let it flow with the current, allowing chance to decide where he would go. But before he had gone very far, he heard Qian's voice calling him. He could just make out Qian running in the mist alongside the riverbank, trying to catch up with him. He pulled over and allowed her to board, then the two continued together until they came to another village, where they passed themselves off as a young married couple.

They lived together in this manner for a number of years, and had two children. But Qian had always been unhappy with the way she had abandoned her father, who was, in spite of his decision to marry her to the merchant, a good and decent man. Finally, she told Zhau that they needed to return to their home village and make amends.

They arranged for a family in their neighborhood to look after their children, then took the boat back up river to their old village. When they arrived, Zhau told Qian to wait with the boat while he went to her father and apologized for their actions.

As Zhau nervously approached his uncle's house, the old man saw him on the path. Instead of the anger that Zhau had expected, his uncle greeted him warmly, asking where he had been all these years, telling him that everyone in the village had been concerned about him.

"But surely all knew that Qian and I had run off together?" Zhau said.

"Qian?" the uncle said. "What do you mean?"

"For the last seven years, we have lived as if married in a village down the river. We even have two children now," Zhau said.

"What nonsense is this?" the uncle said. "Qian never left the village. She fell into a deep coma the same day you disappeared and has been lying in bed ever since. I understood that this was because of her great love for you, and for many years now I have deeply regretted that I had agreed to sell her to that merchant."

Zhau was incredulous, but his uncle took him by the arm, pulling him into the hut, "Come. See for yourself."

Zhau followed his uncle into the hut and there, on a bed, was Qian. Just at that moment, the Qian who had lived all those years with Zhau came up the path as well. The Qian in her bed woke up from her coma and sat up. When the two Qians saw one another, they embraced and once more became a single young woman.

In the koan, Wuzu asks: "Qian's soul was parted from her body. Which, then, was the real Qian?"

Repairs were being made at the temple when Wuzu realized that he would soon die. He went to the gate and observed the progress of the workmen who were rebuilding it. "Do your best," he told them. "I won't come to see you again."

Then he went back to his rooms, There he bathed ceremonially, sat in meditation, and passed away.

## YUANWU KEQIN

Wuzu's principle heir was Yuanwu Keqin, who had been raised in a family of traditional Confucianists and whose formal education included memorizing the Confucian Classics. He was said to have had such a prodigious memory that at an early age he was able to memorize a thousand characters a day. His love of reading eventually led him to examine Buddhist texts. Their content intrigued him, prompting him to seek a teacher with whom he could discuss them. After meeting with several other teachers, Yuanwu eventually visited Wuzu.

He presented Wuzu with his interpretation of the various documents he had studied as well as his understanding of Zen as it had been presented by the other teachers with whom he had spent time. When he was finished, Wuzu remarked: "You've got a problem, you know."

"A problem? What problem do I have?"

"You know too much about Buddhism."

"I know too much!?"

"And you talk too much."

"I talk too much? When one's interested in a subject, isn't it natural to want to talk about it? What's wrong with that?"

"It upsets the stomach," Wuzu said.

Yuanwu was angered by the dismissive manner of the Zen master, and he rose to to take his leave. Before Yuanwu departed, however, Wuzu called to him: "When you fall sick, remember me."

As it turned out, sometime later, Yuanwu became seriously ill, and he realized that none of his learning was of any use to him in answering the questions of life and death. When he recovered, he returned to Wuzu and became his disciple. Under Wuzu, Yuanwu attained awakening.

Yuanwu told his own students, "The heat of a candle flame can't compete with the heat of the sun. The chill of a breeze can't compete with the chill of the moon. The legs of a crane are long, those of a duck, short. The pine is tall and straight; brambles are short and tangled. Geese are white; ravens are black. That's the way it is. When you grasp this, then all things will be your teacher."

*Southern Song dynasty portrait of a Zen priest*

# Chapter Twenty-One

# *WU!*

## Dahui Zonggao

The training undergone by Yuanwu Keqin's disciple, Dahui Zonggao, demonstrates the effectiveness of the koan system that had developed during the Song dynasty. For seventeen years, Dahui studied with several teachers, during which time he had a number of what he called "fragmentary experiences of awakening." But he was not satisfied with the depth of his insight. When he came to Yuanwu's monastery, he heard the master giving a dharma talk about the Tang dynasty Zen teacher, Yunmen Wenyan:

> "A monk," Yuanwu told the assembled monks, "once asked Master Yunmen, 'Where do all the Buddhas come from?' And Yunmen told him, 'The Eastern Mountain walks on water.' But that's not what I say. When I'm asked, 'Where do all the Buddhas come from,' I say, 'A fragrant breeze blows from the south and cools the Dharma Hall.'"

Hearing these words, Dahui later reported, "I felt as if I were cut free from space and time. It was as if a sharp knife had cut the tangled knot of a cord. I was dripping sweat from every pore of my body."

He sought a private audience with Yuanwu and reported his experience. Yuanwu tested the younger man, then acknowledged that he had had a genuine awakening. However, he added: "While it's difficult for people to achieve the level of insight you've attained, you still haven't understood everything yet, as you probably realize. You've died, but now you have to come back to life."

Yuanwu then presented Dahui with this koan: "Being (*u*) and not-being (*wu;* J: *mu*) are like a wisteria vine winding about a tree."

For six months, Dahui meditated on the koan, but every time he came before Yuanwu and tried to offer an explanation of his understanding, Yuanwu stopped him before he could say a word.

"No! It's not like that!" Yuanwu would say.

Slowly the koan came to occupy all of Dahui's attention, and one day, while he was eating, he was so absorbed in the koan that he forgot how to use his chopsticks and let them fall to the floor.

"That's the Zen of the boxwood tree," Yuanwu remarked, referring to the tree from which chopstick wood was harvested.

"I'm like a dog beside a pot of boiling fat," Dahui complained. "It can smell the fat but can't get at it no matter how much it tries. But it can't leave it either."

"You've fallen into a deep pit," Yuanwu admitted. "And you might need to stay there for a while."

Some time later, Dahui asked Yuanwu, "I heard that when you were a student in the assembly of Wuzu Fayen, you asked him to resolve this matter of *u* and *wu*. Is that true?"

Yuanwu admitted he had put the question to Wuzu.

"And what did he say?" Dahui asked.

Yuanwu just laughed.

"It wasn't a private matter, after all," Dahui persisted. "It wasn't secret. You put the question in front of all the monks gathered in the assembly, and they heard the answer as well."

Yuanwu relented, saying, "Very well, I asked my master, 'It's said that being (*u*) and not being (*wu*) are like a wisteria vine wound about a tree. What's the meaning of this?' And he told me, 'You can't picture it however hard you try.' Then I asked, 'And what if the tree is blown over and the vine dies?' Wuzu told me, 'You're still caught up in words.'"

There was a moment's pause, then Dahui laughed aloud. "I understand!" he exclaimed.

Yuanwu then presented Dahui with several testing questions, after which he acknowledged Dahui's attainment. "Today you now know that I haven't deceived you," he told his pupil.

As a result of his own experience, Dahui became an avid advocate of the koan system, which he used as a "skillful means" to help students achieve awakening and then deepen their original insights. For him, awakening was not a single event but an ongoing process.

He told his students that he had had eighteen major awakenings and countless smaller experiences.

"There aren't any words in Zen," he told them. "It's all awakening. When you have awakening, you've got it all."

The koan he most frequently assigned to those who came to him for instruction was Zhaozhou's "Wu!"

Another koan originated with Dahui. He held up his hossu and demanded: "If you call this a staff, you affirm; if you don't call it a staff, you negate. Beyond affirmation and negation, what are you going to call it? Say something!"

In one of his sermons, he told his students: "There's no Buddha other than Mind. It's like a hand and a fist or like water and a wave. A fist isn't anything other than the hand; a wave is nothing other than water. There's no past or future or present in Mind. Words like 'past' or 'future', words like 'Buddha' and 'Mind' are labels, nothing more. So tell me, are the words of the sutras true or not? If not, then we should forget old Shakyamuni with his flapping lips and three-inch tongue. Do what's right without worrying about the past."

## YUELIN SHIGUAN

Like Yuanwu, Kaifu Daoning was a student of Wuzu Fayen. His disciple was Yue'an Shanguo, who in turn was the master of Laona Zudeng. And Laona was succeeded by Yuelin Shiguan.

All of these masters made use of koans, and, in particular, the koan "*Wu*," which was becoming a preferred koan for many teachers in the Rinzai lineage during the Song dynasty. For Yuelin, as for all Zen masters, the goal of Zen was awakening, which results in a deep involvement in life just as it is. However, prospective students often came to Zen because they hoped it would help them escape the difficulties of their lives. As one student put it to Yuelin, "How can I escape the wheel of birth and death?"

Yuelin's curt reply was: "What use is there in escaping it?"

Koans were based upon the spontaneous responses, verbal or physical, Tang masters had made when questioned by their students. Song teachers took the records of these encounters and used them as tools to help their own students. The challenge for the student, as Wuzu's statement to Yuanwu expressed, was to get beyond the words of the koan, beyond the usual patterns of thought and reasoning. As with Dahui when he was so absorbed that he dropped his chopsticks, the student had to become so focused upon his koan that he became one with it—body and mind united.

The actual practice used by these teachers was called *huatou*, which means "the head of a thought." The practitioner reduces the koan to a single word or phrase—such as "Wu!"—which he silently repeats to himself over and over. By doing this with full concentration to the exclusion of all else, the practitioner achieves a state a mind that is before thought.

## WUMEN HUIKAI

Yuelin's most important dharma heir was Wumen Huikai. Huikai had been unable to attain awakening under his first Zen teacher, and so he came to Yuelin's temple in spite of the reputation it had for being a very strict and demanding establishment. He was assigned the koan "Wu!" and struggled with it for six long years. Day and night he absorbed himself in *Wu!*, vowing not to sleep unless absolutely necessary, telling himself he would set his body on fire if he started to doze. To try to stay awake during the night, he walked the corridors of the temple, striking his head against the wooden support columns.

Then one day, as he stood next to the altar where the statue of the Buddha was displayed, he heard a drum being struck, and at that moment all became clear. To commemorate the event, he wrote the following verse:

> From the azure heaven bright with the noon-day sun,
> A sudden crash of thunder!
> All living beings on the Great Earth
> Open wide their eyes,
> Everything in the entire universe
> In a like manner bows the head,
> And [Mount] Sumeru, leaping up,
> Dances a merry *san-t'ai*.[41]

When he later went to Yuelin to have his insight confirmed, the master was dismissive. "What nonsense is this? What demons or spirits have bewitched you?"

Huikai shouted, "Ho!"

Yuelin answered, "Ho!"

And Huikai again shouted, "Ho!"

Yuelin smiled, pleased, and gave Huikai the dharma name Wumen, which means "No Gate."

After completing his training with Yuelin at the age of thirty-six, Wumen went on the traditional pilgrimage. He did not seek fame or students, preferring to lead an obscure life. He let his hair and beard grow, and the clothes he wore were often soiled and poorly mended. He was called "Lay monk Huikai" because of his eccentric appearance. He traveled from monastery to monastery, where he worked in the fields, making no effort to draw attention to himself. But his quiet, humorous manner betrayed the depth of his understanding and potential students took note of him and kept informed of where he went.

He finally settled at a small temple near the West Lake, and although he still did not seek students, they came anyway—from all over China and from as far away as Japan. He assigned the koan "Wu!" to those who asked for instruction. And once they came to awakening through the use of "Wu!" he followed it with several koans by which he sought to guide his students in deepening their understanding.

In 1228, he wrote down the koans he used in a collection he called the *The Gateless Gate* (Ch: *Wumenguan*; J: *Mumonkan*). By "gate," he appears to have meant the type of barrier placed at border crossings. He appended a commentary and a verse to each of the koans.

In the introduction, he explained how the collection came about.

In the year 1228 I was lecturing monks in the Ryusho [Longxiang] Temple in eastern China, and at their request I retold old koans, endeavoring to inspire their Zen spirit. I meant to use the koans as a man who picks up a piece of brick to knock at a gate, and after the gate is opened the brick is useless and thrown away. My notes, however, were collected unexpectedly, and there were forty-eight koans, together with my comment in prose and verse concerning each, although their arrangement was not in the order of the telling.[42]

In spite of his claim that the koans were not recorded in any particular order, he presents the koan "Wu!" [J: *Mu*] as the first in the collection, and his commentary on it is not only longer, it is also more rhapsodic than the commentaries on any of the other koans.

To realize Zen one has to pass through the barrier of the patriarchs. Enlightenment always comes after the road of thinking is blocked. If you do not pass the barrier of the patriarchs or if your thinking road is not blocked, whatever you think, whatever you do, is like a tangling ghost. You may ask: What is a barrier of a patriarch? This one word, Mu, is it.

This is the barrier of Zen. If you pass through it you will see [Zhaozhou] face to face. Then you can work hand in hand with the whole line of patriarchs. Is this not a pleasant thing to do?

If you want to pass this barrier, you must work through every bone in your body, through every pore of your skin, filled with this question: What is Mu? and carry it day and night. Do not believe in the common negative symbol meaning nothing. It is not nothingness, the opposite of existence. If you really want to pass this barrier, you should feel like drinking a hot iron ball that you can neither swallow nor spit out.
Then your previous lesser knowledge disappears. As a fruit ripening in season, your subjectivity and objectivity naturally become one. It is like a dumb man who has had a dream. He knows about it but he cannot tell it.

When he enters this condition, his ego-shell is crushed and he can shake the heaven and move the earth. He is like a great warrior with a sharp sword. If a Buddha stands in his way, he will cut him down; if a patriarch offers him any obstacle, he will kill him; and he will be free in his way of birth and death. He can enter any world as if it were his own playground. I will tell you how to do this with this koan:

Just concentrate your whole energy into this Mu, and do not allow any discontinuation. When you enter this Mu and there is no discontinuation, your attainment will be as a candle burning and illuminating the whole universe.[43]

Wumen's fame and religious stature was such that the emperor called upon him to establish a temple for the "protection of the country." Then, when the country was suffering a persistent drought, the emperor ordered Wumen to preside over a ceremony that it was hoped would relieve the dry period. The story goes that as Wumen began to intone the traditional Buddhist chants, the sky darkened with clouds, and, within minutes, rain started to fall.

As a reward for this service, the emperor bestowed upon Wumen the title "Eye of the Buddha" and presented him with a gold robe. But Wumen preferred to wear the unadorned robes of a simple monk, and—following the example of Baizhang—seeking no special privileges he returned to his own temple, where he continued to work the fields with the other monks.

He became slighter of build as he grew older, and his robes, still tattered and patched, no longer fit him properly. He worked every day, and, to the end of his life, he looked after his personal needs without the assistance of an attendant.

He was seventy-eight years old when he died. His death poem read:

> Emptiness is unborn
> Emptiness does not die
> If you know emptiness
> You and emptiness do not differ.[44]

# Epilogue in Japan

One of the many aspirants who sought out Wumen Huikai was Shinchi Kakushin, who came from the islands five hundred miles east of China that the Chinese referred to as the Land of Wa (the Land of Dwarves). The inhabitants of these islands referred to their country as the Land of the Rising Sun and referred to China as the Land of the Setting Sun.

Buddhism was first introduced to Japan by a delegation of Korean diplomats that visited the court of the Yamato family in 552, a little more than thirty years after Bodhidharma had visited Emperor Wu in China. At that point in their history, the islands were just beginning to be united under a single ruler. Previously, the region had been divided among a number of warring clans. The Yamato established their stronghold in the area now known as Nara Prefecture on the island of Honshu. Their court would have been a very shabby thing compared with the court of Wu. The Japanese were still a culturally underdeveloped people at this time, lacking even a written language.

The Korean diplomats, who were seeking a military alliance, presented the court with a statue of the Buddha as well as copies of sutras that their hosts in all likelihood could neither read nor make much sense of. In spite of that, the Japanese were impressed by the gifts.

By the time of the later Zen patriarchs in China, the political leaders of Japan had acquired a great admiration for Tang culture and sought to emulate it. They adapted the Chinese written characters to their own language; they imported Confucianism, Chinese medicine, music, astronomy, and the Chinese calendar. The architecture of the city of Nara was copied from Chinese models. The Japanese even adapted the example of Chinese bureaucracy. And many families in the upper classes became adherents of a devotional form of Buddhism. Within a short time there were dozens of Buddhist temples on the islands, maintained by coteries of monks and nuns.

Throughout the Tang period, diplomatic missions traveled between China and Japan, and these included monks and scholars who absorbed Chinese culture, philosophy, and religion, in order to bring it back to their own country.

The first recorded Zen student from Japan was named Dosho. He spent time with several meditation teachers in China, including the Fourth Patriarch, Daoxin. In the six hundred years that passed between the lives of Dosho and Shinchi, hundreds of Japanese monks made their way to China, some not surviving the hazards of the journey across the sea. But their zeal was such that they willingly took the chance.

When they returned home, they and their students molded the practice into something uniquely Japanese, just as the Chinese had molded the Indian teaching into something appropriate for their culture. Even more than it had in China, Zen became fully integrated into Japanese culture, and the effects of that enculturation persist to the present.

With men like Dosho and Shinchi, Zen took its second step east.

# Acknowledgments

The author gratefully acknowledges permission to reprint the following material:

- Francis Dojun Cook, excerpts from *How to Raise an Ox: Zen Practice as Taught by Master Dogen's Shogenzo.* Copyright © 1995. Reprinted with the permission of The Permissions Company, Inc. on behalf of Wisdom Publication, www.wisdompubs.org

- Andy Ferguson, excerpts from *Zen's Chinese Heritage: The Masters and Their Teachings, Expanded Edition.* Copyright © 2011 by Andy Ferguson. Reprinted with the permission of The Permissions Company, Inc. on behalf of Wisdom Publication, www.wisdompubs.org

- Albert Low, excerpts from *The World: A Gateway*

- The Rochester Zen Center for their translation of the Heart Sutra

- Shide, ["Up high the trail turns steep"], translated by Red Pine, from *The Collected Songs of Cold Mountain, Revised and Expanded.* Copyright © 2000 by Bill Porter. Reprinted with the permission of The Permissions Company, Inc., on behalf of Copper Canyon Press, www.coppercanyonpress.org.

- John Tarrant and Joan Sutherland for their translation of the *Cantongqi*

- Tuttle Publishing, excerpts from *Zen Flesh, Zen Bones* by Paul Reps and Nyogen Senzaki.

- Excerpts from *Essays on Zen Buddhism,* copyright © 1949 by D. T. Suzuki.  Used by permission of Grove/Atlantic, Inc.

- Excerpt from *Zen: Tradition and Transition*, copyright © 1988 by Kenneth Kraft. Used by permission of Grove/Atlantic, Inc

- Excerpts from *Zen Buddhism: A History—India and China* by Heinrich Dumoulin used with permission from World Wisdom, Inc.

- Excerpts from *Zen Dust: The History of the Koan and Koan Study in Rinzai*, copyright © 1966 by Ruth Fuller Sasaki, reprinted by permission of Harcourt, Inc.

# Appendix

The Wade-Giles and Japanese variants of the Pinyin names used in the text are provided by chapter.

| Pinyin | Wade-Giles | Japanese |
|---|---|---|
| **CHAPTER TWO** | | |
| Huike | Hui-k'o | Eka |
| Jianzhi Sengcan | Chien-chi Seng-ts'an | Sosan Kanchi |
| Dayi Daoxin | Ta-i Tao-hsin | Doshin |
| Daman Hongren | Ta-man Hung-jen | Daiman Konin |
| **CHAPTER THREE** | | |
| Dajian Huineng | Ta-chien Hui-neng | Daikan Eno |
| **CHAPTER FOUR** | | |
| Shenxiu | Shen-hsiu | Jinshu |
| Nanyang Huizhong Guoshi | Nan-yang Hui-chung Kuo-shih | Nan'yo Echu Kokushi |
| Yingzhen | Ying-chen | Oshin |
| Qingyuan Xingshi | Ch'ing-yuan Hsing-ssu | Seigen Gyoshi |
| Nanyue Huairang | Nan-yueh Huai-jang | Nangaku Ejo |
| Heze Shenxiu | Ho-tse Shen-hui | Kataku Jinne |
| **CHAPTER FIVE** | | |
| Mazu Daoyi | Ma-tsu Tao-i | Baso Doitsu |
| **CHAPTER SIX** | | |
| Shitou Xiqian | Shih-t'ou Hsi-chien | Sekito Kisen |

| Pinyin | Wade-Giles | Japanese |
|---|---|---|
| Pangyun "Layman Pang" | P'ang Yun "Layman P'ang" | Hokoji |
| Tianhuang Daowu | T'ien-huang Tao-wu | Tenno Dogo |
| Lungtan Chongzin | Lung-t'an Ch'ung-hsin | Ryutan Soshin |
| Tanxia Tianran | Tan-hsia T'ien-jan | Tanka Tennen |
| Cuiwei Wuxue | Ts'ui-wei Wu-hseuh | Suibi Mugaku |
| **CHAPTER SEVEN** | | |
| Yaoshan Weiyan | Yuen-shan Wei-yen | Yakusan Igen |
| Yunyan Tansheng | Yun-yen T'an-sheng | Ungan Donsho |
| Daowu Yuanjie | Tao-wu Yuan-chieh | Dogo Enchi |
| Chunzi Decheng | Ch'uan-tzu Te-ch'eng | Sensu Tokujo |
| Jiashan Shanhui | Chia-shan Shan-hui | Kassan Zenne |
| **CHAPTER EIGHT** | | |
| Dongshan Liangjie | Tung-shan Liang-chieh | Tozan Ryokai |
| Caoshan Benji | Ts'ao-shan Pen-chi | Sozan Honjaku |
| **CHAPTER NINE** | | |
| Yanguan Qian | Yen-kuan Ch'i-an | Enkan Sai'an |
| Xingshan Weikuan | Hsing-shan Wei-k'uan | Kozen Ikan |
| Dazhu Huihai | Tai-chu Hui-hai | Daiju Ekai |
| Guizong Zhichang | Kuei-tsung Chih-ch'ang | Kisu Chijo |
| Panshan Baoji | P'an-shan Pao-chi | Banzan Hoshaku |
| Shigong Huicang | Shih-kung Hui-ts'ang | Sekkyo Ezo |
| Damei Fachang | Ta-mai Fa-ch'ang | Daibai Hojo |
| **CHAPTER TEN** | | |
| Hanshan | Han-shan | Kanzan |
| Shide | Shih-te | Jittoku |
| **CHAPTER ELEVEN** | | |
| Nanquan Puyuan | Nan-ch'uan P'u-yuan | Nansen Fugan |
| Baizhang Huaihai | Pai-chang Huai-hai | Hyakujo Ekai |

| Pinyin | Wade-Giles | Japanese |
|---|---|---|
| **CHAPTER TWELVE** | | |
| Zhaozhou Congshen | Chao-chou Ts'ung-shen | Joshu Jushin |
| Zui Jiao | T'ieh-tsui Chiao | Tesshikaku |
| **CHAPTER THIRTEEN** | | |
| Huangbo Xiyun | Huang-po Hsi-yun | Obaku Ki-un |
| Changsha Jingcen | Ch'ang-sha Ching-ts'en | Chosa Keijin |
| Hangzhou Tianlong | Hang-chou T'ien-lung | Koshu Tenryu |
| Jinhua Juzhi | Chin-hua Chu-chih | Gutei Chikan |
| Guishan Lingyou | Kuei-shan Ling-yu | Isan Reiyu |
| **CHAPTER FOURTEEN** | | |
| Yangshan Huiji | Yang-shan Hui-chi | Kyozan Ejaku |
| Xiangyan Zhixian | Hsiang-yen Chih-hsien | Kyogen Chikan |
| Chanqing Daan | Ch'ang-ch'ing Ta-an | Chokei Daian |
| **CHAPTER FIFTEEN** | | |
| Linji Yixuan | Lin-chi I-hsuan | Rinzai Gigen |
| **CHAPTER SIXTEEN** | | |
| Deshan Xuanjian | Te-shan Hsuan-chien | Tokuzan Senkan |
| Yantou Quanhuo | Yen-t'ou Ch'uan-huo | Ganto Zenkatsu |
| Xuefeng Yicun | Hsueh-feng I-t'sun | Seppo Gison |
| Qinshan Wensui | Ch'in-shan Wen-sui | Kinzan Bunsui |
| **CHAPTER SEVENTEEN** | | |
| Dingzhou Shizang | Ting-chou Shih-tsang | Joshu Sekiso |
| Sansheng Huiran | San-sheng Hui-jan | Sansho Enen |
| Xinghua Cunjiang | Hsing-hua Ts'ung-Chiang | Koke Zonsho |
| Nanyuan Huiyong | Nan-yuan Hui-yung | Nanin Egyo |
| Fengxue Yanzhao | Feng-hsueh Yen-chao | Fuketsu Ensho |
| Shoushan Xingnian | Shou-shan Sheng-nien | Shuzan Shonen |
| Fenyang Shanzhao | Fen-yang Shan-chao | Fun'yo Zensho |

| Pinyin | Wade-Giles | Japanese |
|---|---|---|
| Shishuang Chuyuan | Shih-shuang Ch'u-yuan | Sekiso Soen |
| Yangqi Fanghui | Yang-ch'i Fang-hui | Yogi Hoe |
| Huanglong Huinan | Huang-lung Hui-nan | Oryo Enan |
| **CHAPTER EIGHTEEN** | | |
| Xuansha Shibei | Hsuan-sha Hsi-pei | Gensa Shibi |
| Luohan Chichen | Lo-han Kuei-ch'en | Rakan Keishin |
| Fayan Wenyi | Fa-yen Wen-i | Hogen Bun'eki |
| Tiantai Deshao | T'ien-t'ai Te-shao | Tendai Tokusho |
| Yongming Yanshou | Yung-ming Yen-shou | Zuigan Ju |
| Daoyun | Tao-yuan | - |
| **CHAPTER NINETEEN** | | |
| Xuefeng Yicun | Hsueh-feng I-ts'un | Seppo Gison |
| Yunmen Wenyan | Yun-men Wen-yen | Ummon Bun'en |
| Muzhou Daozong | Mu-chou Tao-tsung | Bokuju |
| Dongshan Shouchu | Tung-shan Shou-shu | Tozan Shusho |
| Baling Haojian | Pa-ling Hao-chien | Haryo Kokan |
| Xianglin Chengyuan | Hsiang-lin Ch'eng-yuan | Kyorin Choon |
| **CHAPTER TWENTY** | | |
| Huitang Zuxin | Hui-t'ang Tsu-hsin | Maido Soshin |
| Wuzu Fayan | Wu-tsu Fa-yen | Goso Hoen |
| Yuanwu Keqin | Yuan-wu K'o-ch'in | Engo Kokugon |
| **CHAPTER TWENTY-ONE** | | |
| Dahui Zonggao | Ta-hui Tsung-kao | Dai-e Soko |
| Yuelin Shiguan | Yueh-lin Shih-kuan | Getsurin Shikan |
| Wumen Huikai | Wu-men Hui-k'ai | Mumon Ekai |

# Notes

1. D. T. Suzuki, *Essays in Zen Buddhism, First Series* (London: Rider and Company, 1973), 174–75.
2. Peter Matthiessen, *Nine-Headed Dragon River* (Boston: Shambala, 1998), 8.
3. Suzuki, Op. cit, 196–201.
4. D. T. Suzuki, *The Zen Doctrine of No-Mind* (Boston: Weiser Books, 1972), 72–75.
5. Isshu Miura and Ruth Fuller Sasaki, *Zen Dust* (New York: Harcourt, Brace & World, 1966), 268.
6. Translation by John Tarrant and Joan Sutherland of the Pacific Zen Institute.
7. Katsuki Sekida, *Two Zen Classics* (New York: Weatherhill, 2000), 263.
8. Andy Ferguson, *Zen's Chinese Heritage* (Boston: Wisdom Publications, 2000), 95.
9. Sekida, Op. cit, 264.
10. Ibid., 356–57
11. Miura and Sasaki, Op. cit., 305.
12. Ibid., 259.
13. Translation by the Rochester Zen Center.
14. Miura and Sasaki, Op. cit., 297.
15. Sekida, Op. cit., 267.
16. Heinrich Dumoulin, *Zen Buddhism: A History—Indian and China* (Bloomington: World Wisdom, 2005), 225–226.
17. Andy Ferguson, Op. cit., 99.
18. Francis Dojun Cook, *How to Raise an Ox: Zen Practice as Taught in Zen Master Dogen's Shobogenzo* (Boston: Wisdom Publications, 2002), 139–40.

19. Ibid., 140.
20. Will Durant, *Our Oriental Heritage* (New York: Simon and Schuster, 1954), 711–12.
21. D. T. Suzuki, *Essays in Zen Buddhism, Third Series* (London: Rider and Company, 1973), 160.
22. Ibid., 161.
23. Translated by Red Pine (Bill Porter) from *The Collected Songs of Cold Mountain*, Revised and Expanded (Port Townsend: Copper Canyon Press, 2000).
24. Gary Snyder, *Riprap and Cold Mountain Poems* (Berkeley: Counterpoint, 1965), poems 3, 7, 21, and 21.
25. Kenneth Kraft, *Zen: Tradition and Transition* (New York: Grove Press, 1988), 119.
26. Miura and Sasaki, Op. cit., 275.
27. Ferguson, Op. cit, 134.
28. Dumoulin, Op. cit., 215.
29. Ibid.
30. Ibid, 216.
31. Suzuki, *Essays in Zen Buddhism, First Series*, 347–48.
32. Ferguson, Op. cit., 199.
33. Miura and Sasaki, Op. cit., 54–55.
34. Ibid., 271.
35. Suzuki, *Essays in Zen Buddhism, First Series*, 35.
36. Dumoulin, Op. cit., 234.
37. Ferguson, Op. cit., 261.
38. Miura and Sasaki, Op. cit., 55.
39. Sekida, Op. cit, 107.
40. Suzuki, *Essays in Zen Buddhism, First Series*, 286
41. Miura and Sasaki, Op. cit., 204.
42. Paul Reps, *Zen Flesh, Zen Bones* (Garden City, N.Y.: Anchor Books, n.d.), 88.
43. Ibid., pp. 89–90.
44. Albert Low, *The World: A Gateway* (Rutland, Vt.: Charles E. Tuttle Co., 1995), ix–x.

# Bibliography

Aitkin, Robert. *Taking the Path of Zen*. New York: North Point Press, 1982.

Benoit, Hubert. *The Supreme Doctrine*. Eastbourne: Sussex Academic Press, 1998.

Cleary, Thomas. *Timeless Spring*. Rutland, Vt.: Tuttle Publishing, 1980.

Cook, Francis Dojun. *How to Raise an Ox*. Boston: Wisdom Publications, 2002.

Dumoulin, Heinrich. *Zen Buddhism: A History—India and China*. Bloomington, Ind.: World Wisdom, 1988.

———. *Zen Buddhism: A History—Japan*. Bloomington, Ind.: World Wisdom, 1990.

Durant, Will. *Our Oriental Heritage*. New York: MJF Books, 1993.

Ferguson, Andy. *Zen's Chinese Heritage*. Boston: Wisdom Publications, 2000.

Ford, James Ismael. *In This Very Moment*. Newburyport, Mass.: Red Wheel, 2004.

Kapleau, Philip. *The Three Pillars of Zen*. New York: Anchor Books, 1965.

Kraft, Kenneth (ed.). *Zen: Tradition and Transition*. New York: Grove/Atlantic, 1988.

Low, Albert. *The World: A Gateway*. Rutland, Vt.: Tuttle Publishing, 1995.

———. *Zen Meditation Plain and Simple*. Rutland, Vt.: Tuttle Publishing, 2000.

Matthiessen, Peter. *Nine-Headed Dragon River*. Boston: Shambala, 1998.

Miura, Isshu and Ruth Sasaki. *Zen Dust*. New York: Harcourt, Brace and World, 1966.

Omori Sogen. *An Introduction to Zen Training*. Rutland, Vt.: Tuttle Publishing, 2001.

Reps, Paul and Nyogen Senzaki. *Zen Flesh, Zen Bones*. Rutland, Vt.: Tuttle Publishing, 1998.

Rochester Zen Center. *Chants and Recitations*. Rochester: Rochester Zen Center, 2005.

Sekida, Katsuki. *Two Zen Classics*. Boston: Shambala, 2005.

Snyder, Gary. *Riprap and Cold Mountain Poems*. Berkeley: Counterpoint, 2010.

Suzuki, D. T. *Essays in Zen Buddhism, First Series*. New York: Grove Press, 1994.

———. *Essays in Zen Buddhism, Third Series*. Newburyport, Mass.: Samuel Weiser, 1971.

———. *The Zen Doctrine of No-Mind*. Newburyport, Mass.: Samuel Weiser, 1991.

———. *Zen and Japanese Culture*. Princeton: Princeton University Press, 2010.

Tarrant, John. *Bring Me the Rhinoceros*. Boston: Shambala, 2008.

———. *The Light Inside the Darkness*. New York: Harper, 1999.

Watts, Alan. *The Way of Zen*. New York: Vintage, 1999.

# Index of Stories

Baizhang Huaihai,
169–174
  Caring for an ox, 173
  "A day of no work is a
    day of no food," 172
  A fox who had been
    human, 173
  and Mazu, 169
  The sermon is over, 170
  A shout, 170
  "What is it?," 172
Baling Haojian, 278–79
  and Fayan, 262
  *The Three Pivotal Words*,
    279
  and Yunmen, 278
Boatman Monk [see
  Chunzi Decheng]
Bodhidharma, 35–44
  Audience with Emperor
    Wu, 38–40
  First meeting with the
    second patriarch
    (Huike/Sengcan), 41
  Returns west, 43
  A special transmission
    outside scripture, 36
Buddha, 25–33
  Enlightenment, 29
  Flower Sermon, 25
  The Four Signs, 26
  Parable of the man shot
    with an arrow, 31
Caoshan Benji, 134–37
  Commentary on *The
    Five Ranks*, 135
  and Dongshan, 134
  "I'm going but not to
    anywhere different," 135

"It's like a well looking
  at the donkey," 136
"Three cups of the finest
  wine," 136
Changsha Jingcen, 195–98
  Sermon, 197
  "What was it like before
    you met Nanquan?,"
    197
  Where Nanquan went
    after he died, 195
  Who becomes a
    Buddha?, 198
  "Who has concealed
    him?," 197
  and Yangshan Huiji, 196
Chanqing Daan, 214–15
  "I ate Guishan's food and
    shat Guishan's shit," 214
  Riding an ox, 214
Chunzi Decheng [the
  Boatman Monk],
  119–20
  and Jiashan, 121
Cuiwei Wuxue, 105–107
  "Do you need a second
    helping?," 106
  and Tanxia Tianran, 105
  "There's a tall bamboo
    and here's a short one,"
    106
Dahui Zonggao, 296–98
  Sermon, 298
  A staff, 298
  and Yuanwu, 296
  Zen of the boxwood
    tree, 297
Daitzu, 180
Daman Hongren, 55–57

Competition to
  determine Sixth
  Patriarch, 61–65
"How did you choose
  Huineng?," 72
Meets Dayi Daoxin, 56
Meets Huineng, 60
Rebirth, 55
Damei Fachang, 148–50
  An invitation from
    Yanguan Qian, 149
  "Mazu is a senile old
    dotard," 148
Danyuan Yingzhen,
  207–208
Daowu Yuanjie, 116–19
  "I won't say alive; I
    won't say dead," 118
  Parable of the man
    standing on the hill, 117
  and Shishuang Qingzhu,
    118
  and Yunyan Tansheng,
    116
Daoyun, 266
Dayi Daoxin, 53–54
  His heir [Daman
    Hongren], 55
  "It's still with you," 54–55
  Meets Jianzhi Sengcan,
    53
Dazhu Huihai, 142–43
Deshan Xuanjian, 230–234
  Blowing out a candle,
    231
  and Guishan, 232
  and Linji, 234
  and Lungtan Chongzin,
    231

The old woman and the "mind refreshers," 230
and Sansheng, 245
Sermon, 234
Thirty blows, 233
and Yantou and Xuefeng, 235–36

Dingzhou Shizang, 244
and Linji, 224, 244
"Sound the bottom of the river yourself," 244

Dongshan Liangjie, 126–37
Awakening, 129
and Caoshan, 134
Death, 136
The Five Ranks, 133–34
"Go where there is neither cold nor heat," 132
and the guardian diety, 132
and Guishan and Yunyan, 128–30
and the Heart Sutra, 126
and Huizhao Zhanshi, 130
"I agreed with about half and rejected half," 132–33
"Just this is it," 130
and Nanquan, 128
"Three measures of flax," 132

Dongshan Shouchu, 277–78
"Three weights of hemp," 278
and Yunmen, 277

Dosho, 305

Fayan Wenyi, 259–65
and Baling Haojian, 262
Bingting comes for fire, 261
"First, I ask you to practice; second, I ask you to practice," 262
and Luohan, 259–60
No time for repairs, 263

"One has it. The other doesn't," 264
and Shaoxiu, 260
Six Attributes of Being, 265
"You are Echo," 260

Fengxue Yanzhao, 247–50
Death, 249
"I remember Konan in the Spring," 249
"A tortoise crossing the mud leaves traces," 249

Fenyang Shanzhao, 251–52
An invitation from the governor, 251
and Shishuang Chuyuan, 253
"What is Dao?," 251

Fifth Patriach [see Daman Hongren]

Fourth Patriarch [see Dayi Daoxin]

Guishan Lingyou, 200–203
and Baizhang, 200
and Deshan, 232
and Dongshan, 128
How he was chosen the abbot of a new monastery, 201–202
and Yanshan, 208–10

Guizong Zhichang, 143–44
Cutting a snake in half, 143
Mount Kunlun in a poppy seed, 143

Guoshi [see Nanyang Huizhong]

Hangzhou Tianlong, 198

Hanshan and Shide, 153–61

Heze Shenhui, 79–81

Hongren [see Daman Hongren]

Huangbo Xiyun, 192–95
and the crown prince, 193

The disciple should surpass his teacher, 192
False attainment, 194
and Linji, 218
The monk who could walk on water, 193
and Nanquan, 192
There are no teachers of Zen, 195
The value of the written word, 193
and Zhaozhou, 181

Huanglong Huinan, 254

Huineng, 59–67, 72–73
Competition to be named Sixth Patriarch, 61
Death, 80
Meets Hongren, 61
and Nanyue Huairang, 79
"Neither wind nor pennant moves; mind moves," 66
and Qingyuan Xingshi, 78
and Shenxiu's student, 74
and Shitou Xiqian, 94
"Show me your face before your parents were born," 65
Spontaneous awakening, 60
"The teaching of the Buddha is not found in the written word," 72

Huike [Ji], 48–51
Antagonism of other teachers, 50
Death, 51
Meets Bodhidharma, 41
Meets Jianzhi Sengcan (Third Patriarch), 49
Tanlin loses his arm, 49

Huitang Zuxin, 285–287

Huizhao Zhanshi, 130

Jianyuan Zhongxing, 120–22

Jianzhi Sengcan, 51–53

His heir [Dayi Daoxin], 53

Meets Huike, 49

*Xinxin Ming*, 51–53

Jiashan Shanui, 120–22

and the Boatman Monk, 121

Never preached a word of Zen, 121

Jinhua Juzhi, 199–200

One finger Zen, 200

"Say a word of Zen," 199

Jinniu, 221–22

Layman Pang (Pangyun), 100–102

Death, 102

"Hauling water and carrying wood," 101

and Mazu, 90

"Who is it that doesn't understand?," 101

Linji Yixuan, 218–27

Death, 227

and Deshan, 234

and Dingzhou, 224, 244

A hoe, 221

and Huangbo, 218

"I don't pay respects to Buddhas or Patriarchs," 222

and Jinniu, 221

"My awakening is no different from that of the Buddha," 227

Sermon, 225

A true man of no rank, 224

What the Second Patriarch attained from the First, 225

"Who understands?," 224

"Your mind is different from that of the Buddhas and patriarchs," p. 225

and Zhaozhou, 222

Lungtan Chongzin, 230–32

Luohan Chichen, 259

Mahakasyapa, 25–26

Malunkyaputta, 31

Mazu Daoyi, 84–91

and Baizhang, 169

and Damei, 148

Flying geese, 169

Koans, 90

and Layman Pang, 90

"No amount of polishing will turn a tile into a mirror," 84

and Shigong, 146

A shout, 170

Strange words and extraordinary actions, 86

Sun–faced Buddha; Moon–faced Buddha, 91

and Tanxia Tianran, 103

"What is it?," 88

"What is the fundamental meaning of this moment?," 91

"Your own treasure house," 89

Muzhou Daozong, 270–71

Nanquan Puyuan, 164–69

Advice to a governor, 167

Cuts a cat in half, 164

and Dongshan, 128

The god of the fields, 168

A goose in a bottle, 165

"I bought this sickle for thirty small coins," 167

"I'll be a water buffalo and work for the people," 168

"People see this flower as though in a dream," 137

"Possible. Impossible," 165

and Zhaozhou, 178

Nanyang Huizhong [The National Teacher], 73–77

"Build me a seamless tower," 76

Calls his attendant three times, 76

The emperor pulls his carriage, 73

Teaching of "no-mind," 74–76

Nanyuan Huiyong, 246–47

Nanyue Huairang, 79

and Huineng, 79

and Mazu, 84

"Zen isn't sitting or lying down," 79

National Teacher [see Nanyang Huizhong]

Niutou Farong, 54–55

"It's still with you," 55

Pangyun [see Layman Pang]

Panshan Baoji, 144–45

"All are the best," 144

A perfect likeness, 145

Sermon, 145

Qingyuan Xingshi, 78

"Before I studied Zen, mountains were mountains," 78

and Huineng, 75

and Shitou Xiqian, 95

Qinshan Wensui, 235–36

Rumin Zhanshi, 273

Sansheng Huiran, 245

and Deshan, 245

and Xiangyan Zhixian, 245

and Xuefeng, 245

Second Patriarch [see Huike]

Sengcan [see Jianzhi Sengcan]

Shaoxiu, 260

Shenhui [see Heze Shenhui]

Shenxiu, 61–64, 70–71

Competition to be named Sixth Patriarch, 61

Shide and Hanshan, 153–61

Shigong Huicang, 146–48

and Mazu, 146
"Show me the arrow which brings back to life," 147
Taking hold of empty space, 148
Tending an Ox, 147
Shinchi Kakushin, 304
Shishuang Chuyuan, 253–54
and Fenyang, 253
Sermon, 253
Shishuang Qingzhu, 118
Shitou Xiqian, 94–99
Awakening, 95
and Huineng, 94
"In Praise of Sameness and Difference," 98–99
and Qingyuan Xingshi, 95
Shandao's knife, 97
"Who obtained the essential teaching of the Sixth Patriarch?," 96
and Yaoshan, 110
Shoushan Xingnian, 250–51
"If you wish to practice, practice!," 251
A staff, 250
"Why is this blind fellow shouting?," 250
Sixth Patriarch [see Huineng]
Tanlin, 49
Tanxia Tianran, 103–105
Burns a wooden Buddha, 104
Climbs the statue of Manjusri, 103
Death, 105
"Eat when you're hungry; drink when thirsty," 105
and Mazu, 103
Third Patriarch [see Jianzhi Sengcan]
Tianhuang Daowu, 102

"I've never missed an opportunity to show you how to study mind,"102
Tiantai Deshao, 265
Touzi Dadong, 181
Wumen Huikai, 299–303
Death, 303
The Gateless Gate, 301
Wu!, 301
Wuzu Fayan, 287–92
Death, 292
Four koans, 290
Parable of the lesson in burglary, 288
Qian and her ghost, 290
Sermon, 288
and Yuanwu Keqin, 292
Xianglin Chengyuan, 279–80
"Mindfulness without interruption," 280
"Take some and see," 280
and Yunmen, 279
Xiangyan Zhixian, 210–13
A man hanging by his teeth from a tree, 213
and Sansheng, 245
The sound of the bamboo, 211
What Guishan teaches these days, 213
Xinghua Cunjiang, 246
Xingshan Weikuan, 141–42
"I'm not one of 'all beings,'" 141
"If there's no you or I, who is there to see?,"141
"What a fine mountain!," 142
Xuansha Shibei, 258
Enter the sound of the water flowing by, 258
"We make use of it everyday and yet fail to recognize it," 258

Xuefeng Yicun, 235–40
Death, 240
and Deshan, 235, 236
"I came with empty hands; I left with empty hands," 238
"Please have some tea," 238
and Qinshan, 235–36
and Sansheng, 245
"Sitting like a clay Buddha," 237
"What can you learn from the sutras?," 237
"The whole world is like a grain of rice," 239
and Yunmen, 271–72
Yangshan Huiji, 207–10
and Changsha, 196
and Danyuan Yingzhen, 208
Function and substance, 209
and Guishan, 208–209
A mattock, 209
Nothing to say, 209
Rebirth, 210
and Xiangyan Zhixian, 212
Yanguan Qian, 140
"Bring me the rhinoceros," 140
"The Buddha has been dead a long time now," 19
and Damei, 149
Discussing the sutras, 140
Yangqi Fanghui, 254
Yantou Xuanjian, 235–40
and Deshan, 235, 236
His death shout, 239–40
The last word, 239
and Qinshan, 236
"Sitting like a clay Buddha," 237
"What can you learn from the sutras?," 237
Yaoshan Weiyan, 110–116

Death, 115
and Governor Li Ao, 113
"Here is a monk who has something he doesn't understand," 112
His great laugh, 114
"How can you think of not thinking?," 111
How to read the sutras, 111
Koan from *Blue Cliff Record*, 114
Sermon, 115
and Shitou, 110
Yingzhen, 77
Yongming Yanshou, 265–66
Yuanwu Keqin, 292–93
and Dahui, 296
"Grasp this, then all things will be your teacher," 293
and Wuzu, 293
Yuelin Shiguan, 298–99
Yunmen Wenyan, 270–77
and Baling Haojian, 278
"Beating stumps to one's heart's content," 275
Death, 280
and Dongshan Shouchu, 277

A dried shit-stick, 274
and Muzhou, 270
"Rice in the bowl; water in the pail," 275
and Rumin Zhanshi, 273
Sermon, 276–77
A sesame bun, 272
"What made you think you could solve it?," 272
"Why put on your robes at the sound of the bell?," 275
Words are not needed, 276
and Xianglin Chengyuan, 279
and Xuefeng, 271–72
Yunyan Tansheng, 116–18
and Dongshan, 129
Zhaozhou Congshen, 178–88
"After the body has died," 185
An auspicious Image, 178
Awakening, 179
"The cypress tree In the garden," 188
Does a dog have Buddha nature?, 178
And Governor Wang Rong, 185

"He doesn't lack anything," 184
A Hemp robe of seven units, 185
How to read the sutras, 181
and Huangbo Xiyun, 181
If a child of seven has greater understanding, 180
and Nanquan, 178, 179
The old woman of the tea shop, 186
"Please have some tea," 187
The real Buddha resides within you, 182
The Stone Bridge of Zhaozhou, 184
and Touzi Dadong, 181
"Wash your bowl," 17, 183
"The Way is not difficult to attain," 183, 184
"What is the body of Prajna?," 180
"Who is the Buddha?," 187